D0108454

ENGLISH LINGUISTICS
1500—1800

(A Collection of Facsimile Reprints)

Selected and Edited by

R. C. ALSTON

No. 363

THE SCOLAR PRESS LIMITED
MENSTON, ENGLAND
1972

THE HIGH DUTCH
MINERVA
1680

A Scolar Press Facsimile

THE SCOLAR PRESS LIMITED
MENSTON, ENGLAND
1972

THE SCOLAR PRESS LIMITED
20 Main Street, Menston, Yorkshire, England

ISBN 0 85417 890 2

Printed in Great Britain by
The Scolar Press Limited
Menston, Yorkshire, England

NOTE

Reproduced (original size) from a copy in the Bodleian Library, by permission of the Curators. Shelf-mark: Mar. 412.

Nothing is known of the author of this work. It is the first recorded grammar of German written in English, and remained unrivalled until 1731 when Benedict Beiler's *New German grammar* was published. Nevertheless, *The High Dutch Minerva* appears to have gone unnoticed almost since its first appearance. This neglect may be due to the rarity of surviving copies; only four copies of the 1680 edition are known—the copy reproduced here, one in the British Museum, and two in Cambridge University Library, both of which are imperfect. There was a second issue with a title-page dated 1685 of which there is a copy in the British Museum.

All existing copies lack signature C and it seems likely that a mistake in the labelling of the signatures occurred during the original printing since the text is apparently complete as it stands.

Reference: Wing H 1961.

J. R. Turner

a. 3.
des
Adelen
hohteulshe
Sprahkonst
für di
English-
en.

ARTE ET MARTE

A ! Z !

Des
EDELEN
Hohteutſhe

Sprah Konſt

vor di
ENGLISH=
EN.

THE.HIGHDUTCH

MINERVA

A-LA-MODE

OR

A. PERFECT. GRAMMAR
never extant before,

whereby

THE ENGLISH

may both

easily and exactly

learne.

the Neatest Dialect of the German

MOTHER - LANGUAGE

used thoroughout

ALL.EUROPE;

most humbly dedicated

TO HIS ROYAL HIGHNES

PRINCE
RUPERT

COUNT.PALATINE.OF.THE
RHINE

DUKE.OF.BAVARIA.AND.CUM-
BERLAND

VICE-ADMIRAL.OF.ALL.ENG-
LAND

KNIGHT.OF.THE.MOST.NOBLE
ORDER.OF.THE.GARTER
CONSTABLE.OF

HIS.MAJESTIES

CASTLE.AND.HONOUR.OF
WINDSOR
AND.ONE.OF

HIS.MAJESTIES

MOST.HONOURABLE
PRIVIE-COUNCIL
&c.

by

HIS. MOST. ILLUS-
TRIOUS
HIGHNESSES

*most humble and most
obedient servant,*

the Author.

LONDON, printed in L. BRITAIN, and
to be sold at the Rabbets and Harrow in Jack-
sons court Blackfrayer. 1680.

THE
CONTENTS.

THE PROLEGOMENA

doe here comprehend (in lieu of a Preface) fome Teftimonies of feveral great and learned Men concerning the Knowledge of Languages in general , and particularly of the Excellency of the Highdutch

moft

Copious and Significant,
Majeftick and Sweet,
Perfect and Pure,
Eafie and Ufefull,
Antient and Univerfal
Toung.

the Treatife it felf is divided into Three Parts:

GRAMMATOLOGIA

handling of

Letters and Syllables.

𝕬

ETYMOLOGIA

treading of
Words confidered by themfelves
without Conftruction.

ORTHOLOGIA

and

IDIOMATOLOGIA
ſhewe

the Art how to connect Words in writing or ſpeaking good and true Senſe , that we doe not commit either a Solœciſme , or a Germaniſme and Angliciſme.

TESTIMONIA

Summorum quorumdam

Virorum *loco* Præfationis *adducta*

de

Linguarum Notitia *in genere*, *maxime vero de* Germanicæ *infigni* Præftantia.

Francis Bacon *in his XVIII. Esfay*:

𝕳𝖊, 𝖙𝖍𝖆𝖙 𝖙𝖗𝖆𝖇𝖊𝖑𝖑𝖊𝖙𝖍 𝖎𝖓𝖙𝖔 𝖆 𝖈𝖔𝖚𝖓𝖙𝖗𝖎𝖊, 𝖇𝖊𝖋𝖔𝖗𝖊 𝖍𝖊 𝖍𝖆𝖙𝖍 𝖘𝖔𝖒𝖊 𝖊𝖓𝖙𝖗𝖆𝖓𝖈𝖊 𝖎𝖓𝖙𝖔 𝖙𝖍𝖊 𝖑𝖆𝖓𝖌𝖚𝖆𝖌𝖊, 𝖌𝖔𝖊𝖙𝖍 𝖙𝖔 𝖘𝖈𝖍𝖔𝖔𝖑, 𝖆𝖓𝖉 𝖓𝖔𝖙 𝖙𝖔 𝖙𝖗𝖆𝖇𝖊𝖑.

D. E.lm. Caftellus in fua oratione inaugurali *p. m.* 5. in uno idiomate Conditoris noftri celebrare laudes, honoris fummum eft valligium ; in pluribus igitur quanto magis ? enimvero non vir tantum appellandus eft ille unus ac fingularis, fed potius hominum cœtus & Ecclefia. Tot fuftinet perfonas (S. Hieronymi verba funt) quot callet quispiam dialectos. Dona linguarum novae progeniei (Chriftianam intelligo) non antea defuper data fuerunt, quam unigenitus Dei filius illuc afcenderat, in prifti -nam ac primordialem exufcitatus gloriam. Statui exinanitionis atque diminutionis fuæ conveniebat munus conferre prædicationis, non ita πολυγλωττίας, quafi hoc magis inter Chrifti efset Regalia. Fuit fane inter χαρίσματα ad Templi fpiritualis ædificationem fpectantia maxime, nec omnino

vulgaria, intimis ac præ aliis illius κεχα-
ϱιτωμένοις præcipue refervata.

D. Georg. Henilhius *in Præfat. Thefauri:*
Germanica lingua tanta excellit antiquitate, ut
originem ab ipfa Babylonicæ turris ædificatione
ducat; tanta puritate, ut fola virgo illibata di-
cenda fit; tanta amplitudine, ut nullis termi-
nis circumfcribi, fed ubivis potius peregrinari
videatur; tanta denique tum brevitate tum
copia, ut copiam in brevitate et brevitatem
in copia nulla fere dicendi vis nullaque copia
pro dignitate fatis laudare atque extollere
pofsit &c. das ift:

di Teutſhe Haupt - ſprahe iſt di
vortrefflihſte a'm altertume, denn ſi
ire urankunft bei dem Babyloniſhen Turne genommen; di vortrefflihſte an laut-
erer reinligkeit, ſo gar daſs ſi alleinig
di keuſhe unbeflekkte Jungfrawe zu nenn-
en; di vortrefflihſte an weite und ræum-
igkeit, dero grænze unumſloſsen, ſondern vilmer weltweit erſtrekket ſind; di
vortrefflihſte an der kůrze und doh di
vortrefflihſte an der menge, alſo gar daſs
keine kraft noh ůberfluſs.eines wolredend
-en mundes ſattſamlih und nah rɔhter wůr
-de løben und erhœben kœnne diſer (der
Teutſhen ſprahe) ůberflůſsigſte kůrze und
hinwider di kůrzeſte menge und den reih
-eſten ůberfluſs.

Joh. Gorop. Becanus *lib.* 2. *Hermathenæ:*
in Germanica lingua omnia vocabula primo-
genia funt monofyllaba eorumque tanta * *copia*

*ut in ea interpretanda nulla unquam exiſtat
ſententiarum diverſitas, quam frequentem apud
Hebræos eſse nemo diffitetur. hac igitur parte
lingua Germanica Hebraicam vocum copia,
Græcam & Latinam brevitate vincit, in qua
alteram perfeEtiſsimi ſermonis laudem colloca-
mus. ut autem et breviſsima eſset et copio-
ſiſsima, quod mirabile videtur, inde conſe-
cuta eſt·, qvod pluribus conſtet elementis,
quam ulla cœterarum. diphtongos enim plures
multo habet, quam aliæ, & omnes pariter
una conſonante ſuperat, quam duplex digam-
ma licet vocare. quanto autem plures ſunt
literæ, tanto plures erunt earum complexiones
et inde plurium vocum discrimina &c.* Idem
ibidem: *Profecto non video, quid ad laudes
linguæ Germanicæ ulterius addi poſsit. Luci-
diſsima eſt nullaque orationis ambiguitate im-
pedita; eadem rurſum omnium breviſsima;
eadem copioſisſima, qua de parte lucis eſt ori-
go; eadem leniſsima minimaque organorum
moleſtia proferenda; eadem hominem maxime
idoneum reddit ad quamvis aliam et addiſcen-
dam & bene modulandam. numquid aliud
adhuc deſideratur ad ſummam linguæ perfectio
-nem? equidem libenter et obviis manibus her-
bam ei porrigam, qui me docebit, usquam
gentium linguam ejusmodi inveniri, quæ pluribus una dotibus ſit ornata. contra mihi con-
cedi rogo, quod optimo jure poſtularem, ut
pari ratione tantisper mihi liceat ſermoni nos-
tro vernaculo palmam et primas aſserere, dum
quis hæc omnia ſimul in una eademque lingua*

monſtraverit &c. d. i. ih kann warhaftig-
lih niht erſeen, wi mann immermer zu
dem würdigen lobe der Teutſhen ſprahe
ein merers hinzutuen kœnne ; ſi iſt di
helleſte und klærlihſte , wirſet von ſih
weg alles ungewiſse , zweiſinnige und ver
wirrete weſen; ſi iſt di allerkürzeſte und
doh di allerwortreihſte ; ſi iſt ſanft und
gelinde ; ſi flüſset von der zungen liblih
und mit luſt; ſi alleine mahet einen menſh
-en geſhikt und bekwæm allerlei getœn
und ausreden nah-zu ſprehen , und auslænd
-iſhe ſprahen reht zu reden. es ſage einer , wer es kann, ob auh noh was übrig
ſei von der hœhſten vollbommenheit ein-
iger ſprahe ? wollan , ih will überwonn-
en ſein, wa mih einer læren kann, daſs
irgentswa einige ſprahe vorhanden ſei ,
welhe mit mererm kunſtſmukke und beſs
-erer vollkommenheit ausgeziret ſei. i'm
gegenfalle aber kann ih ja mit gutem rehte
fodern, daſs mir ſo lange vergœnnet ſei,
unſerer Teutſhen ſprahe di oberſtelle über
alle zu geben , biſs ein ander aus einer
andren ſprahe vœllig hervorbringen wird
alles das , was ſo vœllig und reihlih inn
unſerer befindlih iſt.   * Simon
Stevin *in Germanica lingua colligit* 2170;
  in Græca vero 265 , & *in Latina* 163.
Claude Duret *en Treſor de l' hiſtoire
des langues de ceſt univers : La langue Alemande eſt un parler ample & copieux de vo-
cables & mots propres & ſignificatifs , & tres-*

🏵 (o) 🏵

idoine à recevoir et former quelque pa-
role que ce soit &c.

Petrus Scriverius de lingua Germanica :

Tael ongelooflick foet, Princes van alle taelen,
geboren om de kroon van anders hooft te halen,
  vol fins, vol defticheits, vol luyfters, lank
        en ruim,
en die wel mifsen kan het over-zeeske fchuim :
tael rick en onvermengt; tael om den toon te tragen;
Godin die niet behooft een wort te leen te vragen
  en halen tot uw hulp; tael van geluckich fchlag,
    die gans Europa dor den taelen trotzen mag;
fchier d' outfte die men vindt, niet o te weder-
        leggen ;
hy booge van de zyn, die will ; wy fullen feggen,
  dat onfe tael de haer fo veel te bovem gaet,
    als van de fwarte nacht de helder fonne ftaet.
en om dat wy den trotz van Vrankrick hier an-
        raken,
  fo fegt haer, dat well eer haer volkeren dus
        fpracken:
    die tael, die daer nu is, di komt van fremd
        gefpuis
    en uit een ander hoeck gefproten, leit daer
        t' huis.

Martin Opiz *in fuo Ariftarcho : in-*
genium verborum noftrorum et tractus
fententiarum ita decens eft, ita felix,
ut neque Hifpanorum majeftati, ne-
que Italorum decentiæ, neque Gallorum
venufta volubilitati concedere debeat.

d. i. es find di woerter, dero fügungen
und kunftmæfig-geordnete fprühe inn der
Teutfhen fprahe fo gefhikklih, fein und

ᛒ

wollſtændig, daſs ſi der Spaniſhen praht,
der Wælthen zirligkeit und der Franzoſen liblihen geſwindigkeit inn keinem
nihts bevor geben.

Becanus *ſupra dictus paſsim in ſuis ſcriptis:*
Lingua Germanorum eſt ſubtilis ſtructura;
admiranda ars & fabrica; res plena mys-
teriis; arcana locutionis et excellentiſsimas
ſignificandi rationes habens. d. i. di Teutſhe ſprahe iſt ein künſtlih ſhœnes gebæu;
eine wunderreihe kunſt und volle gereit
-ſhaft; ein werk voller geheimnüſse;
eine verborgene kraft der rede, da di
reinlihſten und vortrefflihſten urſahen irer andeutungen ſein.

Wenerus, JCtus *in præfat.*

Linguæ Germanicæ dignitas atque ornamen-
tum univerſo jam orbi innotuit; paucis enim
abhinc annis ita crevit, ideoque decorata at-
-que exornata eſt, ut nullius rei et addita-
menti egeat; ea facilitate ac commoditate
ſcribi poteſt, ut neſciam, an non omnibus
aliis anteferenda &c. d. i. di würde
und hoheit der Teutſhen ſprahen iſt numero der ganzen welt offenbar worden;
denn ſi hat biſsanhero innerhalb wenig
jaren inn irer zire und irem ſmukke al
-ſo zugenommen, daſs ſi an keinem mang
-el, und des fremden weſens niht nœt-
ig hat; ſi kann ſo ſhikklih und mit ſolher füglihen leihtligkeit geſhriben werden,
daſs ih meine, ſi ſei dannenhero allen
anderen vor-zu zien.

🎰 (o) 🎰

Goropius : *Linguæ Germanicæ primus
architectus eam dedit literarum pronun-.
ciationem, quæ quam minime vocalia
instrumenta fatigaret, omnem aspe-
ram eorum collisionem, omnem fla-
tum vehementiorem, omnes sibi'os a-
cutiores, omnem ex imis præcordiis
suspirationem, omnia denique quæ ex-
trema, in dentibus, in labiis, vel
in gutture, vel in palato, vel in
lingua videri possunt, diligenter e-
vitans.*

Scrieckius Rodornius Finnius *in suis O-
peribus: Et ut hactenus e Græca et Latina
lingua omnia deducere et probare sunt coni-
ti, tamquam rerum universitas duobus hisce
tantum columinibus niti debuisset, vice nunc
versa, lingua Teutonica per consonantiam
Hebraicam ipsis Græcis et Latinis præluce-
bit, eisque latentem suam originem non tantum aperiet, verum etiam eorum sequaces
in Originibus, Naturæque et rerum Historiis ad unum errantes in viam, vel invi-
ta et reluctante ignorantia reducet &c.* d. i.
wiwol mann sih bisshero ser bemüet,
fast alles und ides aus der Grihifh-und
Lateinifhen fprahe ab-zu leiten und da
-heraus zu beweifen, niht anders als ob
di allgemeinheit der dinge einzig und
alleine dafelbft gegründet wære: fo foll

❀ (0) ❀

dennoh numero i'm gegenteile di Teutſhe ſprahe durh zuſtimmung der Hebræiſhen , den Grihen und Lateinern ſelbſt vorleuhten , und inen niht alleine iren eigenen verborgenen Urſprung und Ankunft entdekken , ſondern ſoll auh ire folger und vertreter, di bifshero inn den Urankünften , inn den natürlihen dingen unꝺ inn dem geſhihtweſen ſæmtlih ge-irret , auh wider allen troz und alle gewalt der unwiſenheit , auf den rehten weg bringen.

Idem : *Sæpe repetivimus , nec ſatis repeti poteſt , totius univerſi antiquiora nomina apud Chaldæos non ſatis proprie , apud Græcos et Latinos nullo modo ſignificari : Hebraice interea et Teutonice omnia propriam ſuam oſtendere eſſentiam et apparentiam.* d. i. diſes haben wir oft beweislih geſagt, kann aber dennoh niht zu'r gnüge geſagt werden , daſs di gar alten namen aller weltſtükke inn der Chaldæiſhen ſprahe niht gar eigentlih, inn der Grihiſh-und lateiniſhen aber gar nihts niht , inn der Hebræiſh-und Teutſhen ſprahe aber auf's eigentlihſte andeuten der dinge vorbild, augenſhein , eigenſhaft und weſen.

Idem: *dum quæro et ſcrutor poſt incredibilem in tali rerum oceano fluctationem , admirandam tandem ſed ſimplicem inter exiſtentias naturales , interque linguam Hebraicam et Celticam , ſive Teutonicam , ſive Scythicam , ſive Belgicam (quæ una eſt)*
de-

detexi confonantiam et convenientiam , et om-
nia fecundum Teutonicum et Hebraicum fig-
nificare. d. i. inn dem ih ſtets nahſinne
und das ſprah‑weſen vo'm anfange biſs
zu'm ende durhdenke ; ſo habe ih denn‑
oh endlih nah ſer vilen zweifelhaften an
‑ſtœſsen erſpûret und entdûkket di wun‑
derreihe verwandnûſs und zuſtimmung
zwiſhen dem natûrlihen weſen und der
Hebræiſh ‑ und Teutſhen ſprahe , und
daſs alles ſeine klare ausdeutung und ver‑
ſtand habe nah deütung der Teutſhen
wœrter.

Cluverius *de German. antiq. lib.* I.
male ac parum perite non modo exte-
ri homines , fed et quidam Germano-
rum a Romanis themata Germanica
deducunt , cum ipſi verius Romani a
Germanis acceperint poſterioribus fe-
culis : quemadmodum et militaris dis-
ciplinæ nonnulla , ut patet ex Vege-
tio et Marcellino et aliis ejus ævi
authoribus , et in his maxime digni-
tatum vocabula , ducatus , comitatus ,
Romanis antea ignota , quæ et ipſa
imperiti noſtri homines a Romanis no,
habere docent &c. Idem ibidem .
fed nec eorum judicium probandum ,
qui ubi aliquod vocabulum in lingua

✿ (o) ✿

Germanica occurrit , quod vel Latino vel Græco vel Hebraico vel Perſico vel alius cujusdam gentis vocabulo ſit par aut ſimile , protinus exclamant , nos illud inde habere &c.

Scrieckius: *notandi ſunt multorum errores , qui , quod multa convenientia invenerint in lingua Græcæ cum Germanica , putarunt ea Germanos a Græis mutuaſse , ignorantia rectæ originis & antiquitatis.*

Olaus Magnus *lib.* 1. *c.* 36. *ab antiquiſsimo tempore cum eſsent Gigantes in terris ſeptemtrionalibus , hoc eſt , longe ante inventas literas Latinas et antequam Carmenta ex Græcia ad oſtia Tyberis et Romanum ſolum cum Evandro perveniret , expulſisque Aboriginibus , gentem illam rudem ac plane ſylveſtrem mores et literas docerent ,* habuerunt Aquilonaria regna ſuas literas. *Cujus rei indicium præſtant eximiæ magnitudinis ſaxa veterum buſtis ac ſpecubus affixa &c.*

Johann. Magnus (*Olai frater*) *lib.* 1. *hiſt. cap. de lit. Goth.*

credendum non eſt , ipſos Aquilonares

omnino carnisse scriptoribus rerum a se magnifice gestarum , cum longe ante inventas literas Latinas Gothi suas literas *habuerint &c.*

Duret : *l' alphabet des lettres des Gots a estè le premier alphabet des premieres & plus anciennes lettres.*

Idem: *vray est, que les histoires d' Hispaigne asseurent, que la langue Gothique estoit du tout semblable a la langue des Celtes : autres affirment , que c' estoit la mesme langue Teutonique &c.*

Wehnerus *in præf. Observ. Cameral.*

lingua Germanica a lingua Latina tum imprimis a literis et notis Latinis omnino aliena ac diversa fuit , utpote quæ proprias ac Romanis incognitas quasdam contineat literas et diphtongos peculiares.

Wolfgang. Iazius *lib.* 8. *de Suevis:* non audiendi sunt, qui ante annos 300. primum omnium linguam Germanicam scribi solitam existimant &c.

Besoldus *cap.* 17. *de natur. populor. Galli quam plurimas voces Latinas addidicerunt , sed ad formam et constructionem Germanicæ linguæ connexuerunt et pronunciarunt , Latinamque dialectum continuis Germanismis deformatam condiderunt. Frustraque* Stephanus

Pasquierus *lib. 7. de recher. c. 2. miratus, unde verba auxiliaria in Gallicam, Italicam et Hispanicam linguam irrepserint &c.*

Idem *cap. 18. Ipsi Galli, unde suas dictiones habent, nesciunt; ideoque in lexicis suis et in etymis indagandis vano nisu mire se torquent.*

Glareanus: *i nunc et pete, citra linguæ Germanicæ peritiam, vocum Gallicarum Etymologiam, quam belli scribentur elenchi?*

Wolfg. Hungerus JCtus *in vind. ling. Germ.*

Nunquam Gallus tam inepte rimaturus hæc efset, si vel mediocrem linguæ Germanicæ haberet cognitionem.

Scrieckius: *antiqua Gallorum et Hispanorum lingua ante adventum Romanorum, per totam Europam varia dialecto fuit Celtica seu Teutonica.*

Martinius *ex Ludovico Carrio: linguam Germanicam veterem Gallorum linguam fuisse satis constat, ut plane sint ridiculi, qui, dum illius linguæ rident antiquitatem, suam sibi maternam linguam irridere se non intelligunt &c.*

Cluverius l. c. si quis peritus paulo diligentius linguam Wallorum, qui adhuc sunt in Anglia, introspexerit, facile illic multa ac innumera vocabula mere Germanica deprehendet.

et paulo inferius: Idem de *Hibernica*
lingua, & item ea, quam in His-
pania *Cantabricam* vocant, judican-
dum cenſeo : nam in hac quoque ple-
raque aut Latina aut Germanica de-
prehendi *&c.* *vid.* Goropius *lib.* 4.
Hiſp. it. Cambdenus, Simon Stevin, Sbrieckius & alii.

Goropius *lib.* 2. *Gall. p.* 26. Quis
ignorat, ſermonem eum, quo nunc
Itali vernaculo utuntur, natum eſse
e Latina et Germanica lingua, qua
Gothi et Longobardi utebantur.

Beſoldus *de linguar. immutat. cap.* 23.
Jus Feudale, quo utimur, abundat uſque me-
ris Germanismis et plures voces Theotiſcas
habet, quæ ab interpretibus antiquitatum Ger-
manicarum ignaris, miſere torquentur, et ex
præjudicio plerumque nobis veræque origini,
per ſententiam quaſi adimuntur. *vid.* Cluverius *lib.* 2. *de antiq. Germ.* & Wolfg.
Lazius *lib.* 10. *de Gothis.*

Scrieckius : *Japhetica ſeu Europæa dia-*
lectus perpetua uſque traditione ad noſtra uſqe
ſecula devoluta eſt, aliqua ut ſit variatio-
ne, ſed fundo quoque manente, adeo ut etiam
hodie Teutones, Belgae, Britanni, Dani et
Septemtriones eo ipſo utantur &c.

Duret *p.* 868. *La Langue de Sueſse eſt*

⁂ (o) ⁂

presque semblable a la langue Gothique, Da-
noise et Nordvegoise, ils ont beaucoup de
mots communs avec les Alemans, veu mesme
que leur langue est issue de la langue Ger-
manique.

quod in Bohemia, Slavonia, Hun-
garia, Transylvania, Polonia, Mos-
covia *&c.* usurpetur lingua Germanica, ex historiis et peregrinatio
-nibus abunde constat ; *Angerius*
autem *Busbequius* in quarta Epist.
Turcica hoc notatu dignum de Tau-
rica Cherfonefo scribit : *non possum*
hoc præterire, quæ de gente accepi,
quæ etiam nunc incolit Tauricam Cher
-fonefum, quam sæpe audiveram ser-
mone, moribus, ore denique ipso et
corporis habitu, originem Germanicam
referre &c.

Albertus Kranzius *in Saxon. lib.* 1.
cap. 1. Saxonum lingua, si ad lucem
veritatis res inspiciatur, sola servat
sinceritatem suæ vocalitatis, ut verba omnia puro sono denunciet, non
inversa stridoribus, non contorta
diphtongis &c.

Duret pag. 828. *les Habitants de*
Saxe se font de tout temps et an-

ciennetè vantez de parler entre touts
les autres Alemands la plus entiere,
pure et diserte langue Alemande.
Juſt. Georg. Schottelius *in ſua Gram-*
matica p. m. 53.

Sicuti ii, qui de literis bene meri-
ti, quando vigilias ſuas candide pro-
ferunt , iniquos Ariſtarchos, atqe
etiam eos (quod deplorandum eſt)
qui in eo genere nunquam verſati
ſunt , ſuſtinere coguntur (ſunt verba hactenus Wolfg. Lazii;) ita fata
-li quadam in Germanos inclementia,
linguæ Teutonicæ ſplendidiſsima
Majeſtas habuit judicem cœcum ; e-
jusdem dulciſsima tonitrua habuerunt
judicem ſurdaſtrum , id eſt , igno-
rantiam hominum exterorum.   Ta-
centibus hactenus Germanis, mus-
ſitantibus iisdem , confitentibus taci
-te et turpiter, relinquentibus decus
hoc patrium mendaciſsimæ aliorum li-
bidini contrectandum , conſpurcan-
dum, conviciandum.   At , ſinent Fata, pellenda tandem cœcitas, excu-
tiendæ tenebræ, conſtringenda rabi-
oſa Dea , cui Tacitus jam olim robur

❀ (o) ❀

parvis magnisque civitatibus commu-
ne tribuit , quæ hactenus ferreo jugo
genium et libertatem Teutiſcæ loque
-læ preſsit; eripienda tandem exteris
injuſta oſtendatio , vindicandum tandem excellens linguæ Germanicæ
vaſtigium.

Druſius *adCriticam* α'φιλόλογον·

Nos, qui (ſublimiori et limatio-
ri)Philologiæ addicti, placentæ
non ſumus , ut omnibus placere
queamus; nec vero eſse debemus,
quum nec nobis omnia placeant.

d. i.   wir, di reht gründlih ſind dem
woerterfleiſ' ergeben,
und inn der toden ſhrift der klugen Alt-
en leben ,
ſind keine kuhen niht , ſo idem munde
ſmekken ;
weil auh niht alles uns gefæll't , was an-
d're hekken.

Votivus Amicorum Adplauſus :

Q.UTINAM·DIGNO.TANDEM.VARO
-NE.FRUATUR
LINGUA.SUÆ.PATRIÆ..CLARA
VENUSTA.BONA!

Grammatologia,

O R

The First Part of Letters and single Syllables.

Chap. I. of the *Orthophonia.*

Sect. I. of the Figure, Number, and Place of the Letters here used.

W
B
P
V
F
D
T
H
J, j
G
K
L
M
N
R
S, ſ
=
Z

single vowels:

A, E, O, I, U
a, e, o, i, u

å, ö, ü

improper dipthongs.

proper dipthongs:

au, åi, åu, ei, eu

aw, åy, åw, ey, ew

improper tripthongs.

w*
b
p
v
f
d
t
h*
y*
g
k
l
m
n
r
s
x*
z*

D

WE have juſt as many vowels as conſonants, if taken right, none more nor any leſs, than you find in the table, thirty ſix in all, placed according to their proper notion, whereof There are five ſingle, and the reſt compound; but Here five double marked with *, and thirteen ſingle.

Sect.2. of the Vowels and their Sound.

Several of theſe letters are otherwiſe pronounced than in Engliſh; as,

A long is pronounced broad, as A before LL in all i. alle; or as AU and AW in aul or awl i. ale.

A ſhort as the Engliſh ſhort O in hot, pot, &c.

E obſcure, as the firſt E in better or never; but E clear, as the laſt of the ſame words; and ſtanding in the end of a ſyllable is onely half expreſſed and half mute, as in French, or as in Engliſh after L and R; e. g. fire-ſcuffle i. feyer-ſhaufel, &c. but over A, O, U not at all, being for it ſelf quite mute, which ſeems to be the reaſon why the High-dutch do not ſeparately ſet this E either before (as the Engliſh in their ea, eo, eu) or after (as ſome of the Latins in their ae, oe) the ſaid vowels, but right over them, as ſome other Latines uſe ſo to incorporate it with thoſe two firſt vowels, that they in the Latin,(and all three in our and the Engliſh tongues) make as one onely ſound, ſo likewiſe one onely character, which two we ſhall now here be forced to make ſhift withall for want of a ſufficient ſtock of our own letters.

Note, the E half-mute, or (as it is called by the French) feminine, is never here to be uſed in a ſubſtantive after another both vowel and conſonant *whatsoever* , *unless it be of the feminine gender or plural number, where (as also in the first person of the definite modes) of necessity it ought to be : e.g.* eine frawe *i. a woman* , eine kræe *i. a crow* , di fee *i. the fea*, di floœ *i. the fleas*, di fnee *i. the fnows* , di ftrafe *i. the ftreet*, eine rofe *i. a rofe*, eine feige *i. a fig, &c. not* fraw, ftras, ros, feig, *&c. fo* der kle *i. trefoil*, der fne *i. fnow*, das roœ *i. roe* , das ftro *i. ftraw* , der has *i. hare*, der will *i. the will*, der jud *or* jûd *i. jew* , der loœb *or* leu *i. lion, &c. not* klee, fnee, roœe *or* rehe, ftroe *or* ftroh, hafe , wille, jude *or* jûde, lewe *or* loœbe.

Some dialects, as the Frankonian, Swabian, and that of the Palatinate , fet this vowel (or instead thereof an H, *efpecially after an* A, O, U, *which are fometimes doubled) before its foregoing confonant, according to their lame pronunciation, not without great confufion of as well numbers and genders, as nouns and verbs : e.g.* lieb *i. love* , ih lieb *i. I love* , feel *i. foul* , keel *i. throat* , hûet *i. hats*, feer *or* fehr *i. fore*, ih fhieb *i. move*, di zier *or* zihr *i. ornament*, ih zier zihr *or* ziehr *i. adorn or make fine and handfom* , die ehr *i. the honour* , ih ehr *i. I honour*, die hahr *or* haar *i. the hairs* , die jaar *or* jahr *i. years*, die zaal *or* zahl *i. number*, ih zaal *or* zahl *i. I pay*, ih zæl *or* zæhl *i. I number or tell* ; ih bohr *or* boor *i. I bore* , een huer *or* huhr *i. a whore, &c. but our dialect hath* libe, (*for* lib *or* lieb *fignifieth an adjective, and as much as* charus *or* acceptus *in Latin*;) fele, kæle, hûte, fere, fhibe, zire, di ere, ih ere, di hare *and* jare, (*becaufe of the Plurality*;) zale, *for* zal *or* zaal *fignifieth a tail* ; zæle, bore, eine hure.

4

O *long as the English* OA *in* throat, oak, *to* groan, &c. *or as* O *in* alone, ſore, dore, ſtore, &c.

O *ſhort as the English* O *in* oven, over, love, &c. never *as in* fore, ſoft, oft, not, &c.

I *long as the English* EE, *e.g. to* feel *i.* filen, wee *i.* wir, heer *i.* hir, beer *i.* bir, &c.

I *ſhort as* I *of the word in i.* inn, ſtill *i.* ſtille, finger *i.* finger, is *i.* iſt, &c.

U *long as the English* OO, *e.g.* too *i.* zu, booth *i.* bude, tooth *i* zan, &c.

U *ſhort as* OO *or* OU *(conſidered in themſelves, without the mixt ſound received from a conſonant following) in* blood *or* bloud *i.* blutt, good *i* gutt, ſtood *i.* ſtunde, could *i.* kunte, foot *i.* fuſs, &c.

Æ *long as the English long* A, *e.g. to* ſhame *i.* ſhæmen, *to* lame *i.* læmen, *to* ſhare *i.* ſhæren, *to* tame *i.* zæmen, *to* lean *i.* lænen, *but* lenen *ſignifies to* lend, &c.

Æ *ſhort as the English* EA, *e.g. to* learn *i.* lærnen, *to* earn *i.* ærnen *or* ærnden, heart *i.* hærz, &c. *or as* A *ſhort in* March *i.* Mærz, ſtarch *i.* ſtærke, ſmart *i.* ſmærz, had *i.* hætte, &c.

This vowel and the clear E *being both of one ſound, are taken oft one for another, and therefore ſome write alſo* ſheren, lenen, lernen, herz, ſmerz, &c. *the which may very well be done in the primitives, but in the derivatives it ſhould always be kept as well in compoſition with another vowel, as ſtanding alone: e.g.* alt *i.* old, ælter *i.* older, di æltern *i.* parents, qſ. the olders, *mas* i. *meaſure,* mæſſen *i. to* meaſure, *apfel i.* apple, æpfel *i.* apples, *adel i.* nobility, ædel *i.* noble, *baur or* bawer *i.* countryman, bæuriſh *or* bæweriſh *i.* clowniſh, *baum i.* tree, bæume *i.* trees, &c. *not as ſome do,* elter, eltern, epſel, edel, beuriſh, beume.

The same is to be observed also of the other two improper vowels, viz. œ *in respect to* e *obscure and* o, *and* û *in respect to* i *and* u, *both in primitives:* e.g. hœben *and* heben *i. to bear or lift up,* shrœkken *and* shrekken *i. to scare,* brœnnen *and* brennen *i. to burn, &c. so* shiben *and* shûben *i. to move,* filen *and* fûlen *i. to feel,* sliffen *and* slûffen *or* slifen *and* slâfen *i. to shut,* rihen *and* rûhen *i. to smell, &c. and in derivatives; e.g.* offen *i. open,* œffenen *i. to open,* tohter *i. daughter,* tœhter *i. daughters,* stro *i. straw,* strœern *i. made of straw,* holz *i. wood,* hœlzern *and* hûlzern *i. wooden,* hure *i. whore,* hûrish *i. whorish,* fufs *i. foot,* fûsse *i. feet, &c.*

œ *both long and short like the English* I, *e.g.* bird, shirt, first, *&c.*

û *both short and long as* M *in Cambro-British or Welch, or as the long* U *in French; but by some it is commonly pronounced as the English* E *long or* I *short in, evil or ill* i. ûbel, *sin* i. sûnde, *mill* i. mûle, *bill* i. hûgel *or* higel, *to fill* i. fûllen, *to kiss* i. kûssen, *&c.*

AU *or* AW *as* OU *or* OW *in English: e.g.* house *i.* haus, *louse* i. laus, *mouse* i. maus, *shower* i. shawer, *sow* i. sawe, *&c.*

ÆI, ÆU, EI, EU, ÆY, ÆW, EY, EW, *sound almost all alike as* I *long and* Y *final in English: e.g. thine or thy* i. dein, *island* i. eiland, *fire* i. feyer *or* fewer, *&c.*

Divers other dialects have as many compound vowels more, proper to every ones pronunciation; as, AI, OI, OU, UI, AY, OY, OW, UY. AA, EE, IE, OO, UU, *&c. but all these we have here (as needless) omitted, provided our spelling natural to our dialect be duly observed.*

Sect. 3. of the Confonants and their Pronunciation.

W *and* Y *are two baſtard letters,* viz. *vowels at their fore part, and confonants at their hinder-part, as being compound,* This *of the vowel* i *and That of* u, *prefixed before the two initial confonants, Here before* i, *and There before* v ; *neither of which (both ſingle and in compoſition) can abide to ſtand after another letter, without being follow'd by a vowel :* e.g. der Mæi *or* Mæyen i. *the May,* freude i. *joy,* ſih frewen i. *to rejoyce,* der tau i. *the dew,* tawen i. *to dew,* &c. *not* Mæy, frewde, taw. *but* W *as a meer confonant may very well ſtand alſo after a confonant, and in the beginning of a word, (after the Engliſh faſhion and pronunciation) which later place* Y *had formerly in our tongue, as well as it has ſtill in the Engliſh.* This *letter we uſe likewiſe in the Greek words for an* v *whereſoever it be, to make them differ from our natives, as the Latins and other learned nations do. they are ſometimes taken one for the other :* e.g. fewer *and* feyer i. *fire,* verdæwen *and* verdeyen i *to digeſt.*

B *after a vowel in the ſame ſyllable, eſpecially before a half-mute* e, *is pronounced as an initial* W *in Engliſh :* e.g. bub *or* bube i. *boy,* beben i. *to tremble,* bleib *or* bleibe i. *ſtay,* &c. *read as if it were written* bu we, be-wen, blei-we.

V *is pronounced by us juſt as by the Engliſh, that is to ſay, ſofter than an* F, *and harder than* V *in French, where it ſounds like our initial* W.

H *(that moſt abuſed letter of all) in the beginning of a ſyllable is a ſingle aſpiration, expreſſed as the Eng-*

lish in these words, that come from ours : e. g. horn,
heart, hunger, hound, &c. never so slightly as in the
original Latin: herb, honour, honest, heir, humour.

This character as a single or soft aspiration ought
(as here shall be taken all possible care) not to be used
after a vowel, as some without reason, nay against
their own manner of pronouncing, too often use to do:
we will write now after our dialect , and as some
of old and still (as well the English as the Low-dutch)
do; e.g. steen i. to stay, Belg staen, geen i. to go, Belg.
gaen, seen i. to see, Belg. sien, schreyen i. to cry,
Belg. schreyen, &c. so rue i. rest, frü or frße i.
early, tuen i. to do, mer or merer i. more, mir i.
to me , dir i. to thee, læte or lœre from lare i.
doctrine, &c. not stehen, gehen, sehen, schrei-
hen, ruhe, frühe, tuhen, mehr or mehrer, mihr,
dihr, lehre or lœhre or old English (in Spencer)
lore. see the foregoing Sect.2. letter E.

Nor after P or T, or any other consonant whatsoe-
ever, except in the Greek words, for the same reason
mentioned above: e.g. Rhetorica, Philanthropia,
Thron.

For as our Ancestors a good while ago left off to
write the H after a P, changing it into F; whereas
the Low-saxonians as well as the Low-dutch and
the English kept onely the P : e.g wafen or waffen,
shaf, hulfe, &c. Engl. weapon , sheep, help. and
of old waphen, shaph, hul ph. whence some still
write Adolph q.d. adel-hûlf, Erphort, &c. so we will
here endeavour (and ought) to follow them in the letter TH, as some already have done before now, retaining onely T and D sufficient for our mouth, not
used to the aspiration of the TH, as there are others,
especially the English and the Arabick : e.g. tuen or

duen *i. to do, Belg.* doen, tewer *or* dewer *i. dear,*
tor *or* dor *i. dore,* taler *(from zalen) i. doller,* rute
or rude *i. rod,* rot *or* rod *i. red, &c.   not as some
write,* thuhen , thewer, thor *or* tohr, thaler *or*
tahler, ruthe *or* ruhte, roth *or* roht.

but H *the double or hard aspiration standing after
a letter in the same syllable (used now by us instead of*
CH, *the Greek words excepted, if you will or must
make use of 'em, e.g.* Christus, Chrysostomus, *&c.)
is pronounced as the English* GH *in, right i.* reht, *sight
i.* gesiht, *flight i.* fluht, *&c. yet somewhat harder
and in the throat, just as the Welchmen their* CH, *or
as the Hebrews their* ה, *and the Grecians their* χ,
*which is (but no more than our letter here) a double
consonant.   see* C.

J, j, *consonant, onely initial, sounds without all
aspiration, as the English* Y *in the beginning of
words : e.g.* jar *i. year,* Jesus , Joseph , jung *i.
young, &c. read as if they were written thus in English,* yaur, Yesus, Yoseph, yoong.

This letter and V *differing both to shape and sound
from the other characters, as well as any of the rest,
are ranked here amongst the consonants, as the Hebrews do their sixth character, and the Armenians
their one and twentieth; which later (viz.) just as ours
hangs down under the line of vowels, and has no stop
over it self.*

G *is pronounced by some as it is in English before*
A, O, U, *and particularly before* e *or* i, *as it is in
these English words that come from ours : e.g. to give
i.*geben, *to begin i.* beginnen, *gests or guests i.*gæste,
gost or ghost i. geist, *a gift or guift given to a bride by
her parents or a dowry i.* ein braut-gift *or* mit-gift,
&c. and always after N: *e.g. to singe i.* singen,

hungry i. hungerig, *&c. where it founds without
all aſpiration, and yet harder than our* J *or the Engliſh* Y ; *but by ſome it is pronounced with a ſmall aſpiration, to make it differ from our* J, *and the double
aſpiration* H; *and yet we do not pronounce it here
neither with the kiſſing tone of the Engliſh in gentle,
general, giant, geometry, or the like words coming from
the Latin, Greek, or other tongues.*

M *after another* M *is changed in ſome dialects of
ours, as in Engliſh into* B, *which the analogy and
derivation does not approve of: e. g.* krumb *or better* krumm *i. crooked*, krümmer *i. more crooked,*
ein kamb *or better* kamm *i. a comb,* kæmmen *i.
to comb*, ein lamb *or* lamm *i. lamb,* di læmmer *i.
lambs, &c. not* krümber, kæmben, læmber.

S *is here always pronounced as by the Low-dutch
or Engliſh* Z *uſed formerly alſo by the old Fran-
konians in the very ſame ſound: e. g.* fuzzo *now*
fuſs *i. foot*, wazzer *now* waſſer *i. water, &c.
whence they of old uſed commonly in the end* ſz *for* ſs,
and tz *for* ts *or now* z. *which ſome ſtill do as well in
writing as printing: e. g.* daſz *i. that,* ſitz *i. ſit, &c.
now* daſs, ſiz. *but never as the ſhort and final* s *of
thoſe Engliſh words that come from ours: e. g. husband, buſineſs, is, wiſdom, &c.*

X *valuing here* HS, *or (as in Engliſh)* KS, *is never uſed by us in the beginning, unleſs of a Greek or
other ſtrange word: e. g.* Xerxes, Xeuxes, &c.

C *before* E *and* I, *likewiſe* T *before an* I *followed
by another vowel, are both pronounced as* TS, *and
elſewhere as in Engliſh ; but we make uſe of them
now onely in Latin, or other words derived from
thence: e.g* contradiciren *i. to contradict,* conclu-
diren *i. to conclude,* concediren *i. to grant, Cicero,*

contradiction, portion, contribution, &c. read *as if they were spelled thus,* contraditſiren, contſediren, Tſitſero, contradictſion, portſion, contributſion ; *not* Siſero, porſhion, *&c. in lieu of theſe two letters , viz.* C *and* T *, when they are ſoft (that is, ſtanding before* E *or* I) *we take as well after a conſonant as before a vowel, the fifth double letter, to wit,* Z *, pronounced now a days as in Italian, or as* TS *in Engliſh ; which two letters both to geminate is not more (though hugely and groſly) abſurd, than it is to double their equivalent (in ſhape ſingle, but in ſound and ſtrength double) character* Z *, or any of the Greek* ζ, ξ, φ, χ, ψ, *and the like of other poliſhed tongues. Therefore we write, e.g.* zuzien *i. to tie together,* zerfezen *i. to cut in pieces,* ſezen *i. to ſet,* fizen *i. to ſit,* kurze hœlzer *i. ſhort woods,* puzen *i. to put : and pronounce as ſome of them were of old written,* tſu-tſien, tſerfets-en, ſets-en, ſits-en, puts-en, kurtſe, hœlts-er. *but not* ſezzen, ſizzen, puzzen, kurzze, hœlzzer, *&c. the which value in pronunciation as much as if they were written after this manner ,* ſetſtſen, ſitſtſen, putſtſen, kurtſtſe, hœltſtſer, *as ſome Cacocriticks baſely uſe to do, out of no other ground and reaſon than being either deceived by the old Frankonian and new Italian tongues, or infatuated by a mere fancy to novelty.*

C *when hard (as it is before* A, O, U, *or a conſonant) is changed here by us, as well before a* K *, as before any of the other letters, into* K *, and* QU *into* KW *, with no leſs reaſon than the Latines do uſe either* C *or* CC *, the Grecians either* K *or* KK *, the Hebrews either a* כ *or* ק *, and we our ſelves either* f, l, ſ, *&c. or* ff, ll, ſſ, *&c. according to the vowel preceding either long or ſhort : e.g.* ein kanker *i. a kanker,*

kærker *i. prifon*, ein kunft-fakk *i. a fack of arts,*
ein kindes-kleid *i. a garment for a child*, eine kræu-
ter-kwelle *i. a well where herbs ufe to grow*, ein
zukker-bækker *i. a confectioner*, *&c.* fo kalb,
korn, kommen, *&c. not as of old and ftill the Eng-*
lifh, calb *i. calf*, corn *i. corn*, commen *i. to come.*

but C *ftanding before the double afpiration* H, *fhall*
henceforward be quite omitted by us, as it was for-
merly by the old Saxonians every where, and is ftill
to this very day by the Englifh after an S: *e.g. a*
fifh, frefh, to wafh, to wifh, &c.

and *immediately after an* S *the letter* H (*followed*
by any other confonant but R *in the fame fyllable*) *fhall*
as well as its C, *and fo both together be left out here,*
as it is done not onely in the forementioned dialects,
but in the Low-Saxonick alfo and the Belgick, to
leffen the tedeous, and more than jewifh and fnakifh
hiffing found of the Swabifh pronunciation, flipt by
degrees from thence as into fome others, fo likewife into
that of ours : e. g. flafen *i. to fleep*, fporren *i. fpur,*
flipferig *i. flippery*, ftall *i. ftall*, fmuzig *i. fmutty,*
fmaragd *i. fmaragd a precious ftone*, fmeifen *i. to*
fmite, ftille *i. ftill*, fnorren *i. to fnort*, fteif *i. ftiff*,
fpreiten *i. to fpread*, fwan *i. fwan*, flav *i. flave*,
fplitter *i. fplitter*, fhrapen *i. to fcrape*, *&c. not*
fchlafen, fchporren, fchlippferig, fchtall, fchmn-
zig, fchmaragd, fchmeifen, fchtille, fchnorren,
fchteif, fchpreiten, fchwan, fchlave *or* sklave *Ital.*
fchiavo ; fchplitter, fchrapen, *as fome either in*
writing or pronouncing love to fpell, perfuading them-
felves, that their words will be the fuller of no leffer
myfteries than grace and emphafis, the fuller they
take both their mouth and their pen.

Those good men both in schools and chanceries, that have the lot to make their whole study, onely business, and daily practice, in nothing else but in spelling letters, and are therefore looked upon by some as Grand-masters of Orthography, most commonly use to write thus: e g. schnaacke, vieh *or* viehe, schwartz, schnee schneh *or* schnehe, *&c. instead of* snake *i.* snail, vi (*of old* fio) *i.* cattel, swarz *i.* swarthy *or* black, sne *i. snow: where every one may see, that almost the moiety of letters is as needless to the good pronunciation, as the fifth wheel would be to a waggon.*

and because not every one has a mind or occasion to bestow time and charges upon searching out antiquities, to acquaint himself with the old spelling, there as well as here used by us, we shall add two examples, but in few words, which will (according to a Spanish proverb) be sufficient for a wise and understanding man, whereas one that's deceived by a false conceit and long use, dotes upon the unproportionable spelling which he is brought up by, will (though convinced) hardly be perswaded by all reasons and books to the contrary, none being so deaf as he that will not hear. Mind therefore how sutable the old spelling (as far as it is here in question) be to the pronunciation of our dialect, when Somner in his Etymologicon cites out of the first book of Beda's History the following words ; ih gefeo othre æ on minum leomum withfeohtende there *æ* mines modes: *and the beginning of the Confession of sins used of old by the German Church, and set before Otfrid's Gospel-book is this;* ih wirdu Gote almahtigen bigihtig inti allen Gotes heilagon, allero suntono, unrehtero githanco, unrehtero worto, *&c. word by word in our dialect,* ih see andre ee (*now* gefez) an meinen glidern

mit- (wider-) fehtende der ee meines mut
-es (*or* gemûtes : *and*, ih werde Gotte all-
mæhtigen beihtig und allen Gottes heiligen,
aller fünden, unrehter gedanken, unrehter
worte ; *in the English word by word :*
I fee an other law of my limbs withfighting
the law of my mind : *and*, I am to God almighty confeffing, and to all Gods holy o-
nes, all fins, unright thoughts·, unright
words. *where in the words* gefeo *and* æ *or*
(*as* Kilian *in his dictionary writes*) ee, *or* (*as* Otfrid *Matth.* 19.)·E. *we fee left out the needles* H
*having after an letter of the fame fyllable, the
found of an hard afpiration,* vs *in* ih, feohtende,
almahtigen, unrehtero *&c. likewife in* urfu-
ah *now* urfahe *i. caufe,* thuruh *now* durh *i.
through,* manflaht *i. manflaughter &c. of the
fame force was this letter alfo in the beginning of a fyllable before a confonant e.g.* hla-
ford *, inftead whereof the English have now
Lord i.* grofer herr, Hrift *i. Chrift, &c. but
afterwards when thofe that love too well either
the immoderate afpiration, or long words and
full lines,* (*to make the reader pay the dearer
for their writings*) *put the fingle afpiration
into the place of the double; this was forc'd
to be changed by divers dialects into divers
other characters,* C, K, CK, HH, HCH, CH,
CHCH, GH, *&c. fo we find e. g.* Crift *and*
Krift *i. Chrift, in Welch* Ghrift Crift Grift
or Chrift, reich *i. rich. Gal.* riche, *Belg.*
ryck, *Ital.* ricco, *and in plur.* ricchi *or* ricche;
ich ic ick *i.* I, boc buch boeck *i. book, &c.
likewife* fprahchlos *and* fprachlos *i. fpeech-*

Œ

less, radalihho *i.honest*, unredihaftlihhiu *i.
that have not reason*, deomuatliho *i. humbly*,
deomuatlihha pigiht *i. humle confession*, ru-
ahchalofe *or* ruahhalofe *i. carelefs ones*, lachen
lahchen *or* lachchen *i. to laugh, &c. fee at
your leafure the books written in the Anglo-faxo-
nick dialect, a good many whereof are kept alfo
here in the Englifh libraries.*

*of thefe confonants confidered hitherto, are
made divers compound ones, fome whereof
being of two fingle letters, have but a fingle
found like a fingle confonant, and ftand onely
in the end of a fyllable after a vowel to make
it fhort e.g.* bb, ff, ff, ll, *&c. never in the beginning as* LL *does in* Spanifh *nor as* DD, FF,
LL *in* Welch. *and fome others, that be as of
different letters, fo likewife of a mixt found,
which they give one another, ftanding onely
either in the beginning of a fyllable e.g.* bl, fr,
ftr, pfl, kw, *&c. or in its end e.g.* md, ng,
rh, lz, fht, *&c. or on both fides e.g.* ft, pf,
tfh, *&c. every one letter of both forts
with its vowel whatfoever ought to be pronounced together, and in one breath, as if it had one
onely character like one of the double confonants.
fee the following fection, and chap.*3. *fect.* 1.

'Tis known, that the Hebrews, *when they
would geminate a confonant made a ftrong
dagefh in the midft of it, and the* Latins *ufed
a great letter inftead of a double e.g.* fuMa,
foSa, *&c. but the* Spaniards *have ftill their
Tilde (as they call it) over the letter* N *onely,
and the* Germans *ufed till now a ftroke over* M *and*
N *when to be doubled e.g.* koñen *i. to come,*

reſien *i. to run, &c.the which we might imitate
alſo in the reſt of the letters, and uſe but a ſingle
le charaɛter marked at the head, this novelty
being not ſo ſtrange to us, as that would be to ſome, if we ſhould find out (and could agree upon)
certain ſingle letters in ſhape , inſtead of the
compound as well conſonants as vowels, made
uſe of hitherto not onely by us, but alſo by all
Europe beſides.*

Chap.II. of the Orthographia.

Seɛt.1. of the Spelling or Compoſiti-
on of Letters into Syllables and
Words.

Ike as all ſublunary things, nay the *Moon*
 herſelf, and the greateſt Empires, ſuffer
their either natural or fatal change ; ſo our and
every other Language has from time to time ſome
alteration. beſides this, our learned Men in the
beginning of writing, and afterwards of printing books, were often forced to yield unto the
unreaſonable proceedings of the *Amanuenſes*
and *Printers*, which they had then as great want
of, as theſe of skill, no leſs than of fit tools
and neceſſary materials ; inſomuch that we ought
not at all to look upon their ſometimes bad ſpelling as a patern for our imitation, but rather
to pity their caſe and to mend their defeɛt. for
the infancy of arts, and the ſcarcity of commo-
dities they then lived in, muſt excuſe them by all
means, but it will not in the leaſt us now, now at
this preſent Age, when all ſciences flouriſh abun-
dantly, and wiſdom does not want any commodity.

*nor plenty knowledge', to order all things hand-
somly according to the ἀκρίβεια and exa'ness
of Arts. We will therefore maigre all opposition, and in spight of envy her self, endeavour as we have begun to purge our writings possi-
bly of their innocent faults, which the injury
of time succeeding made worse and worse, and
are now a days become so grofs and enormous,
that surely neither wife Antiquity, nor the now
living learned world (void of prejudice) will
blame us for a sober and moderate Reforma-
tion (which in its self was not a whit more neces-
fary either in Religion or in experimental Philo-
fophy then this is) undertaken here in our tongue,
the foundation whereof is so well and wisely laid
by its first builder almighty God himself, that
hardly an other language in the whole world
(unlefs perhaps the new Philofophical) can as in
fome other preheminences, fo herein be parallel'd
with it. for here is never a letter wanting, as there
is in that of the Perfians, leaving out fometimes
in writing divers letters, which they add in pronouncing; nor is here any filent or quiefcent,
as we find feveral in the Hebrew, Chaldaick,
Samaritan, and other Oriental tongues; nor fuper-
fluous neither, as muft be in the French, English,
Lufitanick and fome other hybrid fpeeches upon the
account of derivation. in fine, as our letters mentioned in the foregoing chapter, are fufficient
to the expreffion and pronunciation of our dialect; fo we do always pronounce both vowels and confonants, wherefoever we find
them. and becaufe none of thefe is foundable with
-out one of thofe others, as the principal ingre-*

dients of *syllables*; *we do quicken and enliven
each consonant with its next vowel either preceding or following*, *like the Æthiopians,
that never separate any of their seven vowels
from the six and twenty consonants. For
without any doubt, the farther the expression
and sound of a consonant is from its vowel,
the harder is also the way of spelling, especially
for beginners and children, as every one may easily
find it to be true in his own language, as in Hebrew* e.g. Adam, aleph *and* kamez *spells*
A, dalet kamez *and* mem *spells* dam , &c. *in
Greek* e.g. Kyrios , kappa Ypsilon *spells* Ky,
rho jota *spells* ri, omicron sigma *spells* os,
&c. *in English* e. g. double v , ach,
i,ce, ach *spells* which *or* huitsh; er, o, u, ge,
ach *spells* rough *or* ruff, &c. *in French* e. g.
te-e-em-pe-es-sp. tang, &c. *On the
contrary, this must needs be the nearest and the
clearest way of spelling, which expresses the letters, as they found in the very act of composition,
taking the life and strength from the vowel that
they are to bejoyned withall: e. g.* de-e-
es *spells* des ; we-e-es sp. wes, e-en sp.
en; ha-a sp. ha, te-e-er sp. ter ; ka-
sp. ka, be-e-el sp. bel; de-c-er sp. der ;
te-e sp. te, ge-c-en sp. gen. *so likewise,*
fa-a-ag sp. fag , e-et sp. et ; i-ir sp. ir;
re-e-ed sp. red, li-i-ih sp. lih; zu-u sp.
zu ; wa-a-as sp. was ; ma-a-an sp. man;
fo-o-or sf. for, de-c-er sp. der, c-en sp.
en ; mu-u-us sf. mus. *The same is
done also in the compound Consonants, the mem-
bers 1 hereof as in pronunciation, so in spelling*

never *ought to be separated one from the other*
e.g. kwe-e-etſh ſp. kwetſh; ha-a-and ſp. hand,
lu-u-ung ſp. lung , flu-u-uſs ſp. fluſs , ſhæ-
æ-ærz ſp. ſhærz, &c, *but to avoid*
the teadious repetition of the whole ſound of a
compound vowel , we uſe to divide it here in
ſpelling, (though never in pronouncing ſo groſly,
and in writing not a all) taking one part of it to
the precedent conſonant, and the other to the
following, if there be any e.g. pfa-a-u ſp. pfau, ve-
e-en ſp. uen; bræ-æ-u ſt. bræu, ve-e-et ſp. vet ;
          fre-e-iſt. frei, je-e-er ſp. jer.

Sect.2. of Dividing Words into Sylla-
bles.

the common Grammar-Maxim is : qui͜ bene diſtinguit, bene docet *i. he , that diſtin-*
guiſheth well, does teach well; and we may here as
truly ſay: he hath the right knack of a good pro-
nunciation, the very ſoul of a living language,
that well compounds and well divides the letters
and words into ſyllables. *of the ſpelling*
we have treated in the foregoing ſection, but of
the ſeparation of one ſyllable from the other,
we obſerve this conſtant rule : ut vox
componitur , ita divellitur; *that is, as a*
word (both in derivation and in compoſition of
others) is compound, ſo it is divided into
its parts for Analogy, and better pronunciati-
ons ſake e. g. all-ein, über-all, war-um, ver-
aht-en, ent-on-ig-en, be·læſt-ig-et, un-aus-
en-bleïb-lih-er, &c. *where the addition (though*
it ſignifie nothing of it ſelf) muſt be ſounded by
it ſelf as well as either the primitive or the ſingle

word. for those letters (be they single, double, or compound ones) that the right use, and the true pronunciation has joyned, and stand together in the end of a word, the same ought in no wise to be separated one from the other, but may stand together also in the end of a syllable, e. g. trœst-er, hafs-en , kwetsh-ung-en , ver-aht-ung, &c. *likewise note, that considering the feeblenefs of the half-mute* E *never pronounced without an other letters help, it should not (especially being final) be separated from the precedent syllable (as the strength which that* E *relieth upon) to make here for it self a perfect and complete syllable, as it does in meeter, much like to the Sheva of the Hebrews, the sound of both being as swift to the ear, as lightnig is to the eye.* this *general rule is not onely useful here, but necessary also in that compendious way of uniting one word with an other by Hyphen, where the last syllable of the foregoing words (as mente in the Spanish tongue, when two or more adverbs meet immediately) is always elegantly omitted and pronounced afterwards in the last of all, as being the very same e.g.* gereht-weif-und gütig-er Gott , du geb-und erhalt er aller fo-wol ewig-und himmlish-als zeitlih-und irdifh-en dinge *i. just , wife, and good God, thou giver and preferver of all things, as well eternal and heavenly , as temporal and earthly* ; di fo notwendig-als heilfame vorfpreh-und verfœn-ung unferes erlœf-und feligmah-ers wird von allen fromm- und glæubig-en feken gelib-und ge-.

lob-et *i. our Redeemers and Saviours media-
tion and expiation, both neceſſary and profitable
is loved and praiſed by all godly and faithful
ſouls* ; diſes iſt das aller breit-læng und
dikk-eſte ſwert ; jenes aber das etwas
ſmæl-kůrz-und dinn-ere *i. this is the broadeſt,
longeſt, and thickeſt ſword, but that is ſomewhat
ſmaller , ſhorter, and thinner.*

Sect. 3. of the Abjection of Letters, and the Shortning of Words in Writing.

*when You find a word noted with the ſign of
apoſtrophus , you may boldly think that it is put
here in ſtead of an* E, *either alone or with one of
the two like conſonants immediately going before, in which caſe the ſign is commonly left
away e.g.* getren't *or* getran't, gélib't *torne, i.
loved ,* gchoff't *, hoped, des* ſhiff's *, of the
ſhip,* des buh's *i. of the book ,* des ſand's *i. of
the ſand, &c. Elſe without the Apoſtrophus* getrennet, gelibet, gehoſtet, ſhiffes, buhes,
fandes *in diminutivs, and ſometimes
(eſpecially in meeter) in other words it ſtands
alſo (when written, which we ſeldom do here)
in lieu of a ſhort* i : *e. g.* das mæus'gen *i. the
little mouſe,* ein glæs'gen *i. a little glaſs,*
hcil'ger *i. holy,* Teut'ſh *i. Dutch,* befælt'gen
i. to faſten or confirm, überwælt'gen *i. to over-
power, &c. where you ſee it moſt commonly
ſtand before the ſyllable* G E ; *for* mæuſi-
gen, glæſigen, heiliger, befæſtigen, t̃ber-
wæltigen, Teutiſh.

we use likewise or ought to use always *this token of shortning words, when we put away the former letters of the pronouns* derer, irer, *and* es *standing after a verb, and of the definite article especially in the masculine and neuter gender, standing after a preposition* e. g. si leg'ten 'er vike in's gefæng'nifs , *they put many of 'em into the prison for* legeten, irer *or* derer inn das; er rapp't *or* rap't 'er dreye *(scil.* æp'el) mit 'r hand aus 'm korbe , *he took three of 'em (scil. apples) with his hand out of the basket, for* rappete, irer, der, dem ; ir werdet 's glauben, wenn ir 's verfuh't hab't , *you will believe it after you have tried or tasted it, for* es, verfuh-et, habet ; si ging' auf's feld, durh 'n garten, *&c. she went into the field through the garden, for* ginge, auf das, durh den ; *so we say (and should write) for shortness*, i'm *i*. inn dem, zu'm *i*. zu dem, zu'n *i*. zu den, zu'r *i*. zu der, an's *i*. an das, auf's *i*. auf das, unter's *i*. unter das, über'n *i*. über den, über's *i*. über das, *&c. but we never (as the English and the Low-dutch do) take away a letter by the apostrophus, unless there precede some word or other :* e. g. es ist war, es ist *or* wird gefag't *i. 'tis true, 'tis said, Belg.*'t *(for* het) is waar , 'tis gefeyt , *&c. and when* E *or* I *stand betwixt two consonants either of the same or like sound, this elision or crasis (especially without its sign) is not at all to be used, to avoid obscurity of words, the spelling whereof can not distinctly be heard* e g. des haufes *i. of the house*, des shazes *i. of* the *treasure*, der sinnen *i.* of *the senses*, er isset *i. he eateth*, es sneidet *i. it cuts*, du hassest *i.* thou *hatest*, &c. *not* des haus's, shaz's, der sinn'n *or* sin'n, iss't *or* is't, sneit, hast; *where in the two first we do not hear all the letters, and the rest of the words may be mistaken for others*, der sinn *i.* the *sense*, er ist *i.* he *is*, es sneit *or* sneyet *i.* it *snows*, du hast *i.* thou *hast.* so much of the shortning of syllables both in pronunciation and in writing. the abbreviation of syllables and words onely in writing is made by a single stop as in English : e. g.

H. *or* Hl.	heilig, heiliger, &c. *holy.*	
Hr.	herr, *Sir, Master, Lord.*	
Fr.	frawe, *married Lady.*	
Jfr.	jungefrawe, *married*	*mrs,*
	jungfrawe, *unmarried*	
-l.	lih, liher, lihes, &c. *--ly.*	
næml.	næmlih, *namely, viz. to wit.*	
gl.	gleihsam, *qs. or as if it were.*	
d.i.	das ist, *that is.* *(ample.*	
a.z.b.	als zu'm beispile, *as for ex-*	
u.a.m.	und anders mer, *and others more.*	
u.d.g.	und dergleihen, *and such like.*	
u.s.f.		*fort, ferner*
u.s.w.	und so	*weiter* &c.
u.s.f.a.		*fort an*
s.d.1.t.	sie den 1. teil, *see the 1. part.*	
s.d. 2.bl.	sie das 2. blat, *see the 2. leaf.*	
s d 1.s.	sie di 1. seite, *see the 1. side.*	
s.d.3.z.	sie di 3 zeile, *see the 3. line.*	
a ! z !	*a as !the beginning and the end*	

read as if they were written

other abbreviations, proper to several sciences and arts, we omit here, adding onely that of the cabbalistick numeration, common as well to our as to any other language. for as the Hebrews and the Grecians, instead of numeral words used the letters of their alphabets, beginning again after the tenth letter: so the Germans (and the other Western Christians) about some hundred years ago left to write the numeral words in common writing and accounts, using since There the figures 1,2,3,&c. which they learned of the Arabians, and these of the Indians, but in grave writings of concern, and upon certain occasions, they still make use both of the numeral words, and onely of seven peculiar letters of their alphabet, as the Latins did, viz.

Germ.	E,	I,	A,	S,	O,	W,	U,
Latin.	I,	V,	X,	L,	C,	D,	M,
Arab.	1	5	10	50	100	500	1000

as for example,

gib' uns doh, Herr! den ædlen friden wider

or

Gott gibet uns den ædlen friden wider.

where either of the verses does contain the number

1 6 8 0.

Chap. III. of the *Orthotonia*, or the Right Modulating of Syllables and Words.

AS *Orthophonia and Orthographia handle of Letters and Syllables considered in their*

*Effence: fo Profodia treateth of Syllables in their
Quality and Quantity, that is, how to found
and to pronounce the fame right with their natural tone and proper accent, which is to make a
fyliable in a word long or fhort, foft or fharp,
without which the learner cannot know, how to
pronounce the tongue, much lefs to be underftood
when he fpeaks it; whereby he fhall not onely be
difgraced, but driven alfo to beftow longer time
in forgetting that ill touch taken up, than he
might be in going forward in learning ten times
as much. the which being carefully looked unto
at the firft, can not but much adorn the fpeaker,
making himfelf underftood, as well as giving
himfelf exceeding comfort in going forward,
when he knoweth, that he fingeth true harmony,
efpecially when he well obferves the pointing annexed thereunto.*

Sect. 1. of the Quality and Quantity of Syllables, i. of their either foftnefs and length or fharp-nefs and fhortnefs.

*a vowel is then here faid to be long, when we
take longer time to pronounce it ; and fhort,
when fhorter time. Each of the fingle vowels
and of the improper dipthongs is foft and long,
unlefs followed by a double or a compound conjo-
nant ; or elfe in fome particles, and all the final
terminations of polyfyllabicks having but one
confonant, which ends the fyllable, where the
vowel is pronounced fharp and fhort; e.g.*

soft and long:	*sharp and short:*

das *hoc*, lam *lame*, wal **A** dass *ut*, lamm *lamb*,
choice, stal *steel*, haken   wall *wall*, stall *stable*,
hooks, kan *boat*, kal   hakken *dig*, kanne *can*
bare, blasen *to blow*, al   kalt *cold*, verblassen
eel, ale *awle*, sagen *to*   *to become pale*, all *ali,*
say, wagen *wagon or to*   sahen *things*, wahen
venture, faren *to ride.*   *watch*, farren *bullocks*

kæme *came*, læmer **Æ** kæmme *combs*, læm-
lamer, hæsgen *little*   mer *lambs*, hæfsgen
hare, kæler barer, fæl-   *hatred*, kælter *cold*
en *to fail.*   fællen *to make fall.*

den *hunc*, wen *whom*, **E** denn *for*, wenn *when*,
her *hither*, wesen *es-*   herr *fir*, wefsen *whofe*
sence, shelen *to pare.*   shellen *little bells.*

hœle *hole*, grœfer **œ** hœlle *hell*, grœfser
greater, shœfe *laps*,   *greater*, shœfse *shots*,
hœrer *hearer.*   hœrner *horns.*

ofen *oven*, rose *rofe* ›**O** offen *open*, rosse *hor-*
wol *well*, dem sone *to*   *fes*, wolle *wooll*, sonne
the *son*, oder *or*, ih   *sun*, otter *odder*, di
wone *I dwell.*   wonne *pleafure.*

siden *to stede*, ire *her*, **I** fitten *manners*, ih
stil *stiel*, shaubine   irre *I err*, stillen
theatre, ime *to him*,   *appeace*, binne *or*
in *him*, dinen *to ferve*,   imme *a bee*, inn *into*,
wifen *medows*, fig   dinnen *to thinne*,
victory, dir *to thee*,   wiffen *know*, fih *him*
wider *again or tow-*   felf, dirre *dry*, widder
    ard.   ram, gewitter *feafon.*
kåfen *to chufe*, flûf- **û** kûffen *to kifs or a bid-*

ff

or flifen *to flow*, fâlen   *low*, flûffen *or* fliffen
or filen *to fele*, mûter   *flow*, fûllen *to fill*,
more weary, fûr *be-*   mûtter *mothers*,fûrft
fore hâte *bats*.   *prince*, hûtte *hutte*.

das mus *or* mos *mofs*,   U wir muffen *or* mûffen
futer *load*,di bufte *re-*   *we muft*, futter *food*,
pentance, fnuren *fna-*   ih buffe *I bufs*, fnurr
res.   *-en to fnort*.

obferve 1. *thofe words and fyllables*, (*be they
particles or final terminations*, *fignifying of
themfelves nothing*) *from whence no other word
or fyllable can be derived*, *or the vowel whereof* (*if they admit any derivation*) *remains foft
and long*; *they have always one onely confonant e. g.* mis-ver-ftand, unver-ftand-ig,
un-ver-ftænd-ig-er , un-ver-ftænd-ig ere,
un-ver ftænd-ig-er-en ; man *the indefinit
particle ftanding before an imperfonal verb*, des
the definit article i. *of the*, bis i. *untill*, &c. *fo
likewife*, *as we have feen juft before :* das, den ,
wen, her, in &c. *to make the three firft
differ in fpelling*, (*as the reft of them do as
well in pronouncing as fpelling*, *and all together in
fignification*) *from* defs *or* deffen *the demon-
ftrative particle* i. *of that*, ein mann *a man*,
ein bifs *or* biffen *a bit* ; dafs, denn, wenn,
herr, inn, *which laft word has its derivation
in others*, *as* inner *or* innerhalb *and* binnen
within, &c. *it is alfo to be found with a double
N both in old written records and printed
books* ; *but being an eye-fore to fome*, *it may
(when prefix'd before a word beginning with a*

conſonant) *loſe either of the two* N, *as other
particles, without any mark:* e. .g. ingleihen *or*
imgleihen, &c. *but the terminations* inn *and* iſs
or uſs *have now with ſome a ſingle, and then with
others a double* N, or *but the later ſpelling is better,
becauſe they are capable of receiving an other vow
-el,* the *which makes the foregoing* i *or* ů *ſoft
and long, if the following conſonant be not gemi-
nated, as its ſharp and ſhort ſound does require,
contrary to the terminations* en, er, et, &c. e. g.
müll-er, müll-er-inn, müll-er-inn-en; ſhæf-
er, ſhæf-er-inn, ſhæf-er-inn-en ; zeug-
nľſs *or* zeug-niſs, von zeug-näſs-en *or* zeug-
niſs-en, &c. *and that is to be noted every where
in the whole derivation of all other words what
ſoever, as a ſure and infallible rule, how to
know, when and where a ſingle or a double conſonant is to be uſed after ſuch vowels.*

2. *as no compound conſonant of two like letters
may ſtand after an other conſonant in the ſame
ſyllable, e.g.* freind *friend,* feind *feind or
enemy,* find *are,* berg *mountain,* burg *caſtle,*
werfen *tothrow,* und *or (as it was ſpelt formerly
by ſeveral people* unt *and, &c. never* freindt,
feindt, findt, bergk, burgk, werffen, undt *or
(which no body can read)* vnndt
&c. *this and ſuch like unreaſonable and baſe
ſpelling gave occaſion (and its patrons now are
acceſſory) to ſome heinous ſlanders laid upon that
ſweet language: ſo likewiſe no long ſingle
vowel may ſtand either before a double conſonant,
or before a compound one of two like letters,
which later is to be obſerved alſo of any di-*

pthong, as being of its nature long; but if it fall
out, that in derivation of a word they meet in one
syllable, perhaps contrary to the pronunciation
of its dialect, then either the dipthong is changed
into a short vowel, e.g. shaufelen or shoffelen
to scuffle, eine shaufel shoffel or shuffel a scuffle, saufen to drink like a beast, gesoffen
drunken, ein saufer sxufer or siffel a beast-like
drinker or drunken sot, pfeifen to whistle,
gepfifen whistled, smeisen to smite, ge-
smitten smitten, &c. see more of them Part 2.
Chap. 3 Sect 3. not shauffelen, shauffel saust-
en, saufter, or sæuffer, pfeiffen, smeissen;
or the double consonant is turned into its opposite single, e.g. sprahen or sprehen to speak,
Belg. spreken or spreecken, where in our
tongue a or e characteristick is sharp and short,
whence ein gespræh a discourse, eine sprahe a
language, wenn er sprähe when he should say,
&c. where this vowel is still of the same sound
in our dialect; but in others, where it is soft
and long, the words ought to be spelt ein ge-
spræg, eine sprage, sprægе.   and on
the contrary, the single consonant of a soft and
long vowel in another dialect or signification
pronunced sharp and short, ought to be turned into
its opposite double or compound; e.g. der wæg
or weg the way, hin bence, di stad or statt the
city, di stædle or stætte the cities, der steg the
little foot bridge, huner and hünder, chic-
kens, geet hinn-weh go from hence or away,
ih steh'or stehe I prick, &c. which anti-
stæchon or changing letters into others, is very
usual not onely in English and Low-dutch, but

also in the Greek tongue. lastly note, that the apostrophe doth never change either the quality, quantity or accent, much less the letters of a word .g.e. geplag't, gefür't, verſœn't, geleer't, verlor'n, geſin't, getren't, i'm, über'n, &c. where the firſt five are as ſoft and long, but the other four as ſharp and ſhort, as they were before the ſyncopation: geplaget plagued, gefüret leaded, verſœnet reconciled, gelæren learned, verloren loſt, geſinnet mind ed, getrennet torn in pieces, inn dem in the, über' den over the. For the turning the termination of the paſſive participle in endet or ennet, this into ant and the other into an d, is rather an anomaly than ſyncope, and therefore we never uſe here the ſign of the Apoſtrophus, as we doe elſe where.

Sect. 2. of the Quantity of Syllables and Words in reſpect to their Accents, that make 'em either riſe or fall in pro nouncing.

Although we can not paint the tone, nor write the quantity of a ſyllable or word, nor ought we (as ſome preſume) to do ſo much as to expreſs in any of the Europæan tongues the ſigns thereof ; yet they are both the greateſt help to the giving a due ſound to words or ſyllables, and therefore it will be neceſſary, that we endeavour here to

*make appear, upon what syllable (if there be
more than one) the tonick accent is to be placed,
that is to shew, which syllable we must lift
up, and which suppresse in the pronunciation of
polysyllabick words, as we have done in their
lengthening and shortening. mind then but this
one general rule well: Every true both High-
and Low-dutch Radix has its tonick accent,
(and that either soft when the syllable is long,
or sharp when the syllable is short) in the first
syllable, where it still remains both in derivatius
and compounds: e.g.* Gott *God,* goettlih *godly,* goettliher *godlier,* gottes-furht *godlinefs,*
Kœnig *King,* kœniglih *kingly,* kœnigreih
*Kingdom, &c. more examples see in the
whole-second Part. the same holds also in the
compounds of these particles here following,
which for emphasis-sake draw upon themselves
the accent from those words, they are compounded
withall:* ab, after, an, auf, aus, bei, durh,
ein, fæil, fort, fûr, gegen, her, hinn, hinter,
los, mis, mit, nah, nehen, nider, oh, oben,
ober, samt, über, um, un, unter, vor, weh *or*
weg, wider, zu. *but the other inseparable particles leave the tonick accent to the first syllable
of the words, which they are compounded
with:* be, em, ent; er, ge, inn *or* in, re,
ver, zer; *the very same do also some of the separable ones, when they upon certain occasion lose
their emphasis, as* durh, gegen, her, hinn,
um *or* unim, &c. *construed with another such
or like particle; e.g.* durhaus, gegenüber,
hingegen, hergegen, hin wider, umfonft,
zuvor, fûrwar, &c. *so likewife* durh, her,

hinn, hinter, nider, über, um, unter, wider
*&c. construed with verbs either of a special
and emphatick signification, or used in respect and
opposition to its contrary verb* ; *e.g.* ein mann
kann zwar di ganze ftatt inn einer ftunde
durhfáren, aber niht durhgéen; *a man can
in one hour ride, but not go through the whole
city.* ir foltet niht widerréden, was ir
niht zuvorher überléget habet ; *you should
not contradict what you have not before considered well.* er wird feinen feind niht fo
bald umbringen als umringen; *he will not
fo foon kill as furround his enemy.* ein únter-
ríhter *an underjudge,* and unterríhter *a
teacher,* übergében *to deliver up, and* übergében *to give,* úmfhréiben *to write over, and*
umfhréiben *to write about, &c. but have a
care that you do not miftake one compound word
(having the accent in its firft fyllable) for two
fingle ones, the later whereof draws the tonick
accent from the preceding particle upon it felf* :
e.g. fi kommen, dafs fi zúfeen und zúhœeren
wollen, niht aber gefeen oder gehœeret zu
werden ; *they come to fee and to hear, but not
to be feen or heard.* übermorgen *the next day,*
über mórgen will er fih niht bekümmern
he will have no care for to morrow, &c.
be-zeit *or* bei zeit *i. early,* mit reht *i. juftly,*
nebenbei *or* neben bei *i. hard by,* óben-
hinn *i. above, or* oben hinn *i. fimply, &c. in
all the derivative words we have none elfe to
except, but thofe fubftantives that end in* ei *or*
eye, *which have the accent in the laft fyllable
of all e.* g. gafterei *i. feafting,* hurerei *i. whore-*

dom, fopperei *i. foppery,* flaverei *i. flavery,*
bäbereye *i. knavery.* *as several little*
words and prepositive particles seem to lose
their tonick accent like the Encliticks in Greek:
so divers long and compounded ones seem to
have more than one such accent, just as in the
Spanish and the English tongues e. g. ein
únergrúndliher glaubens-artikel *i. an unsear-*
chable article of faith ; di übermæfigen auf-
fneideréyen , *the immoderate boastings and*
braggings, ein únerhört-und únbefhréib-
liher chriften-verfolger , *a cruell persecutor*
of the christians ; der áller-únbarmherzigfte
the most unmercifull ; der áller-únmcnfhlig-
fte *the most inhumane* ; der állerúnbegréif-
ligfte , *the most incomprehensible &c.* *we*
as well as the Grecians and the Latins use to ac-
centuate the Ebrew and other orientall propre na-
mes indifferently either in the last syllabe save one
or save two e g. Elías , Jehóva , Jerúfalem,
Bethlehem &c. . . *but other foreign words as*
well those , that are naturalized in our toung ,
as any one elfe disowned and never or seldom used
by us in good language , doe most commonly keep
here their accent in the very same syllabe , where
they had it before , as in the Greek ein ftratiòt ,
ϛϱατιω'της *or soldier* , Georg , γεωϱγὸς
a propre name , ein *prophet* , πϱοφή-
της , eine académíe *or* académíe . α'κα-
δη μια *or* α'κεδήμεια *&c. in the Latin* di
nature, *natura,* cine perfóne, *perfona,* eine
famílie , *familia ,* purgíren, *purgare,* ftu-
díren , *ftudere &c.* *in the French* monfièur,
madáme , courtefíe , manière *&c. fo likes*

wiſe di majeſtæt, authoritæt, qualitæt, &c.
immediatly coming either from the Italian ma-
jeſtáte, autoritáte, qualitáte ; *or from the
Spaniſh* majeſtàd, authoritàd, qualitàd. *not
as the Engliſh* próphet ácademie, náture,
pèrſon, fámilie, mounſer, mádame, cúr-
tǽſie, mánner, májeſtie, authórity, quá-
lity.

*This conſidered together with our ge-
nerall rule and other obſervations preceding,
will give us ſome ſure marks and certain ſigns,
whereby not only we , but alſo any ſtranger in
our toung may preſently know the moſt part of
our both ſuſpected and other mungrell words from
the true natives.* I. *thoſe, that have a letter
contrary to our truly antient and reformed
alphabet, are either Greek words, as*

C H *e. g chronike, Chriſt chor, &c.*
P H *e.g. phantaſei, Theophil, Philip, &c.*
R H *e.g. Rhetoric, myrrhe, &c*
T H *e. g. thron, Dorothee, theater, catholiſh.*
Y *not ſtanding betwixt two vowels e. g. ſylbe.
or Latin and ſuch that come from thence, as*
C *e.g. cirkel, carcer, policei, ſterance.*
Qu *e.g. conqueriren, queruliren, quæſtion.*
SU *before a vowel e. g. ſuadiren.*
TI *before an other vowell e.g. protection, nation,
Gratian, &c* .2. *they that be otherwiſe ſpelled,
than pronounced in our toung, are moſt
commonly French, though ſome of'em originaly
come from ours e. g. lansquenet* lands-kneht
mareſhall from eine mære *and* ein ſhalk *;laiſſer*
laſſen, *empacquer*, einpakken ; *Saliqua*

from the river di Sale, *Luis or Lodovic from*
der leute weg &c. 3. *those polysyllabick*
radixes of both adjective and substantive
nouns, that have the tonick accent in the last syl-
lable, are either of the Italian, Spanish or of
an other toung coming from the Latin, e.g.
patron, matrone, pistol, parole, instrument,
testament, student, major, profit, polit, dis-
cret, subtil, fatal, pedal, respect, prospect,
comet, planet, nature, persone, and so forth
as many as you will your self, because our lan-
guage is capable to receive any foreign word, if
we had a mind to it. This we have added in
consideration to our language as it was defiled,
not as it is (or at least can be) refined, and ought
therfore to be kept without all such rubbish. for
we as well as Mericus Casau-bonus *(in his book*
of the four Cardinal Languages)disown this bast-
ard way of enriching our toung ,commonly used by
the half-learned Lat *in smatteners ,pettifoggers and*
ignorant travellers, that for want of good skill in
their own toung forget it and (like talking
magpies and prating parrats) use their mouths
to words snatched from other languages unknown
oftentimes as well to themselves as to whome
they write or speake to, underlining almost every
each nativ word with a parole a-la-mode from
France, *or a motto maravigliofo from* Italy, *or*
a Rodomontado *spaventoso that· is in plain* Englifh *an horrible* fpanifh *ly, or else with a nonsen-*
ficall word fetcht from Mexico *or from either of*
the Indies,*and (which is untollerable) if it be a*
scripture-businefs, one or an other either out of
a lasie carelesnefs or not well practiced in the pu-

rity of his mother-toung (wherein his sermon was
to be penned) not only makes speak the forementioned nations with an almost Babylonick confusion of languages ; but he frightens also out of
devotion (if not out of the church and their wits)
that sometimes as plain as unlearned auditory of
his , with the Syrians , Arabians , Æthiopians , Persians and the Turks themselves,
to say nothing of the Latins and the Grecians
or other Heathens and Barbarians. Thus they
studie to become as ridiculous to the Judicious, as
the naked bird laughed at by others in Æsop's
fables , or they strife to imitate a beggar , which
m ending his cloak or coat , takes a patch now
of a gray , now of a blew, now of a red and
now of any other colour , that he can get,
wanting such cloath or stuff , that the whole
garment first was made of , but at last in such
a variety of raggs scarcely to be distinguished
from the rest of the accessory pieces. a notable
couple of the like cento's and tailor cushions
is set abroad at every-ones view at the 135-
142. pages in the description of the fructify-
ing Society , whose most illustrious Head and
Patron resides in High-Saxony at Hall the very
Athens of the most refined Wits and language.
and herein are those so silly and pitiful wretches
of ours the more to be blamed either the
more serious the subject of their set speech is, or
the more their own toung excelles the other languages , from whence they use to begge or rather to robbe that gay gallantrie , without asking
any leav eagerly granted by the Conscript Fathers
to Tiberius Cæsar , that great and as discrete

as learned Roman Monarch , to set one or two Greek words into letters· patent written in the Latin toung for fear its naturall purity should thus be spoiled, which is done in deed by our Popiniays , as far as it layes in their power and corrupted fancy. , wherein we leave them, to satisfy also on the other hand forein enimies of our Heroick language , now the only living headspring of tounges the best furnished store -house of words both in respect to the other three languages. ἀυτογενέσι, and to those , that came from thence , against which manifest truth there start some up out of ignorance partly, partly out of a hatred to what they never learned and therfore never loved , saying, that the Germans as well High-as Low-landers have lost their language or at least the most part of their radixes by shifting their own letters, and by various changing of their spelling , especialy now adayes. to This we answer , that even as a tailor does not shape and cut bodies for clothes , but clothes for the body , and that , which suits one precisely , will be slovenly upon an other : so we write as we pronounce and consequently ought to mend the spelling after the sound pronunciation of the dialect , else they will want proportion , and though we have in former times exchanged some of our old characters with others (differing somewhat from all the rest in the whole world) that are now fitter for writing and printing, as the o'd ones were then for carving and cutting into brass, stone , horn , wood or such like materials , used by our Ancestors in stead of paper ; yet this argueth as litile, that we thereby either spoiled or

loſt our toung and words more than we promo-
ted and poliſhed them, as if one would ſay, that
a Mathematician ſpoiles his eye and loſes his ob-
ject, or a ſoldier his courage and enimy, when
this uſes a ſword and the other a perſpectiv, both
made in forrein parts, but more expedient for
their deſign then thoſe of their own countries
making; or, that a man chargeth the ſubſtance
of his body and of ſome wine by putting
this into an other commodious veſſel leaving
its dreggs behind, and that into an other ſuit
of cloaths, more proper to his limbes. did
not the very ſame, that we doe, ſome other
wiſe and learned nations? pray! look vjon
the Latin letters and amongſt others upon the
H, whether this be not the double aſpiration
of the Grecians, as it was made in former
times, combined afterwards by the middle
crofsſtrok, inſtead whereof the ancient Latins
(Terent. Scaur. II. de Orthograph.) uſed the
letter F, e. g. fordeum, foedus, fariolus &c.
now hordeum, hoedus, hariolus; and the
Spaniards hablar, heno, honda, hermoſo &c.
from the Latin fabulari, foenum, funda,
formoſus. conſider alſo the renouned Syrians,
and though you cannot ſay, that their lan-
guage and words came from Greece, yet you
will and muſt confeſs, that their vowels both
to ſound and ſhape reſemble thoſe of the Gre-
cians, which got theirs from the Phœnici-
ans by Cadmus, adding to them now and
then ſome others mite. nor can there be any
compariſon between our and the Coptick lan-
guages, unleſs it would fall infinitly ſhort of

Ⓖ

its self ; *since the Egyptians took upon them
selves both the yoke and dialect of the Grecians in the time of* Alexander *the Great ,
and of the* Ptolomæ's, *which later did reigne
in Egypt three hundred years together , and
Herodotus tells us in* Euterpe , *that Pfammeti-
chus King of the Egyptians caused to be brought
into his Kingdome no less than thirty thou-
sand Grecians, of the Carian and the Ionian
dialects for the better instruction of the E-
gyptian youth ; but the worst corruption and
the first cause thereof, why the Egyptians received almost all the Greek letters and a great
many words into their own , was the cru-
elty of the tyrant* Cambyses , *who after he had
subjugated their countrie under his dominion
endeavoured to rout together with the pro-
found learning and antiquities of Egypt its very
toung , wherein (viz. in corrupting of the language) he was somewhat imitated by* William
the Norman *after the conquest or rather treatie of* England. *whereas* Allemannie *or
Germanie never tasted any other turnement,
no other tyranny , no other conquest ,
no other injurie then that of time , which
all things temporary are subject unto. for as
the Teutonians are one of the most ancient nations in the world , having their pedigree and
origin from* Noah's *grand child called in the
holy Writ* Afcenas , *and their name either from
their King* Tuifco , *or as some will, from their
old word* Teut *or* Duit *fignifying God , in so
much that they , who pretend to honour our
Houses of* Germany *by fetching them either out*

of the *Trojan* horse or the ruins of *Rome*, doe not knowe, that the ancient *Germans* are of more worth than the *fugitiv Trojans*, and the effeminate *Romans*; as our nation, we say, is one of the renownedst people for antiquity and offspring: so likewise were they never so rude, so wild and so ignoble a crue of vile men, as to lose their mother-toung, as some imagine and upbraid us therwith. for though we can not shewe the *Magna Charta* (if there any was given to our *Grand-sire* coming from the mountains of *Ararath*.) whereby to testify, that our Forefathers as his descendents in blood, had also his toung; yet to be sure they were no beasts, that for want of reason have no language; but having it them, they can not be said to have lost it, becaufe we can not boast of as many antiques and romances, as *Egypt*, *Greece* or *Rome* did before their (now almost utter) decay and before their tounges were kickd out of their own home and turned fagabonds with that of the *Jewes*. yet if the ancient *Germans* be to blame, they are but for modefty, becaufe they would rather doe great and heroick actions worthy to be mentioned by their posterity, then describe them, as being more stout warriors and rough soldiers than soft penmen and smooth courtisans, whereby other nations got this advantage, that they could write of their countriemen, what they should both be and doe (as we reade of *Xenophon* and his *Cyrus*,) when they heard, what others practiced in foraïn countries. the Inhabitants of *Germany* never

went out of their countrie all at once, as
the Ebrewes left Egypt, but they send a-
broad their armies and emissary legions, whereby they enlarged both their language and countrie, as Conquerours use to doe; they kept
their stock at home, where to live upon and
to encrease themselves, alwayes draining up
their children as well in their language as in
military exercises; they had their own wor-
ship and ceremonies, their magistrate and own
Kings by fame and warre well knowne already
in the Patriarchs time; they were afterwards
renowned for victory and valour as well
amongst the Grecians as the Romans, in so
much that there could be made no peace between those two valiant and potent nations,
the Teutonian and the Roman (whose Ea-
gle was then kept up more by the Grecian than
their own mighty power) except by an advan-
tagious treatie confirmed with the heavenly
truth of the holy Gospel it self, and sealed
with the glory of no less then an Empire be-
stowed upon the Germans in such termes,
that their Emperour should be of the Christi-
an Religion on this side, and on the other of
German Blood at least by extraction, wisely
foreseing, that they in success of time by such
meanes and their matchless vertue and undaun
-ted courage would become sovereign masters
what they were then sharers and partners off:
but before this so great and so weighty work
was done, how many expeditions did they make?
how many countries did they overwhelme as a
deluge of a raging sea? how many bloody bat-

tels did they fight ? how often did they pitch
their leaguer in the very heart of the enimies camp ? how many warlike nations did they
conquerre and their countries ranfack ? the
Vandals under Genfaricus posfesfed themfelves
firſt of France , then of Spain , at lenght of
Africk and in Italy of Rome it felf ; the
Franconians and the Burgundians under the
conduct of Pharamond feized that part of
France, where Paris ſtands in , which they
made their Kings refidence, as it is ſtill now
adayes ; the Gothes under Alaricus feized
an other part of it and a part of Italy, the
countrie of Aquitain with the feats of the ancient
Cantabrians and Celtiberians in Spain, from
whence fome came under the name of Scythi-
ans into Scotland (as the Swabians or Sua-
vians into Swedland or Suevia) and ſignali-
zed it with the title of a Kingdome of a
hard and warlike nation , whileſt Alboin with
his Lombards or Longobards laid hold on Gal-
lia Cisalpina ; fome of the Saxons on Siben-
bürgen or Tranfylvanie and others viz. the
Angle-Saxons on this fortunate Iſland of the
unhappy Britains , called now by-and of its
Vanquiſhers England , which together with
Scotland will fufficiently teſtify , how much our
toung has prevailed as well upon their own inhabitans as upon thofe of other countries con-
quered by the Germans , in fo much that
we cannot be faid to have loſt our toung ; yet
if we haue left behind in other countries, fome
words no more ufed by us , why may we not
in cafe of need callſem back as well as o-

*Prince does his soldiers? but when our toung
is styled by some or other a Rough language,
either it is ment of that, which was spoken
before some hundred or thausand years agoe and
in respect to the childish pronunciation of an
effeminate speech ; or that good Gentleman
did never heare speake Germans but peasants
and those perhaps in a Rough dialect indeed.
other objections answered see , if you please,
in the Preface.*

Sect. 3. of the Distinguishing Punctation.

*hither belonges the Pointing , which in respect
of whole sentences and words as membres of
speech , is the same , what there was the
Accentuation in respect of words and syllabes ,
viz. to know , where to make now a longer
and then a shorter stop, when to raise the voice
and when to let it fall &c. according to the
affections or πάθη of the speakers mind,
the names and figures where-of together with
their use and signification explaned at large
in other Grammars we leave out , adding only,
that our Comma is a stroke (/) somewhat long
made as letters in the midst of a line from
the right hand towards the left , whereas the
Latin is a half circle hanging down under the
line of letters.*   *2. the two stops of
diæresis are needless here in our dialect; but
3. the sign of Irony (commonly omitted by
others) is a turned sign of exclamation, and
used when we mean an other thing , than we
speake , as we read in Terence : huic man-*

des, ſi quid recte curatum velis ; euge
bone vir ; ſo likewiſe : er iſt gar ein tapferer held ; ſpoken of a coward , i. he is a
ſtout champion ; ſi iſt di keuſhheit ſelbſten ;
ſpoken of a whore , i. ſhe is the chaſtity it ſelf ;
wir haben uns wakker verantwortet ; i.
ſpoken of a misbehaviour of ours ; i. it is excellently well done by us ;

Here followeth a Pattern of the Ger-
man Pronunciation.

I.

the XII. Articles of the ChriſtianCatho-lick faith.	Pronounce after the Engliſh expreſsion thus :
ih glaube an Gott den va-ter all-mæht-ig-en ſhœpf-er des himm-els und der erd-en. ih glæub' an Je-ſus Chriſt , ſein-en ein-ig-en ſon uns-ern herr'n, der em-pfang-en iſt von dem H. Geiſte , ge-bor-en von der jung-frawen Marie, gelitt -en unt-er Pon-tien Pi-lat-en , ge-creuz-ig-et , ge-ſtorb-en und be-grab-en , ni-der-ge-far-en zu'r hœll-en, am dritt-en tage wi-der-um auf-er-ſtand-en von	ig ghlòu-wey aun Gut dane vàuter, oll-maght -e-ghen ſhœpf-er das him-mels und dare ar-den. ig glibe aun yèi-ſus Chreoſt ſy-nen ine-e-ghen ſoan , ún-ſern herrn,dare em-pfáung-en iſt voan dame by-lee-ghen ghiſtey, ghey-boaren voan dare yòong -frow-en mau-rèe- en, ghe-lit-ten ùn-ter Pun-tſee-en Pee-làw-ten , ghei-crytſee-ghet,ghei-ſtúr-wen und bei-gràu -wen , needer-ghei-fau -ren tſur hèl-len , aum dril-ten tàughey wèe-der-um ouf-er-ſton-den

dem tode , auf-
ge - fa - ren gen
himm -el, fiz - end
zu'r reht-en hand
Gott-es des allmæht-
ig-en va-ters , von
dann-en er komm-
en wird zu riht-en
di.leb-end-ig-en und
di tod-en. ib glaube
an den Hl. Geift ,
eine Hl. Chriftl.
Kirhe , ge - mein-
fhaft der hei-lig-en ,
ver - geb-ung der
fünd-en , auf-er-
fte-ung des Heifh-
es und nah dem
tode ein e-wig-es
leb-en.

voan dame toadey ôuf-
ghei-fau-ren ghan him-
le fits-and ifoor ráght-
en haund gút-tes das
oll - magh - tee - ghen
váu-ters , voan dôn-
nen are cúm-man wird
tfoo ríg-ten dee lá-
wen-dee-ghen und dee
tó a-den. ig glou-wey
aun den hy- lee-ghen
ghyft, iney hy-lee-ghey
kréoftbea-ghey keay ghey
ghey-mixe-fhauft dare
hy-lee-ghen,ver-ghábe
-oung deir fin-den ,
óuf - ar -ftey-oung des
fly-fhes und naug
dame toadey ine ei-wee
-ghes lá-wen.

II.

**the Summe of the Law of God taken
out of Matth. chapt. XXII. v. 37,
38, 39, 40.**

Du folt den Herr-en
dein-en Gott lib-en
von ganz-em herz-
en , von ganz-er
fel-en und von ganz-
em ge-müte. dis ift
das erft-und groefte
ge-bot ; das an-dere
a - ber ift di-fem
gleih : du folft dei-

doo fult den hár-ren
dine en Gutt lee-wen
voan gaunt-fem hárt-
fen , voan gaunt-fer
feil-en und voan gaunt
-fem ghey-mcetey.dis ift
daus arft-und graftey
ghey-bóat ; daus on-
derey äu-wer ift dee-
fem glighe:doo fult dy-

nen næhſt-en liben
als dih ſelb-eſt. an
di-ſen zwey-en ge-
boten hang-et das
ganze ge-ſez und di
Pro-phet-en.

nen nàghs-ten lee-wen
als dig ſel-weſt, aun
dèe-ſen iſwy-en ghei-
hòa-ten hàung-et dàus
gàunt- ſey ghei-ſàts
und dee Pro-phèi-ten.

I I I.

The Lords Prayer.

Unſer vat-er , der
bu biſt i'm himm-el ,
ge-hei-lig-et werde
dein nam ; zu uns
komme dein reih ;
dein will ge-ſhæ-e
wi i'm himmel alſo
auh auf erd-en unſ-
er tæg-lih brot gib
uns heute und ver-
gib' uns uns- ere
ſhuld-en , als wir
ver - geb-en unſ-ern
ſhuld- ig- ern ; und
füre uns niht inn
ver-ſuh-ung , ſond-
ern er-lœſe uns vo'm
übel ; denn dein iſt
das reih , di kraft
und di herr-lig-keit
von e - wig-keit zu
e - wig - keit. A-
men.

un-ſer vàu-ter , darè
doo biſt im him-le, ghei
-hy-lee-ghet mèir - dey
dine naum ; tſoo uns
cům - mey dine righe ;
dine will ghey-ſhà-ey
weq im bim-le , öll-ſo
oug ouf àr-den ; un-
ſer tàg-lee-ghes broat
gib uns hitey und ver-
ghib uns ùn-ſey- rey
ſhòol - den , als weer
ver-gà - wen ùn-ſern
ſhdol-dee-ghern ; und
fèe-rey uns neoght in
ver-ſòo ghoong , zùn-
dern er - lœ -ſey uns
voam è - well ; denn
dine iſt dàus righe, dee
croft und dee herr-lig-
kìte voan èi-wig-kùe
tſoo ei - wig - kùe
àu-man.

Etymologia,

OR

The Second Part of Words considered by themselves without construction.

Chap. 1. *of the Nominal Derivation or Declension.*

Sect. 1. of the Gendre, Motion and Degrees of the Nouns.

N. I. the Gendre and particularly of the Subftantive.

the Gendre of a Subftantive is to be known by three wayes. I. by the auxiliary noun or Article especialy the definit der *,* di *,* das *, which according to its threefold both gendre and termination signifyes a masculine, when it is of the first termination ; a feminine, when it is of the second ; a neutre, when it is of the third termination , as we shall see hereafter. That is the surest way used commonly in dictionaries , but shewing us the gendre only a posteriori or after we know, what article must there be set before a substantive. II. by the signification of the word it self, whereof* *these three* Rules *are to be observed :* 1. *all the propre names of gods, angels both good and bad, men of all dignities, offices and arts, virtues and vices belonging to them ; likewise the names of the quarters of a year, months, dayes, winds, pretious stones, money &c. are of the masculine gendre.* 2.*all the proper names of goddesses, women, dignities, offices, vertues and vices propre to that sex ; as also the names of the rivers, and the fruits of the tree &c. are feminines. except the river* Jordan , Euphrat *or* pfrat, Rhodan , Rein *or* Rhein, Mæin, Po, Nekker ,*and the fruit* apfel, apple, *which are masculines; but the word* weib , *woman or wife would be neutrall.* 3. *all the proper names of the countries, cities, towns and villages, of metalls and minerals, of the letters, of diminutivs and words of number, of the infinitive moods and adjectives used substantively, are of the neutre gendre. except the countries that have the termination* shaft *e. g.* grafshaft , earledome *& c. which are feminines, and the word* stal , *steel a kind of metall propre to the masculine Mars, is as well of the masculine as neuter gendre. This is the most naturall, but too generall way.*

III. *by its finall termination; which is the more speciall way , to be used in a Grammar , especialy for those that have no true and complete dictionary ; and therefore we shall here insist upon it the larger viz. through the whole alphabet* .*fetting betwixt the terminations and the words their naturall gendre indicated by the definit article*, *as ending in*.

B der : ſtab , *ſtaff* , leib , *body &c. except*: das : weib , *wife* , kalb , *calf* , grab , *grave* , laub , *leaf* , *and all that beſides this termina ‑tion have alſo the ſyllable* G E *in their beginning* , *e. g*. gewœlb , *vault* , gewæb , *weaving* , gewerb , *trading &c.*

D der : abend , *evening* , grund , *ground* mund , *mouth &c. except*: di : hand *hand* , gegend , *region* , huld , *favour*, jugend , *youth* , ſhuld , *debt*, tugend , *vertue*, wand , *wall*. das : bad , *bath* , band , *band* , bild , *figure* , eingeweid , *guts* , elend , *miſery* , feld , *field* , geſind , *family*, glid , *limb* , gold , *gold* , kind , *child* , land , *countrie* , leid , *ſadneſs* , lid , *lid* , kleid , *garment* , pfand , *pawn* , pferd , *horſe* , pfund , *pound* , rad , *wheel*, rind , *runt or bullock* , wild , *veniſon or wild beaſts* , end , *end*.

E di : naſe , *noſe* , ſeite , *ſide* , ſeide , *ſilk* , libe , *love* , *&c. except* : der : ſne , *ſnow* , kſe , *threfoly*, *and all that have not the halfmute* E. *but note well* , *that there is never a letter more abuſed both in the meetre and here in the gendre, than the vowel* E, *which abuſe crept in by a bad cvſtom and by the variety of dialects. for ſome of them as the Thuringian , Miſnian , Sileſian &c. add it , when they ſhould not, e. g. in the maſculine and neutre ſubſtantives* : der fürſte ,

der hake , der fame ; das gefihte , das
herze &c. *when they should say and write :*
der fürſt, *prince* , hak , *hook* , fam , *feed*;
das gefiht, *fight* , herz , *heart* ; *whereas some
others as the Frankonian , the Oſter or Voght-
landiſh , and that of the Palatinate , omitte
it both in writing and speaking feminin substantivs, and masculin or neuter adjectivs used
substantively* e. g. der reih , das weis ,
ein ſtub , een kaz, zig, ein ſtund , ru,
nas &c. *when they ought to add it thus :* der
reihe , *the rich* , das weiſe , *the white* ; eine
ſtube , *ſtove* , kaze , *cat* , zige , *she-goat* ,
ſtunde , *houre* , rue , *reſt* , naſe , *noſe. ſee
in the* 1. *part. the* 2. *ſect. of the* 1. *chap.*
F der : aff , *ape* , tropf , *drop* , topf, *pot* ,
    wolf, *walf* , brif , *letter* &c. *except*
das : ſhaf, *ſheap* , ſhaff , *a certain veſſel* ,
          ſhiff , *ſhip.*

G der : ring , *ring* , ſig , *victory* , tag , *day* ,
jüngling , *youngman* , geſang , *ſong* &c *except:*
di : burg , *caſtle* , *and all Denominativs in :*
ung e. g. hoffnung , *hope* , verzweiflung ,
    deſpair , ſendung , *ſending* &c.
das : ding , *thing* , beding , *condition* ,
gelag , *company* , tallig , *tallow* , werg ,
work or tow , aug , *eye* , *likewiſe all Denominativs in* ENG *and* ING *beginning,
with the ſyllable* GE e. g. geding , *bargain* ,
getræng , *throng* , geſling , *ſticking piece* ,
    gemeng , *mixture* , &c.
H der : bauh *belly* , fiſh *fiſh* , tiſh *table* ,
geruh *ſmell* , ſhuh or ſhu *ſhoe* &c. *except*
das : bleh , *tinn* , dah , *datch or tach* , fah,

H

partition , gelah, *laughter* , gelaih or lɤih ,
the feed e. g. of frogs , gemah , *room* , joh ,
yoke , loh , *hole* , peh , *pitch* , reih , *kingdome* , tuh , *cloth* , buh , *book* .   *the
feminins have (or ought to have) their final E,
by some omitted e.g.* di buhe , *beech* , di fahe,
*fake &c.   on the contrary they add often not
only this vowel but the single aspiration also ,
the which never ought to stand in the end of
a word or syllable* , e. g. ftroh , floh , ge-
lahe ; rüh , kuh, vihe *&c.   whereas they
should write :* ftro , flo or flog , gelah,
rue, kue , vi , *which fee in their own place.*
di :   milh, *milk* , marh, *marchionate are
without the E feminin. fee T for T H.*

I. der : Mai, *May* , brei, *porridge &c. except:*
di :   diberei *thievery* , büberei *knaverie* ,
hurerei , *whoredome, and so forth all the nominal Derivativs , receiving sometimes their
finall E. also:* hurereye , dibereye , bübereye,
                fressereye *&c.*

das : ei , *egg* , blei , *lead* , vi , *cattel* ; *likewise all the verball derivativs in* EI *and beginning with the syllable* GE : gefhrei , *haw-
ling* , gefpei , *spitting &c.   not.* gefhreye,
gefhreih or gefhreihe ; gefpeye , gefpeih
                or gefpeihe.

K der :   dank *thank* , drekk *dirt* , hak ,
hook , fakk *fack* , mark *or* markt ,
         market &c.   except :
di : bank *bench* , mark or marh *marchionatus.*
das : volk , *folk* , werk , *work* , ftükk,
part , fhokk , *three score* , mark or *better*
marg , *marrow* , glükk or gelükk , *luck* ,

*fo all the Denominativs of this termination
and beginning with the fyllable* GE *, e. g.* ge-
lenk *, joint ,* gelhenk *,* guift *,* getrænk *,*
drink *,* gemerk *,* token *or* fign *,* gewœlk *,*
clouds *&c. never* gelenke *,* gefhenke *&c.*
L der : al *,* eel *,* efel *,* afs *,* ftegel *,* flail *,*
will *,* will *,* pful *,* pool *,* fattel *faddle,* zæl
or fwanz *,* tail *,* geifel *hoftage* *&c. except :*
di : fakkel *,* torch *or* link *,* gabel *,* fork *,*
geifel *,* whip *,* kahel *,* piece of a furnace *,*
kandel *or* kanne *,* canne *,* nadel *,* needle *,*
kwal *,* torment *,* femmel *,* white bread *,* fihel *,*
fickel *,* fhaufel *,* fcuffle *,* fheitel *,* fheddle *,*
fhifsel *,* difh *or* platter *,* ftaffel *,* ftep *,* trübfal *,* anguifh *,* drangfal *,* diftrefs *,* wal *,* choice *,*
bibel *,* bible *,* fpindel *,* fpindle *,* humani-
el *,* drone *,* néfsel *,* nettle *,* deihfel *pole of
a coach or wagon ,* pærl *,* pearle *.*
das : beil *,* hatchet *,* fell *,* fkinn *,* grakel *,*
quarrel *,* hæil *,* hail or falvation *,* mal *,* meal
or mark *,* mel *meal ,* metall *,* mettal *,* model *,* model *,* œl *,* oil *,* fegel *,* fail *,* figel *,*
feal *,* feil *,* rope *,* fpil *,* play *,* zil *,* mark *to
fhut at ,* kamel *,* camel *. likewife all the
Denominativs of this termination and the initial fyllable* GE *, e. g.* gebell *,* barking *,*
gemal *,* confort *,* getümmel *,* tumult *; &c.
as there be feverall feminins having their* E *,
which is omitted by fome e. g.* nahtigaile *,*
nightingall *,* zale *,* number *,* galle *,* gall *&c.
fo we find both mafculins and neuters written
with it, e. g.* gefelle *,* fellow *,* gehæule *,*
houling *&c. whereof neither fhould be done.*
M der kamm *or* kamb *comb ,* arm *arm ,*

bofom *bofom*, ram or ramen *frame*, traum
dream, tum or dom *dome &c.* except,
di : fham *ar* fhame , *fhame* , tramm or
tramme , *dramm*.

das : lamm or lamb , *lamb* , *and all the*
compounds of the mafculine : tum or dom ,
e. g. fûrftentum , *princedome* , pabftum ,
popedome &c. likewife the denominativs be-
ginning with GE , *as* gewûrm , *vermins* ,
gefwærm, *noife &c.*

N der : beginn , *beginning*, dorn *thorne*,
hàn , *cock*, karn , *cart* , fwan , *fwan*, wein,
wine , kèrn, *kernel &c.* except:
di : birn *pear* , pein *pain* , ftirn , *fore-*
head; and all *the denominativs of that ending*
c. g. kœhin or kœhinn *and fometimes* kœh-
inne , *cookwoman* ; lœbin or lœwinn ,
or lewinne *lionefs &c.*

das : bekken , *bafon*, bein , *bone* , eifen ,
iron, ferken ,*pigg* , fwein , *fwine* , garn,
yarne , hun , *chick* , horn , *horn* , korn
corne, kûfsen , *cufhion or bolfter* , gehirn ,
brains , geftirn , *ftars*, gefpann *couple or*
ftraightening as gefpann ohfen , *couple or yoke*
of oxen, herz-gefpann , *heart-ach* , *likewife*
all diminutivs and infinitivs , e. g. finger-
gen , hændgen , kindgen , *&c. little fin-*
ger, hand, child; efsen *meat*, trinken *drink &c.*
O and œ der : flo or flog , *flea.*

das : ftro *ftraw* , rœ *roe* , wœ *wo.*
P der : karp or karpen , *carp* , klump
or klumpen *lump* , rapp or rappen *black-*
ifh horfe , lapp , *ignorant fellow or rude pup-*
pie , *or* lappen , *ragg or batch &c.* except :

das : geripp *or* geribb *carcass without
flesh*, gefipp *society particularly of a common
crue,* gefupp *drinking or lippling &c.if there
be any more of this termination and the initial
syllable* GE. *but neither of them should have
the feminin E ,* Karpe gefippe *&c.*

R der : hammer , *hammer*, keller *cellar*
leihter , *candlestick*, pfeiler , *pillar* , trihter
funnell, tor *fool , with all the verball substantives in* ER , *e. g.* flæfer , *sleeper,*
kæufer , *cheapman,* rihter *judge &c. except :*
di *:* blatter *bladder* , butter *butter* , feder ,
feather , folter , *rack* , kammer , *chamber* ,
klammer , *holdfast* , klapper , *raddle,* leber,
liver , marter , *torment,* fhulder , *shoulder* ,
stewer *or* steur , *taxes* ; klafter , *fathom* ,
mutter , *mother* , tohter , *daughter* , fwester,
*sister , where the last syllable is allwayes sharp
and short without the* E *feminin ; but when
it is soft and long, we should add the said*
E *both because of the gendre and the pronunci
-ation:* bare , *beere or hearse* , gefare , *danger,*
fhare , *multitude* , gewære , *a word used by
the sellers and buiers* , kere *and* widerkere,
turning and returning , lære *or* loere *doctrin,*
zire *or* zirde *ornament* , gebûre *or* gebirde ,
duty , tûre *or* dûre , *dore* , begire *or* begirde,
desire , kure *or* kœre , *election* , figure ,
figure , fpure , *footstep* , nature, *nature* , rote
rure *the losing of the guts* , fnure , *thread,
or daughter in law* , flure , *piece of ground,*
hure , *whore &c. never :* gefar , lær , zir ,
begir, hur *&c.unless in composition standing
before an other word, as* gefær-lih , *dangerous,*

lær-reih, *full of doctrin*, zir-lih *handsome*,
begirig, *desirous*, hûrish, *whorish*.

das : bir, *beer*, tir, *beast*, har, *hair*,
jar, *year*, par, *pair*, or, *ear*, nadel-œr,
ey of a needle, ror, *gunne*, fiber, *fever*,
biber, *bever*, fuder, *load*, tor *or better*
dor, *dore or gate*, chor, *quire*, waſſer,
water, futter, *fudder or lining*, fenſter,
window, kloſter *cloiſter*, ſilber, *ſilver*, kupf
·er, *cupper*, leder, *leather*, wetter, *weather*, meſſer, *knife*, luder, *extravagancy*,
zukker, *ſugar*, ruder, *rudder or oar of a
ſhip to rowe withall*, ufer, *bank of a river*,
regiſter, *regiſter*, gitter *or* gegitter, *lettice*,
geheur *or* ungeheur, *ſcarecrow*, pflaſter,
plaſter, geſwiſter, *ſiſters and brethren*; ſo
all the verbals beginning with GE, *e.g.* gehœr,
hearing, gewœr *or* gewer, *weapon*, ge-
plærr, *roring*, geſnorr *ſnorting &c.*

S. der : has, *bare*, ſohs *or* fox, *fox*,
ohs *or* ox, *ox*, ſpiſs *or* ſpis, *ſpit &c.* except :
di : gans, *gooſe*, maus, *mouſe*, laus, *louſe*,
nuſs, *nut*, wildniſs, *wilderneſs*.

das : haus, *houſe*, gras *or* graſs, *graſs*,
glás *or* glaſs, *glaſs*, mas *or* maſs, *meaſure*,
mos *or* moſs, *moſs*, ſloſs, *caſtle or lock*;
roſs, *horſe*, taus, *deuce*; eis, *ice*, ſaſs, *fat
or barrel*, loſs, *lot*, reus *or* reuſig, *fa-
got*, wammes *or* wams, *doublet*, as, *dead
corps of a beaſt*, gelæis *or* glæis, *the carti-
loſe*, wahs *or* wax, *wax*, ſo *all the verbals
of that ending and the ſyllable* GE, *e. g.*
geſmæis, *inſects or vermins*, gefæs, *veſſels*,
gefäſs, *buttock*, gefraſs, *feaſting &c.* like-

wise the compounded with the finall syllable
niſs *or* nûſs , *eſpecia'y having in their begin-*
ning the syllable GE , e . g. gefængniſs *or*
gefængnûſs , *priſon*, gedæhtniſs *or* gedæht-
nûſs , *memory &c.* but *without this præfor-*
mativ syllable GE, *they are commonly of both*
the feminin and the neuter gendre e. g. begeg-
niſs , *fortune* , begængniſs , *celebration* ,
verdammnûſs , *damnation* , bildniſs, *form*
or figure &c.

T der : hut , *hat* , rat , *counſel or coun-*
ſellour , bart *or* bard , *beard* , dorſt *or* durſt,
thirſt , ernſt *or* ærnſt , *earneſt* , mut , *cou-*
rage &c. except :

di : armut , *poverty* , *with the other com-*
pounds; antwort , *anſwer* , hut , *cuſtody* ,
ſtatt , *city* , fat , *ſeed* , tat *or* dat , *deed* ,
art , *kind* , aht *baniſhment*, angſt , *anguiſh* ,
axt , *hatchet* , fort , furt , *or* fart , *ford* ,
geſtalt , *manner* , haft , *faſtening or impriſon*
ment , haut , *ſkin* , kraft , *vertue* , laſt , *load* ,
maht , *power* , naht , *night* , praht , *pomp*
or majeſtie , raſt , *reſt* , ſlaht , *ſlaughter* ,
ſorgfalt , *ſorrow* , traht , *faſhion* , braut ,
bride , arbeit , *work* , triſt , *paſture* , gruft ,
grotta , kluft , *that ſpace of two diſtant pla-*
ces , ſhrift , *ſcripture or writing*, vernunft ,
reaſon or underſtandig , welt , *world* , zeit ,
time , zukunft *or* herkunft , *advent or the*
coming near , zunft , *tribe or companie of tra-*
desmen , notdurft , *need or neceſſity*, bronſt ,
heat , konſt , *art* , wut , *madneſs* , luft , *air* ;
aufſiht *or* obſiht , *inſight or care*, friſt , *time* ,
gedult , *patience* , fluht , *flight*, fruht , *fruit* ,

forht *or* furht. *fright or fear*, giht *gout*, lift,
cunning or trick, pfliht, *duty*, fuht *a dis-
ea/e*, fwindfuht, *confumtion*, verziht, *re-
nouncirg and denial of the right and pofsession
of a thing*, zuht, *manners*, poft, *poft*,
bruft, *breaft*, geburt, *birth*, worft, *link
or (black) pudding*, koft, *coft or meat*,
luft, *pleafure* glut, *flame. likewife all Denominativs in* heit *and* keit, *e. g.* erbar-
keit *or* redligkeit, *honefty*, faulheit *or*
trægheit, *idlenefs or lazinefs &c.*

das : wort, *word*, fprihwort. *proverb*,
amt *office*, blat, *leaf*, haupt *(or. hæt)*
bead, haft *or* hæft, *handle or waft*, liht,
light or candle , geriht, *the fefsions or a difh
of meat*, gerûht, *fame or report*, geræt
boush.ld *ftuff or tools* , reht *law or right*,
fheit, *a piece of wood*, gewiht, *weight*,
gediht, *fiaction or poem*; gefiht, *fight or
face*, gleit *or* geleit *and* beleit, *accom-
pagnation*, bret, *board*, zelt *or* gezelt,
apartment or tabernacle , gerift *or* gerûft,
fcaffolt, toht, *wick of the candle*, brot ,
bread, fwert, *fword*, lot, *ounce*, neft,
neaft, hergewett *a word ufed by the Lawiers*,
kraut, *herb*, maut, *fhipmoney*, blut *or* blutt
blood , gut *or* gutt *goods*, geblût *or* ge-
blûtt, *bloud*, gemût *or* gemûtt, *mind*.
U der : bau, *building*, tau *or* daw,
dew, leu *or* lœb, *lion*, fhu *or* fhuh *fhoe &c.
but the feminins have allwayes their final E,
e. g.* di frawe, *woman*, fawe, *fow*, ftrewe,
a bed of ftraw, ræwe, *repentance &c.*

das : gebæu *building*, hæi *or* heu *hay*.

X der Sax *or* Sahs, *Saxon*. ſax or lahs, *ſalmon &c.* but the feminins have or ought to have their character E, e. g. di hei-dexe, *or* eidehſe, *viper*, hexe *or* hehſe, *witch, &c.*

das : wax or wahs, *wax*, crucifix &c. *ſee the lett. S.*

Z der : ſhaz, *treaſure*, ſwanz, *tail*, tanz or danz, *dance*, wiz, *wit*, bliz, *lightening, &c.* but the feminins have all an E e. g. di ſhanze, *ſcaunce*, pflanze, *plant*, ſpize, *point*, ſprůze, *water-enging &c.* *not* pflanz, ſhanz *&c.*

di : Pfalz, *Palatinate, ſeemes to be without the E.*

das : antliz, *face*, geſez, *law or ſtatute*, herz, *heart*, harz or harzig, *roſin*, holz, *wood*, malz, *malt*, ſalz, *ſalt*, ſmalz, greeſe, nez, *net*, raz or ilz, *pol-cat.*

note 1. *the compound words keep the gendre of their laſt part e. g. der* kalbs-kopf, *calfshead*, di hunds-naſe, *dogs-noſe*, das ſhu-leder, *ſhoe-leather &c. except thoſe few, which we have noted already in their own place.*

2. *there be ſome words of two gendres according to the uſe of diverſe countries and dialects, as der and di* : zirat, *ornament*, verhaft *impriſonment*, luft, *aire*, aufrur, *ſedition*, bah, *brook*, un luſt, *diſpleaſure*, funk funken or funke, *ſpark of fire.*

der *and* das : armut, *poverty*, altar, *altar*, eid, *oath*, gift, *poiſon*, gewerb-trading, lærmen or lærm, *tumult*, reih

tum, *riches*, zep ter *or* fcepter, *fceptre*,
fhild, *fhield*, tal *or* dal *dale*, teil *or* deil *part*
or deal, lon *wages*, kan *canow or boat*,
band *band*, hutband, *hatband*, der gemal,
husband, das gemal *or* di gemalin, *wife*.
di *and* das : gelübde *or* gelübt *vow*, er-
kæntnifs, *or* erkæntnûs *knowledge*, bewœg-
nifs *or* bewegnûfs *motion &c. fee the lett. S.*
3. *the gendre diftinguifhes fometimes the fignification of thofe words, that have the fame
fpelling*, e. g. der hut *hat*, di hut *cuftodie*,
der tor, *fool*, das tor *or* dor, *dore or gate*;
der taube *deaf*, di taube *dove*, der
helm *helmet*, das helm, *hilt or handle*;
der ftift *fparable*, das ftift, *diocefs*, der
ort, *place*, das ort, *the fourth part of fil-
ver money*, der ftraus *eftridge*, der *and* di
ftraus, *nofegay*, di wœe, *torment or gri-
ping*, das wœ *woe*, der chor *the muficians*,
das chor *the quire*, der teil *part*, das teil
as hinterteil, *hinderpart*.

4. *we ufe the foreign words commonly in their own gendre* e. g. der :
poet, triumph, doctor, comet, planet *&c.*
di : Philofophie, phantafie, regul, bar-
barei *&c.* das : fecret, protocoll, fa-
crament, parlement, inftrument *&c.*
except : der : method, fyntax, catheder,
kalender, tempel. di : complimente,
marter, lilie. das : creuz, paradis *or*
paradeis, chor *i. quire*.

5. *as the mafculin and neuter A, E, O, of the
Greek, Latin, Spanifh, Italian &c. words
(when we will or muft ufe them) is quite put*

*away in the German , French , and English
tounges , e. g. favor , patron or padron ,
ballon i. football, poet, pom-orance, orange;
glob , diplom, duell &c. so on the contrary Their feminin A is changed Here into a
halfmute E , the which is (or ought to be)
kept allwayes both in pronouncing and in writing as well after a vowell e.g. comœdie, Dorothee &c. where I and E preceding found
by its self , and the finall E founds as that in
kræe or kree , crow , fee , fea , flœe , fleas &c.
as after a consonant e. g. secte , dame , matrone or madrone , trompete marine &c.
except after an L , where this halfmute and
feminin E in our toung is put in the foregoing
vowels place , but the French and the English
keep it still in the words end and pronounce
it , as we doe e. g. fabel , regel , nobel &c.
Fr. fable , regle , noble ; Engl. fable , rule ,
noble.*

n. 2. the Motion particularly of the
Subftantives.

*Many Subftantives fignifying both fexes be-
come moveable by adding to the primitiv and
mafculin , the feminin termination in , inn or
inne , called thence denominative feminine
e. g. fhulter or fhumaher fhoemaker , fhuft-
erin or fhumaherinne fhoemakers wife ;
narr , fool nærrinne , woman-fool ; fneider,
tailor, fneiderinn tailors wife , phantaft , man
fanatick , phantaftin woman fonatick ; lœb or
leu , lion , lœbin or lewin , lionefs &c.
but we muft here as well as in English*

*look more upon the use, then the analogie;
for we say* ohs *ox,* kue *cow, not* ohfin,
oxefs; bokk *he-goat,* zige *fhe-goat, not*
bœkkin, *goatefs;* han *cock,* henne *henne,
not* hæninne, *cockefs &c.*

*To the epicænes, that ferve for both kindes
under one termination (the gendre whereof they
followe) we adde fometimes an other word to
make'em differ one from an other, as to fowls
and birds, when* cocks ein han, *and when*
hennes eine henne *or* fi, *e. g.* difer fper-
ling ift ein han, difer aber eine fi *or* eine henne, *this fparrow is a cock, but that
a henne &c. and to thofe of the fifhes that
are males, we add the word* ·rogener, roan;
to the others milher *qf.* milker; *but to mankind and beafts as well more-footed as four-
footed we add, like the Englifh, the words*
mænngen, weibgen, *male and female.*

Gendre and Motion of the Adjectives.

*R. 1. every adjective has ordinarily three
gendres and as many terminations, which are
taken away after a verbe, when there is neither an exprefs fubftantive nor article, (fee*
R. 4.*) e. g.*

masc.	fem.	neut.	abfol.
ftarker,	ftarke,	ftarkes,	ftark.
ftærkerer,	ftærkere;	ftærkeres,	ftærker.
ftærkefter,	ftærkefte,	ftærkeftes,	* ftærkefte.
hœrender,	hœrende,	hœrendes,	hœrend.
gelib'ter,	gelibte,	gelibtes,	gelibet.
meiner,	meine,	meines,	mein.
difer,	dife,	difes,	dis.

* the superlative loseth only the lett. S according to the R. 2. following.

R. 2. but if one of the demonstrative particles or the definit article ,as well after the verbe as before it , precede an adjective either with its substantive or without it ; we put away only the letter R of the masculin, and the letter S of the neuter adjective whatsoever, that is verbal , nominal or polysyllabick pronominal. e. g. der (diser , jener) reihe mann erbawete das (dis or dises, jenes) kostbare und shoene haus, the (this , that) rich man builded the (this , that) sumtuous and fair house ; welher hut ist der beste ? which hat is the best ? ewerer (or der ewere or ewer hut)ist der besere , und meiner (der meine or mein hut)ist greesser or der groessere , yours is the better one, and mine (or my hat) is the bigger; das ewere pferd war das geswinde, yours was the swift horse &c. this holds also , when adjectius stand in stead of substantivs by the help of the definit article e. g. der gerehte (sc. mensh) mus vil leiden , the just (sc. man) has much to suffer ; di keushe (sc. jungfrawe) blibe bestændig, the chast (sc. mayd) was constant ; das sawere ist bisweilen gesûnder denn das sûsse, the sower thing is sometimes more wholesome than the sweet &c.

R. 3. whereus an adjective in the vocative or exclamative case, and else served either by the indefinit article or an adjective possessive , keeps everywhere the termination er, e , es e. g. libster shaz or libstes herz ! sweet-heart !

I

o du gerehter Gott *! o thou just God!* ein
(mein , difer , jener *&c.*) guter freind,
a (my , this , that &c.) good friend ; eine (eure, iglihe *&c.*) hœeflihe gefellfhaft , *a (your,
every &c.)civill company* ; ein (fein, unfer, ir)
n*z*lihes buh, *a (his, our, her) ufefull book.*
R. 4. *but this (viz. indefinit) article and
the pronominall adjectivs of more than one fyllables lofe here their terminations , as many hereof
are capable , as we have feen already diverfe
examples; and if they doe not or can not lofe
their ending , then the nominal or verball adjectiv lofes its R in the mafculin , and S in
the neutre gendre , e. g.* jener trewe vater,
that faithfull father ; jenes (dis *or* difes*)* ge-
horfame kind , *that (this) obedient child.*

to the motion of nouns belongs their Diminution.

*the nouns as well adjectivs as fubftantivs are
made diminutivs in adding There (to the adjectivs) the fyllable* LIH *anfwering the fyllable
ISH in Englifh e.g.* fwarz fwærzlih , *black
blackifh,* weis weislih , *white whitifh &c. and
Here (to the fubftantivs) the fyllable* GEN
e. g. lhaf fhæfgen , *little fheap,* glafs glæfs-
gen *little glafs,* mann mænngen *little man &c.
and this is done alfo in the propre names of
men and women fometimes not without their
corruption, as in the Englifh and other tounges
e. g.* Hans Hænsgen , *John Jack,* Willhelm
Wilmgen, *William Will,* Fridrih Frizgen,
Frederick, Elifabeth Lisgen *or* Elsgen , *Eli-
abeth Elfe or Betty* ; Katharine Kægen *or*

Thringen, *Katharine Kete &c.* but
we *muſt here in this* rule *as well as anywhere
elſe obſerve the uſe* ; *for we ſay* eine kleine zeit
or glükkſeligkeit, *a ſmall time or fortune &c.
not* zeitgen or zeitlein, glükkſeligkeitgen or
glükkſeligkeitlein.

*here as well of all diminutiv nouns, as of the
moveable ſubſtantivs we have alwayes to obſerve, what we ſhall ſay in the* 6. R. *following.*

n.3 the Degrees of Compariſon.

R. 1. *the degrees of compariſon are formed as
in Engliſh either in adding ſome certain ſyllables to the poſitiv viz. to the abſolute (or as
it ſtands after a verbe without any ſubſtantiv or article) in the abſolute comparativ* ER,
and in the abſolute ſuperlativ ESTE (*to which
is added an* N, *if precede the particle* am) *where
both terminations are of all three gendres* e.g.

der leib ⎱   ⎧ lang, länger, der ⎧ lengſte
di na ſe ⎬ iſt ⎨ dikk, dikker, di ⎨ dikkeſe
das bein ⎰   ⎩ dinn, dinner, das ⎰ dinneſte

a'm ⎧ längeſten ⎱ *the bodie , noſe, legg is
⎨ dikkeſten ⎬ long, thick. thin; longer,
⎩ dinneſten ⎰ thicker, thinner ; the long
-eſt , the thickeſt ,the thinneſt.*

*but to the comparative ſerv ed by the definit arti-
cle, we add yet an* E *in all gendres* e. g.

der ⎧ lange . langere ⎧ leib ⎱
di ⎨ dikke, dikkere ⎨ naſe ⎬ i. e.
das ⎩ dinne . dinnere ⎩ bein ⎰

the ⎧ long . longer ⎱ body.
⎨ thick, thicker ⎬ noſe.
⎩ thin, thinner ⎰ legg.

and to the comparativ accompanied with a fub-
ſtantive and ſerved by the indefinit article, is
added in the maſc. gender ER, in the feminin
ERE, in the neut. ERES, e. g. ewer vater iſt ein gelærter-und weiſerer mann, als
meiner or der meine, *your father is a better
ſchollar and a wiſer man than mine*; ire ſwe-
-ter iſt eine ſchœnere (or ſchœner-) und
reihere jungfrawe dann eure or di ewere
*her ſiſter is a handſomer and richer maid than
yours*; mein hengſt iſt ein hœher-(or hœh
-eres und geſwinderes pferd als ewere mære, *my ſtonehorſe is a higher and ſwifter horſe
than your mare &c.*   the ſuperlativ in the
exclamativ and vocativ caſes, or elſe accompanied with an adjectiv poſſeſſiv or the indefinit article, receives R in the maſculin, and
S in the neuter gendre, e. g. o du grauſam-
ſter widerig ! *o thou moſt cruell tyrant !*
du allerungehorſamſtes kind! *you moſt dis-
obedient child!* unſer tewer-und werteſter
Heiland war ein ſo wol unſchuldigſt-als
gedultigſtes lamm, *our moſt dear and bleſſ-
-ed Saviour was a lamb as moſt innocent as pa-
tient &c.* ſee the foregoing 3. R. n.2.
R.2. or the degrees are made in ſetting before the
poſitiv (eſpecialy of the participles) the words
mer or weniger e. g. mer geſlagen *more
beaten*; weniger beſliſſen, *leſs induſtrious &c.*
and to make it ſignify a ſuperlativ we add the
words ganz, hoh, vil, ſer or the like e. g.
ewer ganz demütiger diner *your moſt humble ſervant* or veſter humiliſmus ſervus ;
ein ſer gelærter mann, *a very learned man*

or vir doctiſsimus *&c. but theſe ſuperlativs
doe ſignify rather excellency than compariſon.*
R. 3. *we uſe to ſet before each of the three
degrees certain particles of intenſion to kighten
their ſignification, as to the poſitive* ſer, gar,
faſt, vil, wol, hoh, überaus; *before the
comparative* weit, noh, vil, mer, noh mer,
etwas, etwas mer; *before the ſuperlative*
aller, zu'm, hoh, a'm, hochſt. *Hither belong
the two particles* ur *and* erz, e. g. ur-alt,
very old or antiquiſsimus, erzbub, *archknave
or ſceleratiſsimus &c. the very ſame is to
be obſerved alſo of ſome ſubſtantivs added to
certain adjectivs ſignifying quality or quantity
e. g.* eine haupt perl, *a very pretious pearle*;
haupt-ſtatt, *a principal city*; welt-land-*or*
ſtatt-kündig, *known in all the world, countrie or citie, Lat. notiſsimus, a, um*; blut-
arm, *very poor, Lat. pauperior Iro or paup er-
rimus*; ſteinreih, *very rich, Lat. ditior Cræſo
or ditiſsimus*, bein-*or* ſtein-hart *very hard*,
honig-ſüſse, *very ſweet as honny*; eſsig-
ſaur, *very ſower as vinegar*; ſne-weis,
very white as ſnow, kol-or-peh-ſwarz *very
black*; blei-ſwer *very havy as lead*; himmel
-hoh *very high as the ſky*; ſonnen-helle *or*
-klar *very light or clear as the ſunne &c.*
R. 4. *three adjectivs only and no more are
irregulars, to wit* gut. good, beſser (*of old
bas*) better, beſt *beſt*; vil *much or many*,
mer *or* merer *more*, meiſt *or* mereſt *moſt*;
wenig *little*, weniger *leſs*, wenigſt *or* minſt
leaſt.

there are ſome adjectives or nouns of like uſe

with adjectivs, *which neither are nor can be compared e. g.* link *left*, rehtish *right-handed*, tod *dead*, lebendig *living*, gœlden *or* gülden *golden*, hœlzern *wooden &c. likewise all numbers and pronouns, e. g.* ein *one*, erst *first*, zwei *two &c.* mein *my*, folh *fuch*, beide *both &c.*

R. 5. *as the abfolute adjectivs of whatfoever degree take the nature of the adverbs, where the comparativ ends in* ER *and the fuperlativ either in* STE, *if goe before it* auf das *or* auf's; *or in* STEN, *when precede* zu'm *(for* zu dem*) or* a'm, *e. g.* er lebet hoh *and* præhtig *he lives high and fumtuously*; er lebet hœher (*or* hoeher) und præhtiger als ein fürft *he lives higher and more fumtnoufly than a prince*; auf's *or* auf das præhtigfte und hœhfte *or* hoeefte, zu'm *or* a'm prrhtigften und hœhften *very high and fumtuously: fo many particles become comparable and adjeftivs in adding the termination of the comparativ and fuperlativ e. g.* unter *under*, der di *or* das untere *the lower*; der, di *or* das unterfte *or* ünterfte, *the lowest of all*; hinter *behind*, der - di - das hintere *that is behind*, weiter hinter *farther behind*, der - di - das affer-hinterfte *the moft fartheft behind*, a'm *or* zu'm hinterften *moft far behind*; bald *foon*, bælder *fooner*, der - di - das fældefte *the foonefs*, aufs bældefte *very foon &c.*

R. 6. *the characteriftick letter* A *either fingle or in a bivowel, as alfo* O *and* U *of the monofyllabick pofitiv in comparifon is changed into* æ, œ, ü, *e. g.* alt *old*, ælter *older*, ælteſte *oldeſt*; faul *lazie*, fæuler *and* der-di- das fäuleſte; hoh *high*, hœher *or* hœer, der -di- das hoehſte *or* hœeſte; rotredd, rœter, der-di-das rœteſte; dumm *dull*, dümmer, der-di-das dümmeſte &c. *but the polyſyllabicks or thoſe, that have more then one ſyllable, are immoveable in their charactériſtick vowels e. g.* tapfer *ſtout*, tapferer, tapferſte; frottig *froſty*, froſtiger, froſtigſte; luſtig *merry*, luſtiger, luſtigſte; aufgeblaſen *lofty or proud*, aufgeblaſener, aufgeblaſenſte; verſuht *tried by experience*, verſuhter, verſuhteſte; willkommen *welcome*, willkommener, willkommenſte; verſluht *curſed*, verſluhter, verſluhteſte &c.

Sect. 2. of the Regular Declenſion.

we have four caſes in both numbers, the firſt whereof is anſwering to the nominativ and vocativ or exclamativ of the Latins, the ſecond to their genitiv or poſſeſſiv, the third to their dativ and ablativ, the fourth to their accuſativ.

Formation of the Singular Number.

the rootword or radix of a noun is the firſt caſe and the fountain, from whence the reſt is derived.

the ſecond caſe is made by adding to the firſt of the maſculin and neuter ſubſtantivs either the letter S, *eſpecially if they end in* EL, EN, ER, e. g. der himmel *heaven or ſky*, des himmels; das getummel *tumult*, des getummels; der regen *rain*, des regens;

der *fegen blefsing* ,des fegens; das haůlen
und weinen *bowling and weeping*, des hæul-
ens und weinens; der pfeffer *pepper*, des
pfeffers; das waffer *water*, des waffers &c.
never himmeles regenes wafferes *&c.* or
by adding the fyllable ES , *when they are ended
in any other confonant or vowell , effecialy in*
SH , S,*X*,Z , *e. g.* der fifh *fifh* , des fifhes;
der lax *or* lahs *falmon* , des laxes *or* lahfes;
das malz *malt* , des malzes *&c. never* des
fifh's lax's *or* lahf's malz's; *whereas in the
other terminations either in meetre or in quick
pronunciation the letter* E *may be omitted e.g.*
der leib *body*, des leibes *or* leib's; der
ftrom *ftream*, des ftromes *or* ftrom's; das
rad *wheel*, des rades *or* rad's *&c. but
allmoft all thofe mafculin fubftantivs , that have
their tonick accent in the laft fyllable and fignify a fenfitiv creature, inftead of* ES *receive
in their fecond cafe* EN *, to which afterwards in conftruction with an other fubftantiv
immediatly following, moft commonly is added
the letter* S, *and the article of the firft cafe is
allways taken away , unlefs both fubftantivs
be combined by hyphen , where the word of the
firft cafe does keep its article , but on the
contrary that , which was of the fecond cafe,
lofes as well the letter* S , *as the article, e. g.*
der Fůrft , herr , foldat , menfh , Tůrk,
has *&c.* das geld des fůrften, des fůrft-
ens geld , das fůrften- geld *the money of
the prince or the princes money*; di fele des
menfhen , des menfhen *or* des menfhens
fele, di menfhen-fele, *the foul of the man*

or man's foul; eine pfode eines hafen, eines hafens (*or* hafen) pfode, eine hafen -pfode, *a foot of a hare or a hares foot &c. to thefe words add alfo the neuter :* hærz *heart. the* mafculins mann, fifh *and perhaps fome others more receive only the fyllable ES*; *but* vater, vetter, bruder, fwager *doe receive either S or N, e. g.* des vetters *or* des vettern, *of the uncle*, des fwagers *or* des fwagern, *of the brother in law.*

fome words having two terminations in the firft cafe, have as many in the fecond, e. g. der nam *or* namen *name;* fam *or* famen *feed;* kuh *or* kuhen *cake;* frid *or* friden *peace;* hak *or* haken *hook;* gart *or* garten *garde;* pofs *or* pofsen *wag or merry trick;* funk *or* funken *fpark;* balk *or* balken *balke;* fnak *or* fnaken *merriander;* lenz *or* lenzen *fpring;* fhatt *or* fhatten *fhaddow;* mæi *or* mæyen *may;* rapp *or* rappen *black borfe;* lapp *or* lappen *botch;* taum *or* taumen *thumb;* ball *or* ballen *ball;* kolb *or* kolben *club;* fnapp *or* fnappen *ftopping,* felfs felffen *rock,* karp *or* karpen *carpe.* des : names, nam's, namens; fames, fam's, famens; frides, frid's, fridens &c.

the feminin termination E, likewife all abfolute both nominall and verball adjectives of what gendre foever and having before themfelves either of the articles, receive N or EN in flead of S or ES, e. g. eine heilige gemeine *a holy communion,* der heiligen gemeinen; di fanfte wolle *the foft wool,* der fanften wollen &c. exc. 1. *the feminin fubſtantivs in E*, *that ſignify* quality, quantity, abundance, weight &c. *keep their termination in the whole ſingular*, *unleſs joined to an other ſubſtantiv by hyphen*, *where they get the letter S, contrary to the maſculins*, *e.g.* di libe *charity*, der libe; di grœſse *great-neſs*, der grœſse; di ſwæhe *weakneſs*, der ſwæhe; di ſwere *heavineſs*, der ſwere &c. *but* di libes-geſhihte *romance of love*; ein libes-kind, *a child of love or begot in love* &c. *theſe and the like adjectivs uſed ſubſtantively in the feminin gendre*, *change their characteris -tick vowels A, O, U, as other moveable ſubſtantives*, *whereof in the foregoing Sect. n. 2. at the end.* exc. 2. *the feminin adjectiv without either of the articles prefixed, ends in* ER, *and the neuter in* ES, *in ſtead of* EN, *which ſyllable ſometimes remaines in the maſculin and neuter gendre*, *e.g.* guten teils *and* gutes teils *the moſt part*, heilſam-en *and* heilſames rats *of wholeſome counſell*, reiſen *and* reifes verſtandes *of a ripe un-derſtanding* &c. einer guten geſundheit *or* guter geſundheit, *of a good health*; gutes *and* guten vermœgens *or* eines guten ver-mœgens, *of a good eſtate*; ſtattlihen anſe-ens *and* ſtattliges anſeens *or* eines ſtattlig-en anſeens, *of a grave authoritie* &c. *the other feminin ſubſtantivs of what ending ſoever being without the finall E, doe keep their termination; but taking it (as ſome doe) they follow the generall Rule*, *e.g.* di hand band, der hand; di ſtatt *city*, der ſtatt; di gerehtigkeit *juſtice*, der gerehtigkeit;

di herrſhaft *dominion* , der herrſhaft; di dinerin *or* dinèrinne *maidſervant* , der di-nerin or dinerinnen; di verrꜩterei *or* ver-rꜩtereye *treaſon* , der verrꜩterei *or* ver-rꜩtereyen ; di erlœſung *redemtion*, der er-lœſung *&c.* *finaly note* , *that the poſſeſsiv* *and relativ adjectiv of the third perſon in all* *three gendres and in both numbres ſtands ſome-*times(*as in Engliſh*) *betwixt two words having* *relation one to the other , eſpecially when either* *of them ſignifyes poſſeſsion e. g.* des fürſten ſein geld *or* des fürſtens gelt *the prince's his* money ; der mutter tohter *or* der mutter ire tohter , *the mother her daughter*; des pferdes zaum *or* des pferdes ſein zaum, *the horſes bridle &c.* *the formation of the* *articles and of the pronouns ſee in the following* *third ſection.*

the third caſe is formed by putting away the *letter* S *of the ſecond , whereſoever it is found;* *the other both adjectiv and ſubſtantiv nouns* *remain here , as they were in the foregoirg* *ſecond caſe , without any other exception than,* *that the adjectivs having neither of the articles* *nor any of the demonſtrativ pronouns before* *themſelves, receive in the maſculin and neuter* *gender an* M, *and in the feminin an* R, *in ſtead* *of their finall* N, *e. g.* er iſt gutem weine und gutem bire *or* dem guten weine und guten bire gewogen , *he loves good wine and* *good beer*; er kœm't von guter (*or* von ei-ner guten) geſellſhaft , *he comes from a* *good company* ; ſi iſt aus berümterem (*or* einem berümteren) geſlehte entſproſsen

al₂ ir , *ſhe cometh from a more renowned kin-*
dred than you &c. *this caſe, when it ſig-*
nifyes the ſixt of the Latins , is allwayes accom-
panied with a prepoſition.

the fourth caſe is like the firſt in all regular nouns
except the maſculin adjectivs , and thoſe maſcu-
lin ſubſtantivs , that have in their ſecond an
N or EN , doe allwayes keep it , e. g. den
menſhen *hominem* ; den loeben *leonem* ; den
pfawen *pavonem.*

Formation of the Plurall.

of the ſecond caſe of the ſingular number is im-
mediatly formed the firſt of the plural 1. *by*
taking away the letter S of the maſculin ſub-
ſtantivs , and the laſt conſonant either N, R,
or S of the indefinit adjectivs in what gendre
ſoever ; *but the halfmute E immediatly fore-*
going is allwayes kept , where it is or ought to
be regularly , e. g. reihe dibe *rich thieves ,*
lange nægel *long nails ,* fromme fürſten
pious princes , ſwere hæmmer *heavie ham-*
mers &c. *note , thoſe ſubſtantivs , that*
have a double termination and ſometimes a
double gendre in the ſingular , have commonly
alſo a double plurail , as der ſhu or ſhuh *ſhoe,*
di ſhue *or* ſhühe ; der tal *or* dal *dale,*
di tale *or* dale , *but* das dal *or* tal , di tæler
or dæler ; der *and ſometimes* das leib *bady,*
di leiber *and (but ſeldom)* leibe ; der menſh
man in both ſexes for mankind , di menſhen ,
men or homines ; *but* das menſh , di menſher;
Gott *God ,* di Goetter; der Geiſt *ghaſt ,*
di Geiſter ; der wald *wood or forreſt ,* di

wælter *and* wælte; der drekk *dirt or mock* , di drekker *or* drekke ; der ort *place* , di œrt-er *and* orte ; *but* das ort *the fourth part of silver money* , di orte; das wort *word* , di worte *and* wœrter ; der *or* di ſtraus *noſegay,* di ſtræuſe *and* ſtræuſer; *but* der ſtraus *or* ſtraus-vogel *eſtridge* , di ſtrauſen; das land *land or countrie* , di lænder *and* lande ; der blokk *or* kloz *block* , di blœkke *and* blœkk-er *or* klœze *and* klœzer ; der pſlokk *plock or wooden nail* , di pſlœkke *or* pſlœkker; der ſtokk *block or ſtick* , di ſtœkke *and* ſtœkker; das ding *thing* , di dinge *and* dinger ; der mann *man or vir* , di mænner *and ſometimes* manne *or* mann e. g. wi vil hat ſi eemænn-er gehabt? *how many husbands had ſhe ?* es ſind drei mænner vor der tûre *or* dûre, *there be three men before the dore.* er hat di veſtung mit dreiſig mannen *or* mann eingenommen , *he has taken the fortreſs with thirty men.* tauſend mann (*or* manne) zu roſse *or* zu pferde , *thouſand horſemen;* hundert mann (*or* manne) zu fuſse *hundred footmen, not* mænner , pferden , roſsen , fûſsen. 2. *by adding to the feminin ſubſtantivs of whatſoever termination either the letter* N, *or the ſyllable* EN, *if it be not there allready , where , as alſo in the definit adjeſtivs , it is alwayes kept e. g.* di ritterlihen taten *or* daten , *the heroick actions or deeds* ; di hellen kwellen , *the clear welles;* di fûſsen freuden und ſiheren ruen , *the ſweet joyes and ſecure reſts ;* di leihten federn , *the light feathers* ; di adlihen tugenden *the noble virtues* , di kleineren ſweſtern *the less sisters &c. except* di sawe *sow*, di sawen *and* sæwe ; di kue *cow*, di kūe ; di magt *maidservant* , di mægte ; di lust *pleasure* , di lūste ; di hand *hand* , di hænde ; di wand *wall*, di wænde ; di zunft *tribe or companie of tradesmen* , di zunften *and* zūnfte . *with all those that have the* dipthong AU *e. g.* di braut *bride*, di bræute ; di maus *mouse* , di mæuse ; di laus *louse*, di læuse. *but* di mutter *and* di tohter *mother and daughter keep here their singular termination*, di mütter, di tœhter. 3. *either by taking quite away the letter* S *of the second singular case in the neuter substantives of what sort soever e. g.* des shafes *of the sheap*, di shafe ; des bedinges *of the condition*, di bedinge; des werkes *of the work* , di werke ; des reihs , *of the kingdome*, di reihe ; des spiles *of the play*, di spile ; des jars *of the year* , di jare ; des roßes *of the horse*, di roße ; des brotes *of the bread*, di brote , *and so forth all that are not amongst the following. or by changing the final* S *of the second singular into* R, *in these words here following*, das : weib *wife*, des weibes *of the wife*, di weiber *the wives &c. so* kalb *calf* , grab *grave* , bad *bath* , rad *wheel* , glid *limb* , lid *lied or song*, augenlid *eyelied* , bild *figure* , feld *field* , band *band* , land *land or countrey* , kind *child* , rūnd *runt or bullock* , shild *shield* , dah *tatch* , fah *partition* , gelah *laughter* , gemah *room* , loh *hole* , bloh *block* , tuh *cloth* , buh *book* , volk *folk* , dal *or tal* dale , maul *mouth*, tum *or* dum *tome with its compounds e. g.* reihtum *riches*, herzogtum *dukedome &c.* hun *pullet*, horn *horn* , gestirn *constellation or stars*,

korn *corne*, gehirn *brains*, fafs *barrell*, flofs
lock or caftle, reus *branch or bau*, glas *glafs*,
taus *deus*, wams *doublet*, haus *houfe*, as *car-
defs*; amt *office*, bret *board*, gut. *good*, ge-
mut *mind*, haupt *head*, kraut *herb*, liht *candle
or light*, neft *neaft*, fwert *fword*, fheit *piece
of cleaven wood*, holz *wood*. *but fome of them
have both* E *and* ER , *as* das gefiht *face*, di-
gefihte *and* gefihter ; gefleht *kind or fort*,
geflehte *and* geflehter ; fah *partition*, fæhe
and fæher ; pfand *pawn*, pfande *and* pfænder;
band *band*; bande *and* bænder; land *countrey*,
lande *and* lænder ; gewiht *weight*, gewihte
and gewihter *&c.*

*there are alfo fome (but very few) which in their
plurall receiv the fyllable* EN , *viz.* des ores
of the ear, di oren ; des herzes *or* herzen *of
the heart*, di herzen: *but* (*according to our
foregoing 3th. R.*) *all diminutivs and that end in*
EL, EN, ER , *likewife all numericall and abfolute adjectivs being of all gendres , as alfo the
infinitivs ufed for nouns , remain here , as they
were in the firft cafe of the fingular e. g.* das fhæfgen ift geſhoren, *the little fheap is fhoren*, di
fhæfgen find geſhoren *the little fheep are fhoren*, zwei bekken find verkauft *two bafons are
fold*, di flægel find zerbrohen *the flails are
broke*, di wafser fteen hoh *the waters ftand
high*, vir mandel *three fcore &c.* *yet fome of thofe
immoveable both mafculin and neuter fubftantivs
efpecially in* EL *or* ER *doe receive now and then
in grave writings an* E, *becaufe of the emphafis
e.g.* das gewæfser *flood of water*, di gewæfs
-ere, der Keufer *Emperour*, di Keufere *&c.*

Of the *Infinitius* used *Substantively* and
therefore stiled (by the most ingenious Author of
the Philosoph. Lang. p. 445.) participle substantives, note, that they have a double sense and
signification e. g. das essen, das graben they
signify 1. either the object of the act or fact
(there of eating) as the former word das essen
meat, or the effect of our action (here of digging
or graving) as the later does der graben the,
and these (as many there be in use, which their
signification will tell us) have a plural number
di essen the dishes of meat, di graeben or gra-
bene graves or ditches; but when they signify 2.
the very act or fact (as here of eating and graving) it self, then they are never used in the plurall, and instead hereof is taken the verball noun
in ung, if there be any need of e. g. das bedanken or danksagen thank or thanksgiving,
di bedankungen or danksagungen never di
bedanken or danksagen.

as in all the Doctrin of Derivation, so
especially here in the formation of the
plurall and its cases we must alwayes observe,
where to change the characteristick vowels U, O,
and A both single and in the dipthong AU, into
their improper bivowels û, oe, ae or aeu; this is
done here in all the plurall cases of all substantives
here not excepted e. g. der fuss foot, di füsse
feet, der son son, di soene sones; der shos lap, di
shoese laps; der vater father, di väter fathers; di hand hand, di haende hands; das haus
house, di haeuser houses; di maus mouse, di maeuse
mice &c. except all those, that in their plurall
end I. in EN or N of what gendre soever e. g. di

namen *némes*, di fonnen *funnes*, di oren *eares*,
&c. 2. *in* ENDE *or* UE *of the mafculins*
e. g. di abende *evenings*, di fhue *fhoes &c.*
3. *in* NDE, FE, LE, RE, SE, TE,
LZE *of the neuters*, *e. g.* di bande *bands*,
di fhaffe *tubs*, di male *meals*, di jare *years*,
di mafe *meafures*, di tahte *or* tohte *wicks*
of candles, di falze *falts*, di malze *malts*
&c. likewife di tage *dayes*, di arme *arms*,
di baftarde *baftards*, di grade *degrees*,
di ale *eels*, di tale *or* dale *dales mafculins*,
and di johe *yokes*, *with fome other neuters*
ending in E, *the which doe not change their*
charafteriftick vowell-
the fecond and fourth cafes have the very fame
termination, that has the firft of that number
in all manners of nouns, degrees and gendres,
diftinguifhed one from an other either by the
prepofed articles or the indeclinable particles,
except the indefinit adjectives receive here an R
through all gendres e. g.

erliher $\begin{cases} \text{mænner} \\ \text{frawen} \\ \text{kinder} \end{cases}$ *of honeft* $\begin{cases} \text{men.} \\ \text{women.} \\ \text{children.} \end{cases}$

unlefs they be preceded by an exceptive or re-
ftrictive particle as etlih, manh, vil, ein-
-ig *and fuch like*; *for then they feem to*
follow alfo the foregoing common rule e. g. et-
liher heiligen *and* heiliger mænner gedank
-en *the thoughts of fome holy men*, yiler
frommer *and* frommen frawen gebete *the*
prayers of many pious women, der gehorfam
manher gottfocrhtigen *and* gotsforrhtige,

kinder *the obedience of many godly children &c.*
note here by the by, every substantiv both of
the singular and plurall second case may
very handsomly be combined with the other
of the first by the token hyphen , the
which (though it be seldom used here in
this composition) commonly either gives or
takes away the lett. N or S in the singular, where
of see the second case of the precedent number
e.g. der buh-hændler *book-seller*, for der
hændler der büher *or* des buhs *the seller of*
the books or book; ein shaf-hirt *a shep-heard,*
for ein hirt der shafe *a heard of the sheep*; ein
kirh-turm *a church steeple*, for ein turm der
kirhen *a steeple of the church*; ein gold-smitt
or silber-smitt *a gold-smith or silver-smith*, for
ein smitt des goldes *or* silbers *a smith of gold*
or silver &c. but sometimes we doe keep either
of the aforesaid letters e. g. ein kriges-her *an*
army, di wolfes -milh *wolfs-milk &c. and some*
times we keep the plural termination e.g. ein
büher -freind *a freind of books*, ein kinder-
moerder *a murtherer of a child or children &c.*
more examples see in the 3: Sect. of the III. chap.
of this II. Part.

the third case is formed by adding to the end of
the first (having not allready this termination)
the letter N ; but all nouns , that have it, admit
no difference of cases here, being declined or
rather distinguished one from an other by the
prepositiv particles just as in English

f.g. { den / or / von } erlihen { männern / frawen / kindern } { to or / of the / honest } { men. / women / childrē.

finaly here *is* to be noted , *that there be severall
Substantivs (known by the use and signification,)
which have no plurall numbre , not so much for
want of a regular formation , as because they
are of no other but singular , propre and peculiar signification , the which becoming plurall,
that is generall and common , gives also to the
words the plurall termination , e.g.* das salz
salt , di salze *salts* ; der eſſig *vinegar* , di
eſſige ; das feyer *fire* , di feyere *fires* , di
keuſhheit *chaſtity* , di keuſhheiten *chaſtities* ;
der Hans *John* , di hanſen *Johns &c.* *on
the contrary there be plurals without the
singular e. g.* di æltern *or* eltern *parents,*
di alpen *the alpes* , di leute *the people* ,
di Staten *the States* , di hundes- tage
the dogs - dayes , di franzoſen *the French
pocks* , di blattern *the ſmall pocks* , di troe-
bern *the huſks* , di maſern *the maſels* ,
&c. and yet we ſay alſo ein ſtat *a ſtate,
but in an other ſignification ;* eine blatter *a bladder or bliſter* , ein hundes - tag
one of the dogs - dayes.

the foraign words follow the *Declenſion of
the nativs* , either with *their own final
termination or without it e.g.* des Plutar-
ches *or* Plutarchen ſpruh *Plutarchs ſentence* , Cicero's *or* Xenophons büher *Ci-
ceroes or Xenophons books* , Petrarchas
or Petrarchens verſe *Petrarchs Poems* , i'm
H. Evangelium des Evangeliſten Marcus
or Lucas *in the holy Goſpel of Mark or Luke* ,
di Sirenen *the marie-maids* , di Amazonen
the Amazons.

Exampels of Declenfion in Regular Nouns.

I. the Indefinit Article before
Singular Masculins.

Cafe

I. ein treuer vater, kneht, menſh,
II. eines trewen vaters, knehtes, menſhen
III. einem trewen vater, knehte, menſhen
IV. einen trewen vater, kneht, menſhen,

    a faithfull father, ſervant, man.
    Singular Feminins.

I.
IV. } eine rehte mutter, ſihel, hand.

II.
III. } einer rehten mutter, ſihel, hand.

    aright mother, ſickle, hand.
    Singular Neutres:

I.
IV. } ein kleines kind, herz, horn.

II. eines kleinen kindes, herzen, horns
III. einem kleinen kinde, herzen, horne

    a little child, heart, horn.

Plurals of All three gendres together:

I. { trewe vater, knehte, menſhen.
  { rehter mütter, ſiheln, hænde.
IV. { kleine kinder, herzen, hœrner.

II. { trewer væter, knehte, menſhen.
  { rehte mütter, ſiheln, hænde.
  { kleiner kinder, herzen, hœrner.

III. { trewen vætern, knehten, menſhen
  { rehten müttern, ſiheln, hænden.
  { kleinen kindern, herzen, hœrnern

II. the Definit Article before 1. *masculins*, 2. *fœ-*
minins and 3. *neuters.*

I {
1 der trewe vater, kneht, menſh.
2 di rehte mutter, ſihel, hand.
3 das kleine kind, herz, horn.
}

II {
1 des { trewen vaters, knehtes, menſhen
3 { kleinen kindes, herzen, horns.
2 der rehten mutter, ſihel, hand.
}

III {
1 dem { trewen vater, knehte, menſhen.
3 { kleinen kinde, herzen, horne.
2 der rehten mutter, ſihel, hand.
}

IV {
1 den trewen vater, kneht, menſhen.
2 di rehte mutter, ſihel, hand.
3 das kleine kind, herz, horn.
}

All three Genders together.

I, IV { di { trewen væter, knehte, menſhen.
di rehten mütter, ſiheln, hænde.
kleinen kinder, herzen, hoerner.
}

II. der { trewen vater, knehte, menſhen.
rehten mütter, ſiheln, hænde.
kleinen kinder, herzen, hoerner.
}

III. den { trewen vätern, knehten, menſhen.
rehten müttern, ſiheln, hænden.
kleinen kindern, herzen, hoernern.
}

III. Proper names of

men:	*women:*	*cities :*	*countries:*
I. Georg,	Katharine,	Hall,	Sahſen.
II. Georgs, n;	Katharinen,	Halles, Sahſens.	
III.Georgen,	Katharinen,	Halle,	Sahſen.
IV.Georgen,	Katharinen,	Hall,	Sahſen.

*all the proper names may be declined alſo with the
definit article e.g.* der Samuel, di Marie, das
Jæn, *but then the feminins have no N in the IV.
caſe, as* di Katharine &c. *not* di Katharinen.

Sect.
the Irregular De
expressed in this
ned after that
in His
Gram-

the Personals.

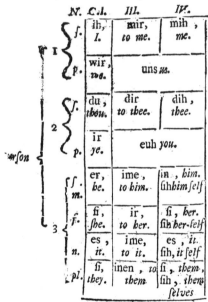

	N.	C.I.	III.	IV.
1 f.		ih, *I.*	mir, *to me.*	mih, *me.*
1 p.		wir, *we.*	uns *us.*	
2 f.		du, *thou.*	dir *to thee.*	dih, *thee.*
2 p.		ir *ye.*	euh *you.*	
3 f. m.		er, *he.*	ime, *to him.*	in, *him.* fih *himself*
3 f. f.		fi, *she.*	ir, *to her.*	fi, *her.* fih *her-felf*
3 n.		es, *it.*	ime, *to it.*	es, *it.* fih, *it felf*
3 pl.		fi, *they.*	inen, *to them.*	fi, *them,* fih, *them felves*

Person

3. *of*
-clenſion , jointly
Table , faſhio-
of D. Wallis
learned
mar.

the Poſſeſsives.

G. maſc.	foem.	neut.
meiner.	meine.	meines.
my , mine.	*m y , mine.*	*my, mine.*
unſer, un-ſerer.	unſere, unſer.	unſer, un-ſeres.
our , ours.	*our , ours.*	*our , ours.*
dein,dein-er.	deine , dein	dein,dein-es
thy, tvine.	*thy, thine.*	*thy,thine.*
ewer, ew-erer.	ewere , ewer.	ewer, ew-eres.
your yours.	*your yours.*	*your, yours.*
ſein ſeiner	ſeine,ſein.	ſein,ſeines
his hisne	*his , hisne.*	*his , hisne.*
ir,irer.	ire, ir.	ir, ires.
her, her s.	*her , hers.*	*her , hers.*
ſein , ſein-er. *its.*	ſeine ſein. *its.*	ſein,ſeines *its.*
ir irer.	ire, ir.	ir, ires.
their theirs.	*their theirs.*	*their theirs.*

N.	Caſ. I.	III.	IV.
Interrogivus of a perſon			
s. m.	wer? who?	weme?	wen?
	welher?	welhem?	welhen?
	which?	to whom?	whom?
f.	wer? who?	weme?	wen?
	welhe?	welher?	welhe?
	which?	to whom?	whom?
a thing			
n.	was?	weme?	was?
	what?	to what?	what?
	welhes?	welhem?	welhes?
	which?	to which?	which?
both P. all g.	welhe?	welhen?	welhe?
	which?	to whome?	who or
	who		which?
Demonſtrativus of a perſon			
s. m.	der, this	deme, diſ-	den, this
	diſer, that	em, jenem	diſen, that.
	jener, the	to this &c	jenen the
	other.		other.
f.	di, this.	der, diſer	di, this.
	diſe, that.	jener to	diſe, that.
	jene the	this &c.	jene, the
	other.		other.
a thing			
n.	das, this	deme diſ-	das, this.
	diſes, that	em jenem	diſes that.
	jenes, the	to this &c.	jenes the
	other.		other.
both P.	di, those.	denen, diſ-	di, those.
	diſe, jene	en jenen	diſe, jene
	the others	to those	the others
		others,	

wes? wefsen ? *whofe ? of*
welhes *?* welhen ? *what*
man.

---

wes ?   wefsen ? *whofe ? of*
    welher ? *what wo-*
man?

---

wes ?   wefsen ? *of what*
welhes *?* welhen ? *thing ?*
whereof?

---

welher ? *whofe ?*

---

defs, defsen. *of this.*
difes , difen. *of that.*
jenes, jenen. *of the other.*

---

der, dero. difer, jener.
of this. of that.   of the other.

---

defs, defsen. difes, difen.
    jenes, jenen.
of this, of that , of the other.

---

der , derer, dero. difer , jener.
of thefe. of thofe. of the other.

as the firſt number or the beginning of all the numbres ein or einer; eine; ein or eines, one , by forſaking its numerical ſignification becomes the indefinit article anſwering the Engliſh A or AN, in the plural einige any or ſome : ſo the perſonal and Demonſtrativ der , di , das that , loſes its emphaſis of demonſtration and becomes an auxiliar adjectiv of the definit nouns or the definit article , the declenſion of both we have ſeen in the end of the next foregoing ſection. m. kein or keiner nullus, f. keine nulla , n. kein or keines nullum ; m. ider or ein ider , f. ide or eine ide, n. ides or ein ides every; m. idweder or ein idweder, f. idwede or eine idwede, n. idwedes or ein idwedes, everyone; m. igliher or ein igliher , f. iglihe or eine iglihe , n. iglihes or ein iglihes, each; m. ein anderer or der andere, f. di or eine andere, n. ein anderes or das andere, an other or the other; m. ſelbiger or ſelber, and derſelbige or derſelbe, f. ſelbige or ſelbe and diſelbige or diſelbe, n. ſelbiges or ſelbes and dasſelbige or dasſelbe, that or the ſame; m. manher, f. manhe, n. manh or manhes ſome or many; the duall beide both, and the plurall etlihe or einige ſome or any, are all declined as the demonſtrative diſer, diſe , diſes; but note only , that the mentioned words ſerved by either of the articles have in their third ſingular caſe the termination N in ſtead of M, and in the ſecond they take N in ſtead of S, e. g. eines menſhen geld or des einen menſhens geld iſt ſo gut als des.

anderen, *the money of one man is as good as
that of the other* ; gebet idem *or* idwedem
and einem iden *or* einem idweden was fein

ift, *give every one what is hisne &c.*
iderman *or* ein iderman , *everybody* ;jeman
and imann (*of old* ieman *and* iaman qs. i-ein-
mann) *fomebody* ; nimann *or* niman (*of old*
ni+a-mann *or* nieman qs. niht ein mann *i. no
man or) no·body , are all three ufed only in the
fingular of both fexes and declined regularly.*
etwas , iht, ihts *or* ihtwas, *fomewhat
or ought , nihtes or nihts nothing or
nought , neutre fubftantives ufed only in the
fingular are immoveable as well , as the follow
-ing adjeEtivs of all gendres and numbres:*
So, *who or which is ufed as the relative*
welher, e, es, *but never after a prepofition:*
felbeft , felb'ft , felb'ften , felber , felb-
felb'ft *or* felb-felb'ften *for the better demon-
ftration and the greater emphafis are commonly
added as adjeEtivs to all manners of fubftantivs, like the word* felf *or* own-felf *in Englifh;
where this is a fubftantiv e.g. my felf* ih felber
not mein felber *&c.*   wafer *or* waf-
erlei , *when they afk , doe fignify which or
of what fort and nature* ; *elfe they denote whatfoever. the later receives fometimes alfo the
plurall termination.*

the poffefsivs ftanding before halben *or*
wegen , *receiv a* T , *e.g.* meinet wegen *for
my fake* , euret halber *or* halben *for your
fake &c. but when either* mein, dein, fein *&c.
or* meiner deiner feiner *&c. is to be ufed ,
fee the* 1. *Sect. of that chapt.* N. 3. R. 3.

Chapt. II. of the Verball Derivation or Conjugation.

We have only Two definit moods viz. Reſt and Oblique , whereof the former comprehends the narrative, indicative, interrogative &c. of the Latins , and the later denotes their con-- and ſubjunctive, conditionall and permiſsive , potentiall and optative , imperative and adhortative &c. Either of them hath no more than two ſingle tenſes , the reſt being circumſcribed, whereof the firſt perſon is denoted here by the numb. 1 , the ſecond by 2, and the third by 3 , to avoid the teadious repetition of the perſonall particles.

Sect. I. of the Auxiliar Verbes and thoſe of the Greater Anomaly.

I. Haben , *to have.*

Reſt *Mood.* Preſent *Tenſe.*

N. S.
1. habe, *have.*
2. haſt, *haſt.*
3. hat, *hath.*

Pl.
1 3 } haben } *have.*
2. habet

Imperfect.

S.
1 3 } hatte , *had.*
2 hatteſt, *hadſt.*

P.
1 3 } hatten } *had.*
2. hattet

Perfect.

S.
1. habe
2. haſt
&c.
} gehabt.

have
haſt had.
&c.

Morethenperfect.

$$S. \begin{cases} 1.\text{hatte} \\ 2.\text{hattelt} \\ \mathcal{C}c. \end{cases} \text{gehabt.} \begin{cases} had \\ bad\beta \\ \mathcal{C}c, \end{cases} had.$$

Futur.

$$S. \begin{cases} 1.\text{werde} \\ 2.\text{wirlt} \\ \mathcal{C}c. \end{cases} \text{haben.} \begin{cases} \text{\textit{shall}} \\ \text{\textit{wilt}} \\ c. \end{cases} \text{\textit{have.}}$$

fee the IVtb. verbe werden.

tbe compound and paulo-mox-futurs are eafily
to be formed as well here as elfewhere.

Oblique *M.*   *Prefent.*

$$S. \begin{cases} 1 \\ 3 \\ 2. \end{cases} \begin{array}{l} \text{habe, } have. \\ \text{habelt, } ba\beta. \\ \text{habe, } bave. \end{array} \quad P. \begin{cases} 1 \\ 3 \\ 2. \end{cases} \begin{array}{l} \text{haben} \\ \text{habet} \end{array} bave.$$

Imperfect.

$$S. \begin{cases} 1 \\ 3 \\ 2. \end{cases} \begin{array}{l} \text{hætte, } bad. \\ \text{hætteft, } bad\beta. \end{array} \quad P. \begin{cases} 1 \\ 3 \\ 2. \end{cases} \begin{array}{l} \text{hætten} \\ \text{hættet} \end{array} bad.$$

Perfect.

$$S. \begin{cases} 1. \text{habe} \\ 2. \text{habeft} \\ \mathcal{C}c. \end{cases} \text{gehabt,} \begin{array}{l} bave \\ ba\beta \\ \mathcal{C}c. \end{array} bad.$$

Morethenperf.

$$S. \begin{cases} \text{hætte} \\ \text{hætteft} \\ \mathcal{C}c. \end{cases} \text{gehabt.} \begin{array}{l} bad \\ bad\beta \\ \mathcal{C}c. \end{array} bad.$$

Futur. I.

$$S. \begin{cases} 1. \text{werde} \\ 2. \text{werdeft} \\ \mathcal{C}c. \end{cases} \text{haben.} \begin{array}{l} \text{\textit{shall}} \\ \text{\textit{wilt}} \\ \mathcal{C}c. \end{array} bave.$$

Futur. II.

S { 1. wûrde } haben. *fhould* } *have.*
  { 2. wûrdeſt }   *wouldſt* }
  { &c. }   &c. }

Inſinit. Preſent.   *Perfeꜩ.*
haben *to have.* haben gehabt, *to have had.*
      Futur.   *Supine.*
haben werden, *to ſhall have,* zu haben *to have.*

Participle Preſent.   *Perfeꜩ.*
habende , *having.*   gehabt , *had.*

II. wollen *to will.*

R. M.   *Preſent.*

S { 1 } will , *will.*   P { 1 } wollen } *will.*
  { 3 }   { 3 }
  { 2 willſt } *wilt.*   { 2. wollet }
  {   wilt }

                 Imperfeꜩ.

S { 1 } wolte, *would.* P. { 1 } woltë } *would*
  { 3 }   { 3 }
  { 2. wolteſt *wouldſt.*   { 2 woltet }

                 Perfeꜩ.

S. { 1. habe }   *have* }
   { 2. haſt } gewolt.   *haſt* } *would.*
   { &c. }   &c. }

                 Morethenperfeꜩ.

S. { 1. hatte }   *had* }
   { 2. hatteſt } gewolt.   *hadſt* } *would.*
   { &c. }   &c. }

                 Futur.

S. { 1. werde }   *ſhall* }
   { 2. wirſt } wollen.   *wilt* } *will.*
   { &c. }   &c. }

O. M.   *Prefen*.

$$S \left\{ \begin{matrix} 1. \\ 3. \\ 2. \end{matrix} \right. \left\{ \begin{matrix} \text{wolle, } will. \\ \text{wolleft } wilt. \\ \text{wolle } be\ willing. \end{matrix} \right. \quad P. \left\{ \begin{matrix} 1. \\ 3. \\ 2. \end{matrix} \right\} \left\{ \begin{matrix} \text{wollen} \\ \text{wollen} \\ \text{wollet} \end{matrix} \right\} will.$$

the reft of this and the Infinit moods is declined as the precedent verbe , which may be noted alfo in the following words , where and
whenfoever we leave fomewhat out ; for we
have No Defectivs at all.

III. Sein *to Be*.

M. R.   *Prefent*.

$$S. \left\{ \begin{matrix} 1.\ \text{bin, } am. \\ 2.\ \text{bift, } art. \\ 3.\ \text{ift, } is. \end{matrix} \right. \quad Pl. \left\{ \begin{matrix} 1. \\ 3. \\ 2. \end{matrix} \right\} \begin{matrix} \text{find} \\ \text{feid} \end{matrix} \right\} are.$$

Imperfect.

$$S. \left\{ \begin{matrix} 1. \\ 2. \\ 3. \end{matrix} \right\} \begin{matrix} \text{war } was. \\ \text{wareft } waft. \end{matrix} \quad Pl. \left\{ \begin{matrix} 1. \\ 3. \\ 2. \end{matrix} \right\} \begin{matrix} \text{waren} \\ \text{waret} \end{matrix} \right\} were.$$

Perfect.

$$S. \left\{ \begin{matrix} 1.\ \text{bin} \\ 2.\ \text{bift} \\ \&c. \end{matrix} \right\} \text{gewefen.} \begin{matrix} have \\ haft \\ \&c. \end{matrix} \right\} been.$$

Morethanperf.

$$S. \left\{ \begin{matrix} 1.\ \text{war} \\ 2.\ \text{wareft} \\ \&c. \end{matrix} \right\} \text{gewefen.} \left\{ \begin{matrix} had \\ hadft \\ \&c. \end{matrix} \right\} been.$$

Futur.

$$S. \left\{ \begin{matrix} 1.\ \text{werde} \\ 2.\ \text{wirft} \\ \&c. \end{matrix} \right\} \text{fein. } \begin{matrix} fhall \\ wilt \\ \&c. \end{matrix} \right\} bee$$

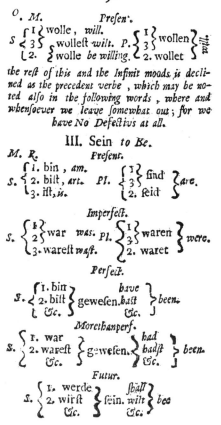

O. M.   *Present.*

S. { 1 } ſei or { been.
   { 3 } ſeye, { bee.
   { 2 } ſeyeſt, beeſt.   P. { 1 } ſein } *be.*
   { ſey } bee.   { 3 }
   biſs   { 2. } ſeid

Imperfect.

S. { 1 } wære, *were.*   P. { 1 } wæren } *were.*
   { 3 }   { 3 }
   { 2. wæreſt, wert. }   { 2 wæret }

Perfect.

S. { 1. ſeye } geweſen.   *have* } *been.*
   { 2. ſeyeſt }   *haſt* }
   { &c. }   &c.

Morethenperfect.

S. { wære } geweſen.   *had* } *been.*
   { wæreſt }   *haſt* }
   { &c. }   &c.

Futur. I.

S. { 1. werde } ſein.   *ſhall* } *bee*
   { 2. wirſt }   *will* }
   { &c. }

Futur. II.

S. { 1. würde } ſein.   *ſhould* } *bee.*
   { 2. würdeſt }   *wouldſt* }
   { &c. }   &c.

note, when you put the participle preterit of the principall verbe betwixt the two auxiliars of theſe futurs, you have alwayes the paulo-max -futures, as you may ſee here and imitate it both in the foregoing and the following verbes.

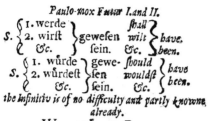

Paulo-mox F*utur* I. *and* II.

S. {
1. werde
2. wirft
&c.
} geweſen
ſein.
{
ſhall
wilt
&c.
} *have.*
been.

S. {
1. würde
2. würdeſt
&c.
} gewe-
ſen
ſein.
{
ſhould
wouldſt
&c.
} *have*
been.

the Infinitiv *is of no difficulty and partly* knowne
already.

IV. werden *to* Become.

this word hath *ſeverall ſignifications, which* in
*Engliſh muſt be expreſſed by diverſe words,
ſignif,ing ſometimes neutropaſſively as much as
to* Become, *and ſometimes as much as to* Be,
where it is *the auxiliary of the* Paſſives, *as
we ſhall ſee ; but often it* denoteth *nothing
elſe but the time to come both in* activ, paſſiv
and neutrall futurs.

M. R.   Preſent.

S {
1. werde *become.*
2. wirft *becomeſt.*
3. wird *becometh.*
} P {
1
3
2. werdet
} werden {
become.
}

Imperfect.

s {
1
3
2. wurdeſt, *becameſt.*
} wurde, *became.* p {
1
3
2. wurdet
} wurden {
became.
}

Perfect.

S. {
1. bin
2. biſt
&c.
} worden. {
am
art
&c.
} *become.*

Morethenperfect.

S. {
1. war
2. wareſt
&c.
} wor-
den {
was
wert
&c.
} become.

Futur.

S. { 1. werde / 2. wirſt / &c. } werden. { ſhall / wilt / &c. } become.

M. O. *Preſent.*

S. { 1 / 3 werde / 2 werdeſt / werde } become. P. { 1 / 2 werden / 3. werdet } become.

Imperfeƈt.

S. { 1 / 3 würde *became.* / 2. würdeſt, *becameſt* } P { 1 / 3 würden / 2. würd et } became.

Perfeƈt.

S. { 1. ſei / 2. ſeiſt / &c. } worden. { been / beeſt / &c. } become.

Morethanperfeƈt.

S. { 1. wære / 2. wæreſt / &c. } worden. { were / wert / &c. } become.

Futur. I. and II.

S. { 1. werde *and* würde / 2. werdeſt *and* wür- / deſt &c. } werden.

S. { ſhall and ſhould / wilt and wouldſt / &c. } become.

Paxlo-mox-futur I. and II.

S. $\begin{cases} \text{1. werde } and \\ \text{würde} \\ \text{2. werdeſt } and \\ \text{würdeſt} \\ \textit{&c.} \end{cases}$ $\begin{cases} \textit{ſhall } and \\ \text{wor-} \textit{ſhould} \\ \text{den } \textit{wilt } and \\ \text{ſein. } \textit{wouldſt} \\ \textit{&c.} \end{cases}$ $\begin{cases} \textit{been} \\ \textit{be-} \\ \textit{come.} \end{cases}$

V. Sollen *to Shall.*

this word ſignifyeth alwayes a neceſſity or obligation, but never a futurition, as it does in the Engliſh and the Lowdutch toungs.

R. M.   *Preſent.*

S. $\begin{cases} 1 \\ 3 \\ 2 \end{cases}$ $\begin{cases} \text{ſoll, } \textit{ſhall.} \\ \text{ſolt} \\ \text{ſolſt} \end{cases} \textit{ſhalt.}$ P. $\begin{cases} 1 \\ 3 \\ 2. \text{ ſoll et} \end{cases} \begin{cases} \text{ſollen} \\ \end{cases} \textit{ſhall.}$

Imperfect.

S. $\begin{cases} 1 \\ 3 \\ 2. \text{ſoltſt} \textit{ſhouldſt.} \end{cases} \text{ſolteſhould.}$ P. $\begin{cases} 1 \\ 3 \\ 2. \text{ſoltet} \end{cases} \begin{cases} \text{ſolten} \\ \end{cases} \textit{ſhould.}$

Perfect.

S. $\begin{cases} \text{1. habe} \\ \text{2. haſt} \\ \textit{&c.} \end{cases} \text{geſolt.}$ $\begin{cases} \textit{have} \\ \textit{haſt} \\ \textit{&c.} \end{cases} \textit{ſhould.}$

Morethanperfect.

S. $\begin{cases} \text{1. hatte} \\ \text{2. hätteſt} \\ \textit{&c.} \end{cases} \begin{cases} \text{ge-} \\ \text{ſolt.} \end{cases}$ $\begin{cases} \textit{had} \\ \textit{hadſt} \\ \textit{&c.} \end{cases} \textit{ſhould.}$

Futur.

S. $\begin{cases} \text{1. werde} \\ \text{2. wirſt} \\ \textit{&c.} \end{cases} \textbf{ſollen.}$ $\begin{cases} \textit{ſhall} \\ \textit{wilt} \\ \textit{&c.} \end{cases} \textit{ſhall.}$

O. *M.* Pre*sent.*

S. $\begin{Bmatrix} 1 \\ 3 \\ 2 \end{Bmatrix}$ folle , *shall.* foll*est* , *shält.* P $\begin{Bmatrix} 1 \\ 3 \\ 2 \end{Bmatrix}$ $\begin{Bmatrix} \text{follen} \\ \text{follet} \end{Bmatrix}$ *shall.*

*the Imperfe*ct *is like that of the Re*ct *mood ,
and the re*st *is known either by the foregoing
or the regular Formation.*

VI. kœnnen, *Can.*

R. *M.* Pre*sent.*

S. $\begin{Bmatrix} 1 \\ 3 \\ 2 \end{Bmatrix}$ $\begin{matrix} \text{kann , } can. \\ \text{kan}st \text{, } can\text{ß}. \end{matrix}$ P. $\begin{Bmatrix} 1 \\ 3 \\ 2 \end{Bmatrix}$ $\begin{matrix} \text{kœnnen} \\ \text{kœnnet.} \end{matrix}$ $\Big\}$ *can.*

*Imperfe*ct.

S $\begin{Bmatrix} 1 \\ 3 \\ 2 \end{Bmatrix}$ $\begin{matrix} \text{konte } could. \\ \text{kont}est \ couldst. \end{matrix}$ P. $\begin{Bmatrix} 1 \\ 3 \\ 2 \end{Bmatrix}$ $\begin{matrix} \text{konten} \\ \text{kontet} \end{matrix}$ $\Big\}$ *could.*

*Perfe*ct.

S. $\begin{Bmatrix} 1. \text{ habe} \\ 2. \text{ haft} \\ \&c. \end{Bmatrix}$ gekont. $\begin{Bmatrix} have \\ haft \\ \&c. \end{Bmatrix}$ *could.*

*More*thenperfe*ct-*

S. $\begin{Bmatrix} 1. \text{ hatte} \\ 2. \text{hattest} \\ \&c. \end{Bmatrix}$ gekont. $\begin{Bmatrix} had \\ hadst \\ \&c. \end{Bmatrix}$ *could.*

Futur.

S. $\begin{Bmatrix} 1. \text{werde} \\ 2. \text{wirst} \\ \&c. \end{Bmatrix}$ kœnnen. $\begin{Bmatrix} shall \\ wilt \\ \&c. \end{Bmatrix}$ *can.*

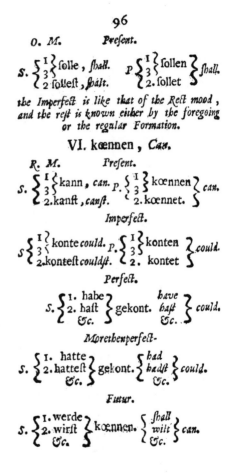

O. *M.*   *Prefent.*

$$S \begin{cases} 1 \\ 3 \\ 2 \\ \end{cases} \begin{matrix} \text{kœnne} \\ \text{kœnneſt} \\ \text{kœnne} \end{matrix} \; can. \; P \begin{cases} 1 \\ 3 \\ 2. \end{cases} \begin{matrix} \text{kœnnen} \\ \text{kœnnet} \end{matrix} \; can.$$

Imperfeƈt.

$$S. \begin{cases} 1 \\ 3 \\ 2. \end{cases} \begin{matrix} \text{kœnte} \; could \\ \text{kœnteſt} \; couldſt \end{matrix} \; p \begin{cases} 1 \\ 3 \\ 2. \end{cases} \begin{matrix} \text{kœnten} \\ \text{kœntet} \end{matrix} \; could.$$

VII. Mœgen *to may.*

R. *M.*   *Prefent.*

$$S. \begin{cases} 1 \\ 3 \\ 2. \end{cases} \begin{matrix} \text{mag} \; may. \\ \text{magſt} \; mayſt \end{matrix} \; P \begin{cases} 1 \\ 3 \\ 2. \end{cases} \begin{matrix} \text{mœgen} \\ \text{mœget} \end{matrix} \; may.$$

Imperfeƈt.

$$S. \begin{cases} 1 \\ 3 \\ 2. \end{cases} \begin{matrix} \text{mohte} \; might. \\ \text{mohteſt} \; mighſt. \end{matrix} \; P \begin{cases} 1 \\ 3 \\ 2. \end{cases} \begin{matrix} \text{mohten} \\ \text{mohtet} \end{matrix} \; might.$$

Perfeƈt.

$$S. \begin{cases} 1. \; \text{habe} \\ 2. \; \text{haſt} \\ \&c. \end{cases} \begin{matrix} \text{ge-} \\ \text{moht} \end{matrix} \begin{matrix} have \\ haſt \\ \&c. \end{matrix} \; might.$$

Morethenperfeƈt.

$$S. \begin{cases} 1. \; \text{hatte} \\ 2. \; \text{hatteſt} \\ \&c. \end{cases} \begin{matrix} \text{ge-} \\ \text{moht.} \end{matrix} \begin{matrix} had \\ hadſt \\ \&c. \end{matrix} \; might.$$

Futur.

$$S. \begin{cases} 1. \; \text{werde} \\ 2. \; wirſt \\ \&c. \end{cases} \begin{matrix} \text{mœgen} \end{matrix} \begin{matrix} ſhall \\ wilt \\ \&c. \end{matrix} \; may.$$

L

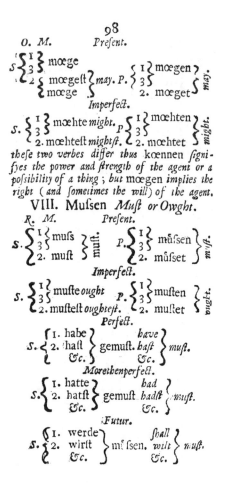

O. M.   *Present.*

$S \begin{Bmatrix} 1 \\ 3 \\ 2 \\ \end{Bmatrix}$ mœge
mœgeſt
mœge $\Big\}$ *may.* P. $\begin{Bmatrix} 1 \\ 3 \\ 2. \end{Bmatrix}$ mœgen
mœget $\Big\}$ *may.*

Imperfect.

S. $\begin{Bmatrix} 1 \\ 3 \\ 2. \end{Bmatrix}$ mœhte *might.*
mœhteſt *mightſt.* P $\begin{Bmatrix} 1 \\ 3 \\ 2. \end{Bmatrix}$ mœhten
mœhtet $\Big\}$ *might.*

theſe two verbes differ thus kœnnen ſignifyes the power and ſtrength of the agent or a
poſsibility of a thing ; but mœgen implies the
right (and ſometimes the will) of the agent.

VIII. Muſsen *Muſt or Owght.*

R. M.   *Present.*

S. $\begin{Bmatrix} 1 \\ 3 \\ 2. \end{Bmatrix}$ muſs
muſt $\Big\}$ muſt. P. $\begin{Bmatrix} 1 \\ 3 \\ 2. \end{Bmatrix}$ mūſsen
mūſset $\Big\}$ *muſt.*

Imperfect.

S. $\begin{Bmatrix} 1 \\ 3 \\ 2. \end{Bmatrix}$ muſte *ought*
muſteſt *oughteſt.* P. $\begin{Bmatrix} 1 \\ 3 \\ 2. \end{Bmatrix}$ muſten
muſtet $\Big\}$ *ought.*

Perfect.

S. $\begin{Bmatrix} 1. \text{ habe} \\ 2. \text{ haſt} \\ \&c. \end{Bmatrix}$ gemuſt. $\begin{matrix} \textit{have} \\ \textit{haſt} \\ \&c. \end{matrix} \Big\}$ *muſt.*

Morethenperfect.

S. $\begin{Bmatrix} 1. \text{ hatte} \\ 2. \text{ hatſt} \\ \&c. \end{Bmatrix}$ gemuſt. $\begin{matrix} \textit{had} \\ \textit{hadſt} \\ \&c. \end{matrix} \Big\}$ *muſt.*

Futur.

S. $\begin{Bmatrix} 1. \text{ werde} \\ 2. \text{ wirſt} \\ \&c. \end{Bmatrix}$ miſsen. $\begin{matrix} \textit{ſhall} \\ \textit{wilt} \\ \&c. \end{matrix} \Big\}$ *muſt.*

O. M.   *Preſent.*

S. { 1 3 } mîſſe { 2 { mûſſeſt { mâſſe } (muſt.)   P. { 1 3 } mûſſe { 2. mûſſet } (muſt.)

Imperfeſt.

S. { 1 3 } mûſte { 2. mûſſeſt } (ought.)   P. { 1 3 } mûſten { 2. mûſtêt } ought

IX. Laſsen *to let or Grant , likewiſe to Cauſe or Bid.*

R. *M.*   *Preſent.*

S. { 1. laſſe *let.* { 2. læſſeſt *letteſt.* { 3. læſſet *let.*   P. { 1 3 } laſſen { 2. laſſet } *let.*

Imperfeſt.

S. { 1 3 } lieſſe *let.* { 2. lieſſeſt *leiſt.*   P. { 1 3 } lieſen { 2. lieſet } *let.*

Perfeſt.

S. { 1. habe { 2. haft { &c. } gelaſſen { *have* { *haſt* { &c. } *granted.*

Morethenperfeſt.

S. { 1. hatte { 2. hatlſt { &c. } gelaſſen { *had* { *hadſt* { & c. } *granted.*

Futur.

S. { 1. werde { 2. wirſt { &c. } laſſen { *ſhall* { *wilt* { &c. } *grant.*

Θ. *M.*   *Prefent.*

S. { 1, 3 } lafse } 2 lafseft } *let.*   { 1, 3 } lafsen } 2. lafset } *let.*

X. Dærfen *to Dare or May.*

R. *M.*   *Prefent.*

S. { 1, 3 } darf *dare.*   2. darfeft *dareft.*   P. { 1, 3 } dærfen } 2. dærfet } *dare.*

Imperfect.

S. { 1, 3 } darfte *durft.*   2. darfteft *durftoft.*   P. { 1, 3 } darften } 3. darftet } *durft.*

Perfect.

S. { 1. habe, 2. haft, &c. } gedorft.   { have, haft, &c. } *might.*

Morethenperfect.

S. { 1. hatte, 2. hattft, &c. } gedarft.   { had, hadft, &c. } *might.*

Futur.

S. { 1. werde, 2. wirft, &c. } darfen   { fhall, wilt, &c. } *dare, may.*

O. *M.*   *Prefent.*

S. { 1, 3 } dærfe *may.*   2. dærfeft *mayft.*   P. { 1, 3 } dærfen } 2. dærfet } *may.*

Imperfect.

S. { 1, 3 } dærfte } 2. dærfteft } *durft.*   P. { 1, 3 } dærftē } 2. dærftet } *durft.*

some dialects *use* in this verbe *sometimes* O *or* U *in* stead *of an* A , *and* œ *or* ů *instead of an* Æ. to the greater anomaly *is also brought the following verbe, though it be con-strued with other verbs by the help of the particle* zu *to* e. g. er weis zu heuheln *be knows to dissemble.*

XI. Wissen, *to Know.*

M. R. *Present.*

S ⎰ 1 ⎱ weis ⎰ know ⎱ P. ⎰ 1 ⎱ wisse ⎰ know.
  ⎱ 3 ⎰   ⎱ knoweth ⎰   ⎱ 3 ⎰ wisset ⎰
  ⎰ 2. ⎰ weisest ⎰ knowest   ⎱ 2. wisset ⎰

Imperfect.

S. ⎰ 1 ⎱ wuste *knew, wote.* P. ⎰ wusten ⎰ knew.
   ⎱ 3 ⎰   ⎱ wustet ⎰
   ⎱ 2. wustest *knoweft.*

Perfect.

S. ⎰ 1. habe   *have*
   ⎱ 2. hast ⎰ gewust *haft* ⎱ known.
   ⎱ &c. ⎰   *&c.* ⎰

Morethenperfect.

S. ⎰ 1. hatte   *had*
   ⎱ 2. hatst ⎰ gewust *hadst* ⎱ known.
   ⎱ &c. ⎰   *&c.* ⎰

Futur.

S. ⎰ 1. werde   *shall*
   ⎱ 2. wirst ⎰ wissen. *wilt* ⎱ know..
   ⎱ &c. ⎰   *&c.* ⎰

O. M. *Present.*

S. ⎰ 1 ⎱ wisse   P. ⎰ 1 ⎱ wisse ⎰ know.
   ⎱ 3 ⎰ know.   ⎱ 3 ⎰ wisset ⎰
   ⎱ 2. wissest ⎰   ⎱ 2. wisset ⎰
   ⎱ wisse   ⎰

Imperfect.

S $\left\{\begin{matrix}1\\3\end{matrix}\right\}$ wúſte $\left.\begin{matrix}\\\end{matrix}\right\}$ *wiſt,* P. $\left\{\begin{matrix}1\\3\end{matrix}\right\}$ wúſten $\left.\begin{matrix}\\\end{matrix}\right\}$ *wiſt,*
 $\left.\begin{matrix}2.\end{matrix}\right.$ wúſteſt $\left.\begin{matrix}\\\end{matrix}\right\}$ *knew.* 2. wúſtet $\left.\begin{matrix}\\\end{matrix}\right\}$ *knew*

the reſt goes after the Analogie.

Sect. 2.   of the Regular Formation.
1. of the Activs.

the reſt preſent *is* formed of the indefinit
(*as the prime and principal verb (signi-*
fying more directly the notion of action) by
putting away the letter N *in the firſt ſingular*
and adding inſtead therof the two letters ST
in the ſecond , and the Letter T *in the third*
ſingular , as alſo in the ſecond plurall ; but
the firſt and third perſons of the greater num-
ber are like the infinitiv , which here in our
dialect has the finall N*. e. g.* eſsen, freſsen
&c. uſed alſo in the Belgick eeten , freeten;
in the Allemannick æſsan, fræſsan; *in the An*
-gleSaxonick etan , fretan ; *whereas others*
omitte it , as the Turingick geæſe, gefræſse;
the Sileſsan æſsæ , fræſsæ ; *and the Engliſh*
to eate, to frette.

R. M.   *the Preſent.*

S. $\left\{\begin{matrix}1.\text{ libe } \textit{love.}\\2.\text{ libeſt } \textit{loveſt.}\\3.\text{ libet } \textit{loveth.}\end{matrix}\right.$ P. $\left\{\begin{matrix}1\\3\end{matrix}\right\}$ liben $\left.\begin{matrix}\\\end{matrix}\right\}$ *love,*
   2. libet $\left.\begin{matrix}\\\end{matrix}\right\}$

the Imperfect

hath the ſame addition of terminations in the
ſecond ſingular and in the whole plurall, receiving beſides theſe everywhere before the
finall characteriſtick vowell of both numbers the
ſyllable ET thus

S. $\begin{Bmatrix} 1 \\ 3 \end{Bmatrix}$ libete *loved.*   P. $\begin{Bmatrix} 1 \\ 3 \end{Bmatrix}$ libetē $\Big\}$ *loved.*
    2. libeteſt *lovedeſt*   2. libetet

*the very ſame conjugation has the oblique mood
in both tenſes, except in the ſecond ſingular
of the preſent the two letters ST are taken away,
when we beſeech or command, elſe not; the
like apocope ſuffers alſo the third of the ſame
number and tenſe in what ſignification ſoever
by putting away the letter T, as in Engliſh, thus*

O. M.   Preſent.

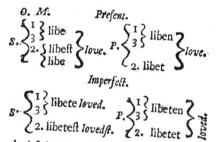

S. $\begin{Bmatrix} 1 \\ 3 \end{Bmatrix}$ libe $\Big\}$ *love.*   P. $\begin{Bmatrix} 1 \\ 3 \end{Bmatrix}$ liben $\Big\}$ *love.*
   2. $\begin{Bmatrix}$ libeſt $\\$ libe $\end{Bmatrix}$ 2. libet

Imperfeſt.

S. $\begin{Bmatrix} 1 \\ 3 \end{Bmatrix}$ libete *loved.*   P. $\begin{Bmatrix} 1 \\ 3 \end{Bmatrix}$ libeten $\Big\}$ *loved.*
   2. libeteſt *lovedſt.*   2. libetet

the infinit preſent is uſed with the particle zu,
Engl. To, *Low - D.* Te, *in ſtead of the
Latin gerundy and ſupins e. g.* zu liben, *Engl.
to love, Lowd.* te beminnen, *Lat.* amatum,
amatu, amandi. *but where and when this
particle before an Infinitiv is to be uſed elſe,
every one knowes not ignorant of the Engliſh
toung. we uſe the infinit preſent alſo with
the neuter article in ſtead of the verball ſubſtantive ſignifying an aſtion e. g.* das liben

amatio seu actus amandi or the act of love;
von dem liben , *ab or de actu amandi &c.*
in stead whereof we may forme from thence an
other verball substantiv in ung , *as the Eng-*
lish in ing , *having the same signification as*
the foregoing hath e.g. di krœnung *or* das
krœnen *the crowning or coronation*; di ker-
ung und wendung *or* das keren und
wenden *the turning &c. but he , that doeth*
this action , is expressed by the substantiv of the
termination ER , *e.g.* ein trinker *a drinker,*
ein eser *an eater,* ein anklæger *an accuser.*
we doe decline our participles activ and passiv,
of that present by adding There the letter D
e. g. libend , *loving* ; *and Here by turning*
N into T , where (as in the Greek toung e.g.
γέγονα , γὲγεαφα *&c. or in old English ,*
as we have many remainders , for instance in
Chaucer yeboren , yeleaped *&c. where G is*
turned to Y) we must in the head of the theam
set the preformativ syllable GE, in Lowdutch
GHE , *e. g.* gelibet *loved. standing before*
a substantiv , they both receiv the termination
ER , *and are declined as other adjectivs e.g.*
libender. gelib'ter.
those, that have a separable preposition before
themselves, receive the syll. GE *after it e.g.* un-
ge-offen-baret *unrevealed,* lôs-ge-sprohen *ab-*
solved , ab-ge-shüttelt *shaked off &c. the*
very same is to be observed of the particle zu
to (when it makes a Supine or Gerundy) al-
wayes giving to the foregoing separated prepo-
sition the token of division e. g. nah-zu forsh-
en *to inquire after* , wider-zu geben *to give*

again , auf - zu blafen *to blow up &c.*
but all the verbes beginning with Be, Ent, Em,
Er ; Ver , Zer , (*as alfo* wider *and* über
*when they lofe the tonick accent) are without
this addition of the fyll.* GE , e. g. begonn-
en *begunne* , entleibet *killed* ; erlœfet *re-
deemed,* vergefsen *forgotten*; zerrifsen *toren*;
überwæltiget *overpowerd* , widerfprohen
contradicted &c. Efsen *to eate has* gegefs
-en *eaten in ftead of* geefsen. *in meetre
and vulgar language is ufed fometimes* gefsen,
gangen , kommen *for* gegefsen gegangen
gekommen , *and everywhere both in meetre
and oratory or profe we fay well* mûfsen foll-
en wollen dœrfen mœgen kœnnen *con-
ftrued with an exprefs infinitiv e. g.* ir hættet mir's fagen follen *you had fhould tell me
of it &c. but the regular participles* gemuft
gefolt gewölt gedorft gewoht gekont *are
ufed without an infinitiv e. g.* warum afet
ir niht ? ih habe niht gedorft gewolt gekont *&c. why did you not eate ? i durft not,
i would not, i could not. fee the VI. R. in the
irreg. form. of the lefs anomaly.*
the Latin participles in RUS *and* DUS *are
circumfcribed as in Englifh e. g. lecturus* ein
-er der da lefen wird *one that will read or
goes to read &c. verba legenda* di vor·zu le-
fenden worte *or* di worte fo da follen (mûfs-
en) vorgelefen werden *words that fhall be read.
fo likewife the perfect tenfe and the more-
than-perfect are formed of the participle
preterit added to its propre auxiliar verbe , as
in Englifh , e. g.*

R. M.   *Perfect.*

S. $\begin{cases} 1.\ \text{habe} \\ 2.\ \text{haft} \\ \mathscr{C}c. \end{cases}$ gelibet $\begin{cases} have \\ haſt \\ \mathscr{C}c. \end{cases}$ loved.

Morethenperfect.

S. $\begin{cases} 1.\ \text{hatte} \\ 2.\ \text{hatteſt} \\ \mathscr{C}c. \end{cases}$ gelibet $\begin{cases} had \\ hadſt \\ \mathscr{C}c. \end{cases}$ loved.

O. M.   *Perfect.*

S. $\begin{cases} 1.\ \text{habe} \\ 2.\ \text{habeſt} \\ \mathscr{C}c. \end{cases}$ gelibet $\begin{cases} have \\ haſt \\ \mathscr{C}c. \end{cases}$ loved.

Morethenperfect.

S. $\begin{cases} 1.\ \text{hætte} \\ 2.\ \text{hætteſt} \\ \mathscr{C}c. \end{cases}$ gelibet $\begin{cases} had \\ hadſt \\ \mathscr{C}c. \end{cases}$ loved.

Inf. M.   *Perfect.*

gelibet haben *to have loved.*

but the neuters receiv the auxiliar of the paſsivs

      e. g.

R. M   *Perfect.*

S, $\begin{cases} 1.\ \text{bin} \\ 2.\ \text{biſt} \\ \mathscr{C}c. \end{cases}$ geſtanden $\begin{cases} ſtood. \\ ſtoodſt. \\ \mathscr{C}c. \end{cases}$

Morethenperfect.

S. $\begin{cases} 1.\ \text{ware} \\ 2.\ \text{wareſt} \\ \mathscr{C}c. \end{cases}$ geſtanden $\begin{cases} ſtood. \\ ſtoodſt. \\ \mathscr{C}c. \end{cases}$

O. M.   *Perfect.*

S. $\begin{cases} 1.\ \text{ſei} \\ 2.\ \text{ſeiſt} \\ \mathscr{C}c. \end{cases}$ geſtanden $\begin{cases} did \\ didſt \\ \mathscr{C}c. \end{cases}$ ſtand.

Morethenperfect.

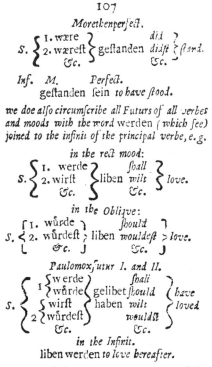

S. {
1. wære
2. wæreſt
&c.
} geſtanden {
did
didſt
&c.
} ſtand.

Inf. *M.* *Perfect.*
geſtanden ſein *to have ſtood.*

*we doe alſo circumſcribe all Futurs of all verbes
and moods with the word* werden *(which ſee)
joined to the infinit of the principal verbe, e. g.*

in the rect mood:

S. {
1. werde
2. wirſt
&c.
} liben {
ſhall
wilt
&c.
} love.

in the Oblique:

S. {
1. wûrde
2. wûrdeſt
&c.
} liben {
ſhould
wouldeſt
&c.
} love.

Paulomox̃futur I. and II.

S. {
1 {
werde
wûrde
} 2 {
wirſt
wûrdeſt
&c.
} gelibet {
ſhall
ſhould
wilt
wouldſt
&c.
} haben {
have
loved
}

in the Infinit.
liben werden *to love hereafter.*

*we never uſe in good language to circumſcribe
the ſingle tenſes, as the Engliſh doe, e. g.* ih
lahe *not* ih tue lahen *i doe laugh*, er lahe-
te *or* er flûſe *not* er file ein lahender *or*
ſlafend *he fell a-laughing or a-ſleepe*, ih
komme *not* ih bin kommrend *or* ein komm-

ender *i am a-coming*, hœret ir ? feet ir?
not duet ir hœeren ? duet ir fœn ? *doe*
you heare ? doe you see ? fo ih will lefen *not*
ih bin geend zu lefen *i am going to reade*,
was wolte ih doh fagen? *not* was war ih
geend zu fagen ? *what was i going to fay ?*

II. of the Paſſives.

the paſſives uſe *everywhere the auxiliary*
werden *and* fein. *e. g.*

R. M.   Prefent.

S. { 1. werde / 2. wirſt / &c. } gelibet { *am art &c.* } *loved.*

Imperfect.

S. { 1. wurde / 2. wurdeſt / &c. } gelibet { *was waſt &c.* } *loved.*

Perfect.

S. { 1. bin / 2. biſt / &c. } gelibet worden. { *have haſt &c.* } { *been loved.* }

Morethenperfect.

S. { 1. war / 2. wareſt / &c. } gelibet worden { *had hadſt &c.* } *been loved.*

Futur.

S. { 1. werde / 2. wirſt / &c. } gelibet werden { *ſhall wilt &c.* } *be loved.*

O. M.   Prefent.

S. { 1. werde / 2. { werdeſt / werde } &c. } gelibet { *been beeſt bee &c.* } *ioved.*

Imperfect.

S. { 1. wûrde 2. wûrdeft &c. } gelibet { *were* *wert* &c. } *loved.*

Perfect.

S. { 1. fei 2. feift &c. } gelibet worden { *have* *haft* &c. } { *been* *loved* }

Morethenperfect.

S. { 1. wære 2. wæreft &c. } gelibet worden { *had* *hadft* &c. } { *been* *loved* }

Futur. I. and II.

S. { 1 { werde wûrde } 2 { werdeft wûrdeft } &c. } gelibet werden { *fhall* *fhould* *wilt* *wouldft* &c. } *be love*

Paulomoxfutur I. and II.

S. { 1 { werde wûrde } 2 { wirft wûrdeft } &c. } gelibet worden fein { *fhall* *fhould* *wilt* *wouldft* &c. } { *have* *been* *loved* }

Inf. M.   *Prefent.*

gelibet werden *to be loved.*

Perfect.

gelibet worden fein *to have been loved.*

Futur.

werden gelibet werden *to be loved hereafter.*

in stead of these two later tenses which we formed here and elsewhere , is alwayes used as well by us as the English the Obliqve mood with the particle dáß *that, either expressed or understood , both here in the passive and in any other verb.*

Supine and Gerundie.

gelibet zu werden *to be loved.*

Participle.

gelibet *loved.*

III. *of the Reciprocks.*

the Reciprock and Neuter verbes are after the same manner (that is either as the Ativs or as the Passivs) conjugated, where the Neuter - Ativs or Reciprocks use the auxiliar haben *to have, e. g.*

Present.

S. $\begin{cases} 1. \text{ frewe mih } \textit{rejoice.} \\ 2. \text{ frewest dih } \textit{rejoicest.} \\ 3. \text{ frewet sih } \textit{rejoiceth.} \end{cases}$

P. $\begin{cases} 1 \\ 3 \end{cases}$ frewen $\begin{cases} \text{uns} \\ \text{sih} \end{cases}$ $\Big\}$ *rejoice.*

2. frewet euh

Imperfect.

S. $\begin{cases} 1 \\ 3 \end{cases}$ frewete $\begin{cases} \text{mih} \\ \text{sih} \end{cases}$ *rejoiced.*

2. frewetest dih *rejoicedst.*

$$P. \begin{Bmatrix} 1 \\ 3 \end{Bmatrix} \text{ freweten} \quad \begin{Bmatrix} \text{uns} \\ \text{ſih} \end{Bmatrix} \Big\} \textit{rejoiced.}$$
$$2. \qquad \text{frewetet euh} \Big\}$$

Perfect.

$$S. \begin{Bmatrix} 1. \text{ habe mih} \\ 2. \text{ haſt dih} \\ \&c \end{Bmatrix} \text{gefrewet} \quad \begin{Bmatrix} \textit{have} \\ \textit{haſt} \\ \&c. \end{Bmatrix}$$

Morethenperfect.

$$P. \begin{Bmatrix} 1. \text{ hatte mih} \\ 2. \text{ hatteſt dih} \\ \&c. \end{Bmatrix} \text{gefrewet} \quad \begin{Bmatrix} \textit{had} \\ \textit{hadſt} \\ \&c. \end{Bmatrix}$$

Futur.

$$S. \begin{Bmatrix} 1. \text{ werde mih} \\ 2. \text{ wirſt dih} \\ \&c. \end{Bmatrix} \text{frewen} \quad \begin{Bmatrix} \textit{ſhall} \\ \textit{wilt} \\ \&c. \end{Bmatrix} \textit{rejoice.}$$

IV. of the neuter - paſsivs.

*but theſe to wit the neuter-paſsivs (none of
them as Neutres excepted) we decline with
the auxiliary ſein in the Preterits , and with
werden in the futurs. which theſe verbes
be , we will note on their forehead with the
letter N in the enſuing table of the leſs anomaly,
where they , as many there are irregulars , oc
-curre with their ſignification , needleſs here
to be ſet down , but the regulars are thoſe
that follow* bœrſten *to burſt ,* erblaſsen *or*
verblaſsen *to become pale,* errœten *to bluſh,*
erſtarren *or* verſtarren *to become ſtiff for
cold or amazement ,* erſtaunen *to ſtart back
and be aſtoniſhed ,* n. ſegeln *to ſail ,* n. ſtürz-
en, *to fall down,* verarmen *to become poor,*
verblinden *to become blind ,* verblāen *to loſe
or ſhed the flowers,* verfaulen *to rotte ,* ver-*

lairen *to become halting* , vernarren *to be-come like a fool* , verfmahten *to languishe* , verftummen *to become dumb* , verwefen *to decay*, zerlehfen *to gape or chink* , *n.* zerreifen *to goe in pieces*, *n.* zien *to betake himself from one place to an other.* *mind well, that* we fayd in the rule *neuter passives as*

neuters. for *fome of them are often alfo activs fignifjing a tranfitiv action , and then they are declined in their preterits with the activ auxiliary e. g.* zerreifen *fignifyeth active-ly to teare in pieces , but neutraly to goe in pieces &c.* likewife we fay er ift vo'm pfer -de geftûrzet *(neutraly)* he *is fallen beadlong from the horfe , and (actively)* fi haben in von dem pferde geftûrzet *they have pulled him from the horfe.*

V. of the Imperfonals.

the *imperfonals are formed as in Englifh thus e. g.* es regnet, es fneyet , es weet , *it raineth , it fnoweth , it bloweth* ; mann faget men fay , es gezimet uns, es gefællet uns, es beluftiget uns tugendhaftig zu fein *it bekoveth us , it pleafeth us , it delighteth us to be vertuous.*

VI. of the Derivativs.

we doe *circumfcribe the derivativ verbes of the Latins , as the Inchoativs or augmentativs with the word* werden *e. g.* ih werde gros, fett, ftumpf *or* dumm , *i growe tall or great , fatt , dull ,* Lat. grandefco , pinguefco , hebe -refco ; es wird tag, finfter *or* naht *it groweth day dark or night, Lat.* diefcit, tenebrafcit, noctefcit *&c.*

the Frequentativs we circumfcribe with the word oft, often , ofters *or* fleifig *e. g.* ih befuhe often *i vifit often,* ih erfuhe fleifig *i befeech freqvently &c. that is in Latin* vifito, rogito.

the Diminutivs are circumfcribed either with the word wenig *or* ein wenig *e. g.* ih trinke ein wenig *i fup a little,* ih finge ein wenig *i fing a little or chirp &c. Lat.* forbillo, cantillo. *or with fetting the fyllable* EL *or* LE *before the later characteriftick vowel e. g.* lahen *to laughe ,* læheln *to fmile;* fprengen fprengeln *or* fprenkeln *to fhrinkle ,* klingen klingeln *to make a little noife with the bells ,* kûnft -eln *to imitate an art by little and little &c. which termination* EL *or* LE *was ufed antiently alfo in the Subftantivs , e. g.* hûndel *or* hûnd -le bifsel *or* bifle *&c. but now it is grown quite out of fafhion in good language. for we fay* hûndgen *little dog ,* bifsgen *little bit. fee P.*
II. *chap.* I. *Sect.* 1. *n.* 2.

this is the only One conjugation of all our Verbes , a very little differing from that of the Low - dutch and the Englifh, as you may eafily guefs and judge of the compound tenfes and other moods , when you look on the two fingle ones of the reft to be had in each of them , the terminations whereof together with their characteriftick vowel we have here added as an overplus in the next following table:

High-dutch.	Low-dutch.	English.
	Present.	

	High-dutch	Low-dutch	English
S. { 1.	E.	1. E.	1. E.
2.	EST.	2. EST.	2. EST.
3.	ET.	3. ET.	3. ETH

P. ⎰1⎱ EN. ⎰1⎱ EN. ⎰1⎱ E.
  ⎱3⎰   ⎱3⎰   2
  2. ET. 2. ET. 3

Imperfect.

S. ⎰1⎱ ETE. ⎰1⎱ EDE. ⎰1⎱ ED.
  ⎱3⎰   ⎱3⎰   ⎱3⎰
  2. ETEST. 2. EDEST. 2. EDEST.

P. ⎰1⎱ ETEN. ⎰1⎱ EDEN. ⎰1⎱ ED
  ⎱3⎰   ⎱3⎰   2
  2. ETET. 2. EDET. 3

Sect. 3. of
the Less Anomaly in Verbes.

Those verbes, that are declined irregularly in few persons and tenses (following everywhere else the regular formation) meet all together in the ensuing table , where the first person , we have set down only , will shew , how the rest are formed , when we observe these few rules here following.

R. 1. *the halfmute* characteristick *E before* T *and* ST *may everywhere be syncopized either alone , if precede an inseparable consonant ; or with one of two like consonants e. g.* er lib't *he loveth ,* ir lib'tet *ye loved ;* gelib't *lov'd ,* du siht'st *thou fightest ,* er slaht *or* slaht *-et he killeth ,* verdam't *or* verdammet con-

demned , er fæl't or fællet *he falles* , es
shallet or shal't *it sounds &c. this being done*
as well in the regular as the irregular verbes
of all sorts , used commonly for shortness both
in meeter and familiar discoursing , is rather
to be called a Syncope than anomaly ; but the
following Rules doe belong only to the verbes
in hand , which must be well observed.

R. 2. *such irregulars to wit verbes of the*
less anomaly change their characteristick vowel
in the 2. and 3. singular of the rest present as
A *both single and in the dipth.* AU *into* Æ ,
e. g. ih slafe , du slæfest , si slæfet ; ih
saufe , du sæufest , er sæufet *from* slafen
to sleepe, saufen *to drink as a beast &c.*
E *both long and short into* I , *e. g.* ih lese , du
lisest , er liset , *from* lesen *to reade* ; ih feh
-te , du sihtest , er siht *or* sihtet , *from* seht
-en *to fight.* *the very same is done also in*
the 2. singular of the oblique mood when we
beseech or command e. g. sihte du *fighte thou,*
lise du *reade thou,* ise du *eate thou &c.*
O *into* œ , *e. g.* ih komme, du kommest
and kœmmest , er kommet *and* kœmmet
or kœmt *from* kommen *to come.*
u *into* eu , *e. g.* ih lüge, du leugst , er
leugt *from* lügen , *to tell a lye &c.*

R. 3. *the like changing of letters into others*
is in the imperfect of both definit moods, as
also in the preterit Participle, which particu-
larly turneth very often the termination ET *into*
EN *as in English. for in both numbers of*
the rest Imperfect we change
A *single and long into* U , *e. g.* ih grabe

i digg or *carve* , ihgrube , du grubeſt &c.
AU *and* A *ſhort into* I *long and ſometimes
into* O *ſhort e. g.* ih lauſe *i runne* , ih life
and loffe , du lifeſt *and* loffeſt &c. ih halte
i hold , ih hilte , du hilteſt &c.

ſhort ⎰ E I ⎱ ⎰ *into* A ⎱ ⎰ helfe *i helpe*, halfe *holp.*
⎨ ⎬ ⎨ *e. g.* ⎬ ⎨ ſinge *i ſinge*, ſange *ſong.*
long ⎱ O U ⎰ ⎱ ih ⎰ ⎨ komme *i come* kame *came.*
⎩ tue *i doe* , tate *did.*

æ ⎱ *indif-* ⎱ *into* O *and* ⎰ wæge woge wuge.
û ⎰ *ferent* ⎰ *in ſome di* ⎨ flûſse floſse fluſse.
-alects in
e ⎱ *long* ⎰ *to* U *e. g.* ⎰ ſhere ſhore ſhure.
œ ⎰ ⎱ ih ⎰ ⎩ ſwœre ſwore ſwure

from wægen *to weigh* , flûſsen *to ſhut* , ſher-
en *to ſheare* , ſwœren *to curſe.* *except* geb
-en *to give has* ih gabe du gabeſt ; ſeen *to
ſee* , ih ſae du ſaeſt ; ſteen *to ſtande* , ih
ſtande , ſtonde , ſtunde ; geen *to goe* , ih
ginge *or* gange , du gangeſt *or* gingeſt.
EI *into* I , *and* EY *into* Y *or* I *e. g.* ih
ſhreye *crye* , ih ſhrye ; es ſneyet *it ſnow*
-eth , es ſnye *or* ſnie ; ſleiſen *to whet* , ih
ſliffe ; beiſen *to bite* , ih biſse ; ſtoſen *to
thruſt* , ih ſtiſe; bleiben *to ſtay* , ih blibe;
ſhreiben *to write* , ih ſhribe; weiſen *to
ſhowe* , ih wiſe du wiſeſt &c. *but* weiſ-
en *to whiten is regular. beſides this we have
yet* ar *other irregularity here* , *when* ing *and*
enk *is changed into* ah *e. g.* bringen *to bringe* ,
ih brahte *i broughte* , du brahteſt ; denk-
en *to thinke* , ih dahte *i thought* , du daht-
eſt &c.

finaly note here *as well as in both fingle tenfes of the Oblique, that the double confonants and the compound ones of like letters are alwayes changed into the oppofite fingle ones as often as the preceding vowel becomes long in pronouncing* e. g. ih bakke *of old* bahe *or* bache *i* bake, ih fize *of old* fitfe *or* fitze *i* fite, *Imperf. R.* ih buge *or* buke *i baked*, ih fafe *i fate*; *Imperf. Obl.* ih büge *or* büke, ih fæfe *&c.* *on the contrary they* (*the fingle confonants*) *are changed into doubled or compound ones*, *if this* (*the foregoing vowel*) *be fhort* e. g. ih reite *i ride*, ih ritte; ih beife *i bite* ih bifse, *many exampels more we finde in this and in the following Rule*, *as alfo Part* 1. *chap.* 3. *fect.* 1. *n.* 2.

R. 4. the charact-eriftick vowels:

a, o, u	of the Imperfeſt reſt are changed in that of the ob-lique into	x, œ, ih, ü̇	as	aſe; æſe fohte;fœhte floſse;flœſse fluſse,flüſse. ſworeſwœre ſwure ſwüre

from eſsen *to eate,* fehten *to fight,* flüſen *to flowe,* flüſsen *to fhut,* fwœren *to curfe or fweare.*

R. 5. *thofe irregulars, that have for their characteriftick vowel either A, E clear, O or U in the indefinit prefent, keepe it in the participle preterit and change the regular T into N* e. g. flafen *to fleepe,* geflafen; geben *to give,* gegeben; feen *to fee,* gefeen; ftofen *to thruft,* geflofen; tüen *to doe,* ge

tun, *as the Franconians in their dialect still say,
in lieu whereof we use* getan. *but* E, *when
obscure in pronunciation, is changed into an* A
e. g. steen *to* stande, gestanden; geen *to
goe*, gegangen; shæren *to shave or sheare
is better spelled with an* æ *then* e, *and has
therefore* geshoren *according to the following
rule.*

au	*are changed into an* O.	{saugen *to sucke*, gesogen; saufen *to drinke as a beast*, gesoffen &c.
æ		wægen *to weigh*, gewogen; gebær-en *to bring forth*, gebo-ren &c.
i	*with the termina-tion* EN *e. g.*	{shiben *to move*, geshoben; kisen *to chose*, gekosen &c.
œ		hœben *to lift up*, gehoben; swœren *to sweare* gesworen &c.
û		bìgen *or* bigen *to bowe*, gebo-gen; rûhen *to smell*, geroh-en &c.

thither is to be referred ershallen *to resound,*
ershollen; *but* ligen *to laye down has* gelegen.

Ei *is turned to* I, *and* EY *to* Y *or* I, *but
the short* I *in our dialect is changed into* O,
*as we have seen just now; whereas in others
into* U, *e. g.* smeisen *to smite*, gesmissen;
shreyen *to crye*, geshryen *or* geshrien;
rinnen *to rinne*, geronnen *or* gerunnen;
gewinnen *to winne*, gewonnen *or* gewunn-
en; finken *to finke*, gesonken *or* gesunk-
en; zwingen *to force*, gezwongen *or* gezwungen; sizen *to sit hath* gesessen; *but*

bringen *to bringe*, gebraht; denken *or ge-*
denken *to thinke*, gedaht.

the regular termination ENDET *is commonly*
changed into AND, *and* ENNET *into* ANT
e. g. senden *to fend*, gesendet *and* gefand;
pfænden *to take a pawn* , gepfændet *or*
gepfand ; bekennen *to confejse* , bekennet
and bekant ; trennen *to teare in pieces*,
getrennet *and* getrant *& c. fee the following*
table. but blenden *to blinde hath only* geblend
-et *not* gebland ; *on the contrary we fay*
commonly gebrand *burnd* ; *feldom* gebrennet
or gebronnen.

R. 6. *as the regular : fo the irregular com-*
pounded with the feparable Prepofitions (follow
-*ing the fimple ones in all their irregularity)*
are to be divided thus I. *in both the regular and*
irregular fingle tenfes of the rect mood and,
when we command or befeech, of the Oblique
the (feparable) prepofitions become poftpofi-
tions, that is, they are taken away from the
head of the verbes and fet after them and their
following nouns e. g. der befelig-haber gabe di ftatt auf *the governour delivered the*
town , from aufgeben ; keret (wendet)
das ftunden-Glafs um *turne the houre-glafs ,*
from umkeren *or* umwenden ; trinket es
alles aus *drinke it all off , from* austrinken;
kere ftraks wider um *goe back prefently or*
ftraights. 2. *but elfewhere as well here in*
the rect , when the prepofition lofeth its empha-
fis , and in any other fignification of the oblique
as alfo in the infinit prefent , pafsiv and activ
participles , likewife in both verball nouns ,

K2

*the prepositiv particles keepe their place e. g.
er widerleg'te seinen gegenteil he refused
his antagonist, der feind begerete, dass der
Herzog nah überlesung des brifs di vestung aufgæbe the enemy demanded, that the
duke would deliver the fortress, after he had
seen over the letter &c. unless the conjunctiv particles dass, so, wann &c. (which usualy
precede the oblique mood) be omitted; for then
we followe the former observation e. g. sæe
ih meinen bruder wider! in stead ih wûnshe or wolte God, dass ih meinen bruder
widersæe! i wish or would to God that i should
see my brother again! see the regular formation
of the participle passiv, and to make us the
surer in the other particular irregularities, here
omitted: let us hasten to their common table,
where we have to note, that when there be
more then one word, the first is used in our
dialect, and the other in others.*

TABLE
of
the Irregular Verbes.

Present definit.	*Imperfect rect.*	*Particip. preterit.*
ih bakke.	bakkete	gebakken,
i bake.	buge.	gebakket.
bedarfe.	bedarfte,	bedarft,
have need of.	bedorfte.	bedorft.
befele *commande.*	befale, befole.	befolen.
befleise *endeavor.*	beflisse.	beflissen.
beginne. beganne, begonne.		begonnen,
beginne.	begunne, begonte.	begunnen.

beife. *bite.*	bifse.	gebifsen.
belle.	balle, bolle,	gebollen
barke.	bellete.	gebellet.
berge. *bide.* barge, borge.	geborgen.	
betrüge. *deceive.* betroge.	betrogen.	
bewœge.	bewœgete,	bewœget,
move.	bewoge.	bewogen.
bige, beuge. bigete, bügete	gebogen, ge-	
bœge, büge. boge,	bœget, ge-	
bowe, bende. beugete.	beuget.	
bite. *pröffer.* bote, bitete.	geboten.	
bin. *am.* wäre, war.	gewesen.	
binde. bande, bonde,	gebonden,	
binde. bunde.	gebunden.	
bitte. *pray.* bate.	gebeten.	
blafe. *blowe.* blife, blafete.	geblasen.	
n. bleibe, *remaine.* blibe.	gebliben.	
n. { bœrfte, *bufte.* bœrftete. geboœrftet		
borfte } borftete. gebofften.		
brate. bratete,	gebraten,	
rofte. brute.	gebratet.	
n. brehe, *breake.* brage.	gebrohen.	
brenne. brande, gebrand,	gebrennet,	
burne. brennete.	gebronnen	
bringe. *bringe.* brahte.	gebraht.	
darf. darfte, dorfte.	gedarft, gedorft,	
dure. durfte.	gedurft, dœrfen.	
dekke. dekkete,	gedekket,	
cover. dekkte.	gedakkt.	
dinge. dingete, donge.	gedinget, ge-	
hire. dunge.	dongen, gedungen	
n. { drenge. drange.	gedrongen,	
dringe. dronge.	gedrungen,	
thringe. drunge.	gedrenget.	

denke. *thinke*. dohte.   gedaht.
dreſhe. *threſhe*. draſhe, droſhe. gedroſhen.
eſſe. *eate*.   aſe. gegeſſen, gefſen.
n. falle. *falle*. file.   gefallen.
fange.   finge, funge,   gefangen
catche.   fangete.
n. fare. *fare*, *ride*. fure.   gefaren.
fehte.   fohte,   gefohten.
fighte.   fehtete.   gefehtet.
fire } *carrie*. firete, für- gefüret, gefir
füre }   te, furte.   -et, gefirt.
finde.   fande, fonde,   gefonden
finde.   funde.   gefunden.
flehte.   flohte,   geflohten,
weave, knit. flehtete.   geflehtet.

n. { flüge / flige } *flye* floge, fluge   geflogen.

n. { flie / flüe } *runn away*. floe.   gefloen, geflon.

n. { fliſe / flüſe } *flowe* floſse.   gefloſsen.

forhte mih. forhte,   geforht,
am afraid. foerhtete.   gefoerhtet.
freſse. *frette or* fraſe.   gefreſsen.
eate as a beaſt.

n. { frire / friſe } *freeſe*. frore, gefroren,
    froſe.   gefroſen.
gebe. *give*. gabe.   gegeben, geben.
gebære. *beare or bring forth*. gebare geborn.
gedenke, bedenke, verdenke &c. *see*. denke.
gefalle, befalle, verfalle, zerfalle &c. *see*
       falle.
gefriſe, gefrire. *fee* frire, friſe.
geen. *goe*. ginge. gegangen, gangen.

n. es gelinget. es gelonge. gelongen.
it comes to pafs. es gelunge. gelungen.
gelte. *am efteemed.* galte, golte. gegolten.
n: genæfe. *recover.* genafe. genæfen.
genæfe. *enjoye.* genofse. genofsen.

n. { gerate. gerite, gerûte, geraten
   { gefhee. gerute; gefhae, gefheen,
   bappne. gefhen

n. gefwelle, gefwalle, gefwollen.
   fwelle. gefwolle.

gewinne. *win.* gewanne, gewonne. gewonnē.
gife { *power* gofse, gufse. gegofsen.
gûfe { *out or in.*

gleife. glifse, geglifsen,
glifter. gleifsete. gegleifet.
n. gleite. *flide.* glitte, gleitete. geglitten.
glimme { *glowe.* glomme, geglommen.
glumme { glûmmete. geglummet.
grabe. *digg, carve.* grube. gegraben.
greife. *touch.* griffe. gegriffen.
greine. grinne, gegrinnen.
groxe. greinete. gegreinet.
habe. *have.* hatte. gehabet, gehabt, gehat.
halte. *bold.* hilte. gehalten.
n. hange. hange, hinge, gehangen.
  bange. honge, hunge. gehænget.
hawe. hibe. gehawet, gehawen,
bewe. hawete. gehiben.
heifhe. hifhe, geheifhen,
demand. heifhete. geheifhet.
heife. *bidde.* hife. geheifen.
henge. hangte, gehenget,
bange. hengte. gehanget.
helfe. halfe, holfe, geholfen.

belpe.   hulfe.

hœbe.   hœbete ,   gehaben ,

lift up.   hube.   gehoben.

kann.   konte.   gekont,   gekœnt, ge-

can.   kunte.   kœnnet, kœnnen.

kænne ⎰ *knowe*   kante ,   gekant ,

kenne ⎱   kennete.   gekennet.

kife ⎰ *chufe.*   kifete ,   gekifet

kife ⎱   kofe.   gekofen.

n. klimme klimme.   geklomben ,

climbe. klimbete.   geklimbet.

klinge.*found.* klange , klonge. geklungen,

knæte ⎰ *kneade* knate   gekneten ,

knete ⎱   knetete.   geknetet.

kœre. *chufe.* kore , kœrete. gekoren,

n. komme. *come.* kame.   gekommen.

n. kribe. *creepe.* krohe.   gekrohen.

n. kwelle. kwalle , kwolle. gekwollen.

     foke or flote out of a well.

lade.   lude ,   geladen ,

lode , lead. ladete.   geladet.

lafse. *let , leave.* life,lifse. gelaffen.

laufe.   life ,   gelaufen,

leape . runne. life.   geloffen.

leide. *fuffer.* litte , leidete. gelitten.

leye. *lend.* lie , leyete. gelyen , geleyet.

lefe. *reade ,gather.* lafe. gelefen.

lige. *laye.* lage.   gelegen.

luge. *lye.* luge.   gelogen.

mag. *may.* mohte.   mœgen , gemoht.

male. *griade.* mole . mule. gemalen.

meide. *fhunne.* meidete , mide. gemiden.

mæfse ⎰ *mei-* mafe ,   gemæfsen.

mefse ⎱ *fure.* mefsete.   gemefset.

muſs.	muſte.	gemuſt,
muſt.		gemüſset.
næme. *take.* name.	name.	genommen.
nenne.	nante,	genant,
næme.	nennete.	genennet.
pfeife. *whiſtle.*	pfiffe.	gepfiffen.
pflege. *uſe to-*	pflage, pfloge.	gepflogen.
preiſe.	priſe,	gepriſen.,
praiſe.	preiſete.	gepreiſet.
ræhe.	ræhete.	gerohen,
revenge.	rohe.	geræhet.
rate. *gueſſe*	rite, rute,	geraten.
or adviſe.	rätete.	
rehe.	rohe,	gerohen,
ræke.	rehete.	gerehet.
reibe. *rubbe.*	ribe, reibete.	geriben.
ſ. reiſe.	riſse.	geriſsen.
goe in pieces.		
ſ. reite. *ride.*	ritte.	geritten.
rihe $\}$ *ſmell.* rûhe	rohe.	gerohen.
ringe.	range, ronge.	gerongen.
wringe.	runge.	gerungen.
ſ. renne.	rante.	gerant,
runne.	rennete.	gerennet.
ſ. rinne. *ſtow.*	ranne, ronne.	geronnen.
ruſe $\}$ *call.* ruffe	rûſe,	geruſen.
	ruffete.	geruffet.
ſaufe. *drinke bigb.*	ſoffe.	geſoffen.
ſauge.	ſoge.	geſogen.
ſucke.	ſaugete.	geſauget.
ſee. *ſee.*	ſae.	geſeen.
ſende.	ſande,	geſand,
ſende.	ſendete.	geſendet.

ſeye. *ſtraine.*	ſie, fye, ſoe.	geſoen.
ſeze	ſazte,	geſazt,
ſet.	ſezote.	geſezet.
ſhaffe.	ſhuſe,	geſhaffen.
create.	ſhaffete,	geſhaft.
ſhalle.	ſhallete,	geſhallet,
ſound.	ſholle.	geſhollen.
n. ſheide. *depart.* ſhide.		geſhiden.
ſheine.	ſhine.	geſhinen.
ſhine.	ſheinete.	geſheinet.
ſheiſe. *ſhite.* ſhiſse.		geſhiſsen.
ſhelte.	ſhalte,	geſholten.
chide.	ſholte.	
ſhære.	ſhore,	geſhoren.
ſhare, ſhave. ſhure.		geſhüren.
ſhibe } *draw,* ſhobe, ſhnbe.		geſhoben.
ſhúbe } *move.* ſhibete.		geſhibet.
ſhinde.	ſhande, ſhonde.	geſhonden.
pull off the ſkin. ſhunde.		geſhunden.
ſhite, ſhúte.	ſhittete,	geſhütt.
ſhitte, ſhútte.	ſhotte,	geſhutt,
power out or in. ſhitte,		geſhittet.
ſhœpfe.	ſhœpfete,	geſhœpfet,
draw.	ſhapfte.	geſhapft.
ſhreibe. *write.* ſhribe.		geſhriben.
n. ſhreite. *paſse.* ſhritte.		geſhritten.
n. erſhrække. erſhrakke.		erſhrokken.
am ſcared.		
ſhreye { *crye* ſhrie,		geſhrien,
{ *ſhreeke* ſhrye		geſhryen.
n. ſhrumpfe *ſhrink* ſhrumpfete,		geſhrumpfet,
ſhrümpfe ſhrümpfete.		geſhrumpfen.
ſhúſe. *ſhoote.* ſhoſse, ſhuſse.		geſhoſsen.

ſide. | ſode, ſidete, | geſoden,
ſiethe. | ſotte. | geſotten.
ſinge. | ſange, ſonge. | geſongen.
ſinge. | ſunge. | geſungen.
ſinke. | ſanke, ſonke, | geſonken,
ſinke. | ſunke. | geſunken.
ſinne. *muſe.* | ſanne, | geſonnen.
n. ſize. *ſit.* | ſaſe. | geſeſſen.
ſlafe. *ſleepe.* | ſlife, ſlufe. | geſlafen.
ſlage. *beate.* | ſluge. | geſlagen.
ſleihe. *goe ſneeking.* | ſlihe. | geſlihen.
ſleife. *ſharpen, grinde.* | ſliffe. | geſliffen.
ſleiſe. *ſlit.* | ſliſſe. | geſliſſen.
ſlinge. | ſlange, ſlonge, | geſlongen,
devour | ſlunge. | geſlungen.
ſlinke. | ſlanke, ſlonke, | geſlonken
ſwallowe. | ſlunke. | geſlunken.

ſliſe ⎱ *ſoutte or*
ſlúſe ⎰ *conclude.* ſloſe, ſluſe. geſloſen.
ſlúſse ⎰

ſmeiſe. *ſmite.* ſmiſſe. geſmiſſen.
n. ſmelze. *melte.* ſmalze. ſmolze. geſmolzen.

the active is regular.

ſneide. *cutte.* ſnitte. geſnitten.
es ſneyet. ſneite, ſnie. geſneit, geſnien,
it ſnoweth. ſnye, ſneyete. geſneyet, geſnyen.
ſoll. *ſhall.* ſolte. geſolt, ſollen.
ſpeye ⎱ *ſpit.* ſpie, ſpeiete, geſpien, geſpyen.
ſpeye ⎰ *ſhew.* ſpye, ſpeyete. geſpeit, geſpeyet
ſpinne. ſpanne, ſponne, geſponnen.
ſpinne. ſpunne. geſpunnen.
ſprehe. ſprahe, ⎰ geſprohen.
ſpeake. ſprage.
n. ſpringe. ſprange, ſpronge. gſprongen,

ſtringe.	ſprunge.	geſprungen.
n. nee.	ſtande, ſtonde.	geſtanden.
ſtand.	ſtunde.	
ſtehe.	ſtahe.	geſtohen.
ſtich, pricks.	ſtage.	
act. ſtekke.	ſtekkete,	geſtekket, ge-
thruſt into.	ſtakkete,	ſtak't, geſtækket.
n. ſtække. *ſticke.*	ſtake.	geſtækket.
n. ſteige. *goe up.*	ſtige.	geſtigen.
ſtæle. *ſteale.*	ſtale, ſtole.	geſtolen.
n. ſtærbe.	ſtarbe, ſtorbe.	geſtorben.
dye.	ſturbe.	
ſteube. *fly about as duſt.*	ſtobe.	geſtoben.
ſtibe.		geſteubet.

the actv is regular.

ſtinke.	ſtanke, ſtonke.	geſtonken,
ſtinke.	ſtunke.	geſtunken.
ſtoſe ⎫ *puſhe.*	ſtiſse,	geſtoſsen.
ſtoſse ⎭	ſtiſe.	geſtoſen.
ſtrekke.	ſtrekkete,	geſtrekket,
ſtretche.	ſtrak'te,	geſtrakt.
ſtreihe. *touch*	ſtrihe.	geſtrihen.
ſoftly or ſtroake.		
ſtreite.	ſtritte,	geſtritten.
qvarrel.	ſtreitete.	
ſwære.	ſware,	geſworen.
breed filth	ſwore, ſwærete.	
as a ſore doth.		
ſweige. *ſay nothing.*	ſwige.	geſwigen.
ſwelle. *ſwelle.* ſwalle.		geſwollen.
ſwimme.	ſwamme.	geſwommen.
ſwimme.	ſwomme, ſwumme.	geſwummen.
n. ſwinde.	ſwande,	geſwenden.

ſhrinke. ſwonde, ſwunde. gefwunden.
lwinge ſwing. ſwange, gefwongen.
winnowe. ſwonge,ſwunge. gefwungen.
ſwœre; ſweare. ſwore, ſwure. gefworen.
tauhe. tohte. getauht.
am good. tauhete. getoht.
tue *or* due. tate, getan,
doe. date. gedan.
darf. darſte, dorſte, gedorſt,
dare. durſte. gedurſt.
trage. *trudge.* truge. getragen.
treffe. *hit at.* trafe, traffe. getroffen.
treibe. *drive.* tribe. getriben.
trenne. trante, getrant,
ſ. p rate. trennete. getrennet.
n. trœte. *treade.* trate. getrœten.
trife } *droppe.* troſe; getroffen.
triffe }
trinke. tranke, tronke. getronken,
drinke. trunke. getrunken.
beTrige } *deceive.* betroge. betrogen.
beTrŭge }
aſ. verderbe. verderbete. verderbet,
ſpoile. verdarbe. verderben.
n. becomo verdarbe. verdorben.
nought. verdorbe, verdurbe.
vergeſſe. *forget.* vergaſe. vergeſſen.
vergleihe. verglihe, verglihen.
compare. vergleihete. vergleihet.
verlire } *looſe.* verlore, verlure. verloren.
verliſe } verloſe. verloſen.
verſlage,}verſlinge, &c. *ſee* ſlage, ſlinge.
verlœſhe. verlaſhe, verloſhen.
gœ out. verloſhe. verlœſht.

n. {wahſe} wuhſe, wax- gewahſen.
, {waxe} {*waxe* ete, wahſete. gewaxen.
wæge. *weighe.* woge, wuge. gewogen.
walze, wælze. walzete gewalzet,ge-
wallowe. wælzete. wælzet,gewalzen.
waſhe wuſhe, gewaſhen.
waſhe. waſhete.
webe, wæbe. webete, wobe. gewebet.
weave wæbete. gewoben.
weihe. *give place.* wihe. gewihen.
weis. *knowe.* wuſte. gewuſt.
weiſe. *ſhewe.* wiſe. gewiſen.
wende. wande, gewand,
winde, turne. wendete. gewendet.
werbe *e. g.* warbe, worbe, geworben.
ſoldaten. *liſte.* wurbe.
werde. ward, worden,
am, become. wurde. geworden.
wærfe warfe, worfe, geworfen.
throwe. wurſe.
winde garn. wande, gewonden
winde garn. wonde. wunde. gewunden.
will. *will.* wolte. wollen , gewolt.
wûrke. wûrkete gewûrket,
worke. worke. geworken.

zeye. *accuſe.* zie, zye. gezyen, gezin-
verzeye. verzie. verzeyete. verzien , ver-
perdon. verzye. verzeite. zin , verzyen.
n. zergloebe. zerglobe, zerglóben,
gape. zergloebete. zergloebet,
n. zie *goe away.* zoe. zoge. gezogen.
zwinge. zwange , zwon- gezwongen,
force. ge, zwunge. gezwungen.

Chap. III. of
the Etymologia strictly so called.

hitherto of the two definit parts of speech; the
third (being immovable and signifying neither a
certain number nor case nor mood nor person &c.)
is called therfore indefinit particles, added to
those, that are definit and declinable, to say
out some thing, that is either not at all or at
least not sufficiently expressed, the construction
whereof (which is the one only thing here to be
considered) shall be showne in the following
chapter, leaving their signification (not belonging
to a grammar) to a word-book or dictionary,
to make the better speed in the doctrin of derivation, which the particles as well as either the
nouns or verbes are capable off; especially because we see, that others, treating of the German and the English toungs, have but slightly
touched it or left it quite out, which though. if
well understood will give a great help and light
in both languages, having the greatest congruity
one with the other, as we shall see at large anon.

Sect. 1. of
the Homeborne Derivation.

like as the substantivs become adjectivs, these
on the contrary become substantivs, and both of
them become sometimes particles: even so these
all become often verbes, from whence many both
nouns and particles are derived. especially the
substantiv is made an adjectiv in adding either
one of these terminations, or one of the adjectivs, viz.

BAR *e. g.* ere *honour*, erbar *honest*; wonder *wonder*, wonderbar *wonderfull*; dinst *office*, dinstbar *officious*; mannbar *of age*, laug-bar *deniable*, ungastbar *unhospitable or* ἄξεν⊙ *&c.*

IG *e. g.* hoffart *pride*, hoffærtig *proud*; maht *power*, mæhtig *powerfull*; lust *lust*, lustig *lustie*; zorn *anger*, zornig *angry* &c. *so the particle iz now*, izig *present*; gestern *yester*. gesterne *of the yester day*, heite *to day*, heitige *hodiernus*, neulig *not long ago*, der neulige *the new* &c.

IH *or* IHT *e. g.* laus *louse*, laufih *or* laufiht *lousie*; dorn *thorn*, dornih *or* dorniht *thorny*; feder *feather*, federih *or* federiht *feathery*; stein *stone*, steinih *or* steiniht *stony*, drekk *dirt*, drekkih *or* drekkiht *dirty* &c.

LIH *e. g.* hof *court*, hæflih *civill*; furst *prince*, furstlih *princelike*; koenig *king*, koeniglih *kingly*; Gott *God*, goettlih *godly* &c.

EN *e. g.* gold *gold*, gulden *goelden or* golden *golden*; lein *line*, leinen *or* linnen *linnen*; hanf *or* hampf *hamp*, hænfen *made of hamp*; har *hair*, hæren *made of hair*; wolle *wooll*, wollen *wüllen or* wullen: *woollen* &c.

ERN *e. g.* holz *wood*, hoelzern *wooden*; fleish *flesh*, fleischern *made of flesh* &c.

ISH *e. g.* weib *woman*, weibish *womanish*; teufel *divel*, teufelish *divelish*; hoelle *helle* hoellish *hellish*; vi *beast*, viish *beastly* &c.

HAFT *or* HAFTIG *e. g.* laster *vice*, lasterhaft *or* lasterhaftig *vicious*; tugend *virtue*, tugendhaft *or* tugendhaftig *virtuous*: ernst *earnest*, ernsthaft *or* ernsthaftig *serious* &c.

SAM *e. g.* mûe *toile*, mûfam *tailefome*; ftid
peace, fridfam *peaceable*; hæil *hail*, hælfam
found and good; tugendfam *virtuous &c.*

LOS *e. g.* Gottlos *godlefs*; glaub *or* glaub-
en *faith*, glaublos *or* glaubenlos *faithlefs*;
fprahlofe *fpeechlefs*; finnlos *fencelefs*; frucht-
los *fruitlefs &c.*

ARM *e. g.* blut - arm *bloodlefs*; gelt - arm
poor in money &c.

REIH *e. g.* fig *victorie*, fig-reih *victorious*;
wafser-reih *full of water*; kunftreih *arti-
ficiall &c.*

VOLL *e. g.* genade *mercy*, gnaden-voll
or genadenreih *merciefull*; freuden-voll *or*
freudenreih *joy-full*; wünder-voll *or* wun-
derreih *wonderfull &c.*

SÜHTIG *e. g.* flaf-fühtig *given to fleep*;
zank - fühtig *quarrelfome*; gewinn - fühtig
covetous of gain &c.

GIRIG *e. g.* rum-girih *defirous of praife*;
rah-girih *revengefull*; blutgirih *or* blutdœrft
-ig *bloodthirfty. &c.*

*hither are to be brought all the compounds, the
later part whereof is an adjectiv, and the former
a fubftantiv. contrary wife the adjectivs grow
fubftantivs, either when we put away the
faid adjectivs and terminations both in the
alleged and in a good many other examples; or
when we add thefe following terminations.*

HEIT *e. g.* tronken *drunken*, tronkenheit
drunkennefs; vergefsen *forgot*, vergefsenheit
forgetfullnefs; fhœn *beautifull*, fhœnheit
beauty; fwah *weak*, fwahheit *weaknefs*; gleih

like, gleihheit *likeneſs*; træg *or* faul *idle or foul*, trægheit *or* faulheit *idleneſs &c.*

KEIT *e. g.* ewig *everlaſting*, ewigkeit *eternity*; nühtern *ſober*, nühternkeit *ſobriety*; barmherzig *mercifull*, barmherzigkeit *mercy*; gutherzig *goodhearty*, gutherzigkeit *goodheartineſs &c.*

NÜSS *or* NISS *e. g.* gedaht *mentioned*, gedæhtnüſs *memory*; betrûbt *ſad*, betrûbtnis *ſadneſs*; verwand *related*, verwandnis *relation*; gefangen *taken priſoner*, gefængnis *priſon*; ſo verhindern *binder*, verhindernis *binderance*; ærgern *ſcandalize*, ærgerniſs *ſcandal &c.*

SHAFT *e. g.* bereit *or* gereit *ready*, bereitſhaft *or* gereitſhaft *readineſs*; bekant *acquainted*, bekandſhaft *acquaintance*; kund *knowne*, kundſhaft *notice &c.*

TUM *e. g.* reih *rich*, reihtum *riches*; eigen *proper*, eigentum *propriety &c.*

UNG *e. g.* veraht *deſpiced*, verahtung *contemt*; erlæuht *illuminated*, erlæuhtung *illumination*; verlæumd *ſlandred*, verlæumdung *ſlander &c.*

E *or* TE *e. g.* lang *long*, længe *or* længte *length*, ſtreng *ſtrong*, ſtrengte *ſtrength*; gros *great or* groſs, grœſe *or* grœſse *greatneſs or groſneſs*; ſwarz *black*, ſwærze *blackneſse &c.* theſe *and the like terminations are added alſo to other (concrete) ſubſtantivs to make them abſtraƈts or to ſignify the ſtate and condition, which the thing is in, as*

SHAFT *e. g.* freind *freind*, freindſhaft *freindſhip*; geſell *companion*, geſellſhaft *company*;

jungfr. we *maid* , jungfraußhaft *maydenbead*;
bru.ler *brotber*, bruderßhaft *brotberbood &c.*
ȚUM *e.g.* fürftentum *princedome*, chriften
-tum *chriftendome* ; kæifertum *empire* , bis-
tum *or* bißhofftum *bißhoprick ˟c.*

EI *or* EYE *and* (*but feldome*) DEI *or*
DEYE *e.g.* praler *boafter*, pralerei *or* pral
-ereye *boafting* ; reiter *horfeman*, reiterei
borfemanßhip or chevalrie ; fpœtter *mocker* ,
fpœtterei *mockery* ; narr *fool*, narredei *or*
narredeye *jolly or foolißhnes &c.*

ER *and* ERIN *e. g.* Engelland *England*,
Engellænder *Englißhman*, Engellænderin *Eng*
-*lißh woman*; London *London*, Londner *Lon-*
dener , Londnerin *a woman from London*;
Danzig , Danziger , Danzigerin , *and fo*
fortb allmoft all patronymicks. from tbence are
alfo derived adjeftivs in ISH , *ufed commonly*
of irrationall and fencelefs tbings, *as tbe Latin*
adjeftivs in ICUS *e.g.* Spanien *Spain*, ʻpa-
nier *Spaniard* , Spanilher wein *Spanißh*
wine, vinum Hifpanicum ; Indien *Indie* , In-
dier *or* Indianer *Indian*, Indifhe *or* Indiani-
fhe gewürze *ftices brought from tbe Indies*,
aromata Indica *&c. of tbe termination* INN
of tbe feminins, *and* GEN (*in lieu of* LE *or*
LEIN *Į of tbe diminutivs, fee in the doftrin of*
moveable and diminutiv fubftantivs P.II: chap. I.
feft, 1. *n.* 2. *and chap.* 2. *feft.* 2. *about tbe end.*
but tbe terminations E, DE, TE, EL, ER,
FT, LING, NIS, SAL, ST, T, UNG,
are added to verbes, *to make tbem fubftantivs,*
after we have firft taken away the termina-
tion EN *of the infinitiv, as*

E, DE, TE, *e. g.* liben *to love*, di libe *love*; be
-gere *to desire*, begire *or* begirde *desire*; ziren
embellish, zire *or* zirde *embellishment*; gelo-
ben *to vowe*, eine gelübde *a vow*; verlob-
en *to promise*, ein verlobter *or* eine ver-
lobte *a bethroted*, eine verlœbte verlœbnis
or verlobung *a promise of marriage*; sihfrew-
en *to rejoice*, freude *joy &c.*

EL *e. g.* fligen *to fly*, ein fligel *a wing*;
stœkken *to put in*, ein stükkel *or* stihel *an*
iron-crow; winden *to wind or wrap up*, eine windel *a clout or swadling*; spinnen *to*
spinne, eine spinnel *or* spindel *a spindle*.

ER, UNG *e. g.* erretten *or* erlœsen *to*
release or redeeme, erretter *or* erlœser *releaser*
or redeemer, di errettung *or* erlœsung *the*
release or redemtion; versuhen *to tent*, ein
versuher *a tenter*, versuhung *temtation &c.*

FT *e. g.* ankommen *to come nigh*, ankunft
or of old ankumft *coming nigh or advent*;
zusammen-kommen *to come together*, eine
zunft *or* zümft *society or company*; vernem
en *perceive*, di vernunft *or* vernumft *the*
reason &c.

LING *e. g.* sterben *to dye*, ein sterbling
a starvling or carrion; finden *to finde*, ein
findling *a child that is found or a findling*,
saugen *to give suck*, ein sæugling *a suckling*,
müden *to hire*, ein müdling *a hireling &c.*
so of the nouns di lære *doctrine*, ein lærling
a disciple or apprentice; eine kammer *a cham-*
ber, ein kæmmerling *a chamberlain*; lib *dear*,
ein libling *a dareling*; hanf *or* hamf *hamp*,
ein hænfling *a linnet*; hof *court*, ein hœfling

courtier ; jung *young*, jüngling *youngman on younling &c.*

SAL *e. g.* irren *to erie*, irrfal *errour* ; dring-en *and* trüben *to throng and disturb*, drangfal *and* trübfal *vexation and disturbance* ; lab-en *to comfort* ; labfal *comfort &c.*

ST *e. g.* dinen *to serve*, dinst *service* ; ge-winnen *to winne*, gewinst *gain* ; koennen *or* künnen *to can or know*, konst *or* kunst *art* ; broennen *to burne*, bronst *beat* ; goennen *or* günnen *to favour*, gonst *or* gunst *favour &c.*

T *e. g.* faren *or* füren *to carry*, eine fart *or* furt *carriage or load* ; gebæren *to bring forth*, di geburt *birth &c.*

likewise of the cardinall number is derived the ordinall with their adverbes e. g. ein *one*, erst *first* ; erstlih erstlihen erstens zu'm (zu dem) ersten *or* vor's (vor das) erste *first or as the first* ; zwei *two*, zweide *or* andere *second*; zweidens vor's zweide *or* zu'm zweiden *secondly* ; drei *three*, dritte *third* ; drittens vor's dritte *or* zu'm dritten *thirdly &c.*

but the other adverbs in all their degrees either keep the termination of the adjectius e. g. fahte *or* fanfte *soft and softly* ; fahter *or* fæhter fanfter *or* fanfter *softer or more softly* ; a'm *or* zu'm fahtesten *or* fæhtesten fanftesten *or* fanftesten *most softly* ; fleisig *industrious and industriously*, fleisiger *more industrious and more industriously* ; a'm *or* zu'm fleisigsten *or* fleisigster *most very industriously &c.* gut *good has* wol *well*, besser *better*, bestens a'm *or* zum besten aufs beste *best or very well. or they (the adverbs, especially being substan-*

tivs or participles) receive the termination either
LIHEN *or* LIH *in the positiv, to which later*
is added in the comparativ ER *, and in the su-*
perlativ STEN *preceded by the particle* a'm
or zu'm; *or* STE *preceded by* auf's *or* aufd s
e. g. er rihtet (weiſe, weislih *or*) weislih-
en *be judgeth wiſely*, weiſer *or* weiſſliher
more wiſely, auf's weiſſlihſte zu'm *or* a'm weis-
lihſten *moſt or very wiſely*. er tate es (wiſſ-
end, wiſſendlih *or* wiſſendlihen *be did it*
wittingly, zeitlih *or*) zeitlihen *timely*, ſtünd-
lih *or* ſtündlihen *hourly*, tæglih *or* tæglihen
dayly, jærlih *or* jærlihen *yearly*, veræhtlih
or veræhtlihen *ſcornfully &c*. *to the adverbs*
either poſitiv, or ſuperlativ in EN *we adde*
ſometimes an S*, and then here in the ſuperlativ*
thoſe prepoſitiv particles a'm, zu'm *&c. are left*
out e. g. eilends *quickly*, augenblikks *in a*
moment, links *or* rehts *with the left or right*
hand, ſhœnſtens *very fairly*, weiſeſtens *moſt*
weiſely &c. the poſitiv adverbs are alſo made
either by foreſetting, to the abſolute of the Pa-
tronymicks, the particle auf*, or by adding to*
thoſe that ſignify any other quality, the word
weiſe *e. g.* auf Teutſh, auf Engliſh, auf
Spaniſh *&c. after the Dutch, Engliſh, Span-*
-iſh faſhion; erliher weiſe *or* redliher weiſe
honeſtly. the reſt of this Etymologie is made
clear in the declenſions of nouns and verbes,
where the words of the firſt caſe and perſon
are the roots, from whence all the others came.

Sect. 2. of the Forein Derivation.

there is an abundance of Highdutch and Eng-

lifh words , which both in writing and pronouncing are either the same or very like, as you may
well guesse at thofe not few examples cited but
accidentaly here in this small treatice ; but the
revolution of time and diverfity of dialeĉts have
changed the manner both of pronouncing and of
ſpelling in a good many words here omitted.
this mutation muſt needs be done by antiſtœ-
chon and the other grammar-figurs , as we ſhall
endeavour to make appeare.

proſthefis : eine hore or hure *a whore* , ir *to her* ,
erſt *firſt* , oben *above* , band *riband* , eine
kelle *a ſkellet or ſkillet* , der rom or ræm von
der milh *cream* , krazen *to ſcratche* , nifen
to ſueeſe , krabbeln *to ſcrabble* , nagen *to
gnawe* , ein ram or ramen *a frame.*

aphaerefis : ein klomp or klompen *a lump,*
eine kwelle *a welle* , geſlank *lank* , gelůkk
luck , kneipen *to nippe* , erkwikken *to quicken* , ſchnattern *now* ſnattern *to chatter* , ſmel-
zen *to melt* , gewinnen *to winne* , gelibt *loved,*
and thus GE of the participles is alwayes taken
away, which is to be obſerved alſo of all the
other nouns beginning with the ſaid ſyllable e.g.
gereht *right* , gefiht *fight* , gefund *found* , gedanken *thoughts &c.* genug *has enough.*

epenthefis : der donner *the thunder* , ſi *ſhee* ,
ſiſe *or* fis *ſweet* , *Belg.* ſoet; handtwelle *hand-
towell* , wildnifs *wildernefs* , glaſer *glaſier.*

ſyncope : ein hůgel *a hill* , ůbel *evel or ill* ,
oder or, niht *not* , uns *us* , wůnſhen or wůndſh
-en *to wiſhe* , welh *which* , folh *ſuch* , ſweſter
fiſter , unſer *cur* , als *as* , mærgel *marle* ,
ſanft *ſoft &c.*

paragoga: lenen *or* leyen *to lende ,* inn *, into,*
kern *kernell ,* eine burde *a burden ,* ein helm
   a helmet , dapffer *dapper or pert ,*
apocope : eine sunde *a sin ,* der saft *the sap ,*
ih *i;* wir *we ,* ein prister *a priest ,* eine bi-
   ne *a bee ,* ist *is ,* ein kan *canam. or boat*
metathesis : topf *or* top *pot ,* eine butte *a*
   tub , ein ross *a horse ,* eine burste *a brush,*
brennen *or* broennen *to burne ,* forht *fright,*
ein bred *a board ,* der kolb *or* kolben *the*
   club *,* von *Belg.* van *&c.* son *and* san *Engl.*
of &c. which *is done constantly in those words*
that *ende in* LE *,* NE *,* RE *, e. g.* ein koh-
   loeffel *a ladle ,* ein girtel *a girdle ,* eine na-
   nadel *a needle ,* shewenn *to showre ,* feyer
   or feir *fire ,* angel *angle ,* gestolen *stolne.*
*and though a certain rule or standing certainty
can not be prescribed (as we could wish it were)
through the whole language without instances
and exceptions ; neverthelesse we are sure , that
it will helpe us much , when we knowe by those
meanes , how either a German may very easily
turn the English , or an Englishman the High-
dutch words into his own , and thus in half
an houres time get by heart a greater store of them
than he is able to reade over scarce in half a day ;
which seeming hyperbole will soon evanish in the
metamorphosis here following , where to English the High-dutch words , we have to
                                change their*
A, *and* O*, both long ; likewise* Æ *, into* EA*,
e. g.* ein jar *a year ,* klar *clear ,* nae *near ,*
bard *beard ,* befaren *to feare ,* ja *yea ,* mal
or mal *meal ,* lager *or* lager *leaguer ,* larn-

en to leaxne, ein bær or ber a bear, ædel
cable or eible, ſtrom ſtream, anſtatt or in ſtæ-
de in ſtead, eine bone a bean, rot redd,
tret thread, or ear, brot bread, der Oſt the
Eaſt, Oſtwind Eaſt-wind, Oſtern Eaſter.
Æ into A e. g. bekker baker, hætte had,
æpfel apples, gærtener gardener, ſtærke
ſtarth, tære tar, wæſpe waſpe, ſhu-lxiſt ſho-
laſt, umhænge hangings &c.
A ſhort into O and E e. g. belangen to belong, lang long, geſang ſong, mang among,
gedrang throng, gaſt gueſt, raſt reſt, halt-
en to holde, harſh or hæiſher boarſh.
AU and ÆU into EA EW or OU e. g.
hæupt or haupt head, kaufen to cheapen,
draumen or dræumen to dreame, haufen or
hæufen to heape, laufen to leape, raufen or
ræufen to reape, der ſaum the ſeam, taub
deaf, der baum eines wæbers the beam of a
wæver, berauben to bereave, ſhawen to
ſhowe or ſhewe, ſnauze ſnout, ſhaurih ſhowry,
ſlau or wizig ſlow or wittie, untertaugen
to tugge down, blawe blew, hawen to hewe,
der dau the dew, es dawet it thaws, ſawer
ſower, eine laus a louſe, das haus the houſe,
laut loud, das maul the mouth, maulworf molewarp, maulbere mulber-
rie, eine ſawe a ſow, brawen or bræwen to
brewe, mæyen or mæen to mowe, hæulen
to bowle, aus out, faul foul &c. but ſometimes into U O or OO e. g. der ſhaum the
ſtam, ſhaumen or ſhæumen to ſcumme, eine
pflaume a plum, ſauhen to ſucke, ſaufen to
ſuppe, der daum or daumen the thumb, eine

daube *a dove*, ein laub brotes *a loaf of bread*, ein rauber *a robber*, ein raum *a room*, auf up, ſauhen *to ſucke or ſoake* &c.

B *finall or ſtanding before an* F, *in the ſingular nouns commonly into* F, *but in their plurals and elſewhere into* V e. g. ein dib *a thief*, dibe *thieves*, kalb *calf*, kælber *calves*, ein weib *a wife*, weiber *wives*, ein ſhaub *a ſheaf* das leben *the life*, zu leben *to live*, leblih *lively*, ſtab *ſtaff*, ob *if*, halb *half*, ab *of*, ſelb or ſelbſt *ſelf or ſelfs*, ſtreifen ſtræben or ſtreiben *to ſtrife*, ſiben *to ſift*, ſib *ſive*, eine ſalbe *a ſalve*, ſtube *ſtew, or ſtove*, ſterb -en *to ſtarve*, treiben *to drive*, di leber *the liver*, der rab *the raven*, hærbeſt *harveſt*, der abend *the avond or evening*, übel *evel*, wæben *to weave*, ſhaben *to ſhave*, geben *to give*, haben *to have*, liben *to love*, über over; grab *grave*, graben *to grave or carve*, nabel *navel*, ſibene *ſeven*, eben *even*, heben or hœben *to heave*, ſwer zu hœben *heavie*, nabe *nave of a cartwheel* &c. *ſee* P.

CH *after a conſonant and before a vowel in the ſame ſyllable into* H, *but between two conſonants of one ſyllable it is quite taken away both here in our dialect and in the Engliſh* e. g. aſche *now* aſhe *aſhe*, raſch *now* raſh *raſh*, ſhroten *to ſhred*, ſhrœt or krumm *ſhrewd*, ſlabbern *or* ſlappern *to ſlabber*, ſlitten *ſledge*, inn ſhiſer zerſplittern *to ſhiver into ſpliſters or ſplinters*, ſnæppiſh or ſnippiſh *ſnappiſh*, puſhen *to puſhe*, ſhrein *ſhrine or ſcrine*, ſwærm -en *to ſwarme*. *but the Engliſh like the Italians and Spaniards doe turne it, ſometimes*

to C *or* K *e. g.* ſharmezel *or* ſharmûzel
ſkirmiſh, *It. and* Hiſp. ſcaramuccia; •ein buſh
a buſh, It. *and* Hiſp. boſco, *whence an am-*
buſh, Gall. embuſcade; It. *and* Hiſp. embos-
cáda ; ein wiſh *a wiſk*, ſhelten *to* ſcolde,
ſkanze ſcannee *or* ſconce; ſhrapen *to* ſcrape,
eine ſhûppe *a* ſcoop, ſhofsfrei ſcotfree,
ſhreiber ſcrivener, ſhalen einer wage; ein-
nes fiſhes *or* haupts ſcales *of a ballance, fiſh*
or bead; haſel- nuſs-ſhale haſſel-nut-ſhell *or*
ſhale. *ſee the lett.* H ſect. 3. *chap.* 1. *Part.* 1.
and lett. S. *of this ſect.*

D *into* TH *e. g.* ding *thing,* mih dûnket *me*
thinketh, denken *to thinke,* der *or* di *the,* dis
or das *this or that,* durh *thorough,* der mund
the mouth, dann *or* denn *than or then,* der
tod *the death,* bruder *brother,* pfad *path,* bad-
en *to bathe,* das bad *the bath,* eine ſwade gras
a ſwath of graſs . Nôrd *North,* leder *leather,*
ander *other,* dritte *third,* beide *both,* eine
ſheide *a ſheath,* dinne *thinn,* dikk *thick,* eine
heide *a heath,* ein heid *a heathen,* dar *there,*
weder *whether,* dreye *three,* dorn *thorn,*
doh *though,* danken *to thanke,* ein eid *an*
oath, du *thou,* dein *thine,* dorſt *thirſt,* doerſtig
thirſty, &c.

E *long,* Æ *and* EI *often into* EA *and* EE
e. g. heilen *to heale* ; feyer-herd *fire-hearth,*
eine herde *a beard* ; leder *leather,* ſtelen *to*
ſteale, feder *feather,* di ſee the ſea, ſeen *or better*
ſren *to ſee,* ſeen *or better* ſeen *to ſowe,* ſteir-
en *to ſteere* ; ſteyermann *ſteerman,* treden *or*
traeden *to treade,* das wetter *or* watter *the*
weather, das mel *the meal,* ærde *or* erde *earth,*

leiten *to leade*, fpreiten *to ſtreade*, heizen *to heate*, teir or deyer *dear*, teil or deil *deal*. *but ſometimes eſpecially* EI *into* O, OA *or* AI *e.g.* lﳋife *ſope*, geiſt *ghoſt*, meiſt *moſt*, mer *more*, fer *ſore*, greinen *to groxe or groane*, alleine *alone*, das werk *the work*, geis *goat*, bein bone, heis *kot*, ein *one*, einſt or eins *once*, eid oaih, ſtein *ſtone*, ein ſtreih *or* ſtrih *a ſtreak* or *ſtroak*, ſwerd *ſword*, heim *home*, nein *no*, kein *none*, preiſen or præiſen *to praiſe*, regen *rain*, ſtreyen or ſtræyen *to ſtraye &c. and oftentimes into* I, *e. g.* mein *mine*, dein *thine*, pfeife *pipe*, neine *nine*, fein *fine*, wein *wine*, ſweine *ſwine*, ſheinen *to ſhine*, eitel *idle*, eiland *ile*, ſleim *ſlime*, meile *mile*, eiſen *iron*, lein *line*, leim *lime*, kneif *knife*, feile *file*, feilen *to file*, leiht *light &c. but* I *or* EI *finall or* EY *into* Y *or* IE *e. g.* eine ſwein -ſteye *ſwinesſtie*, ſhreyen *to crye*, wi *why*, zweiliht *twielight*, bei *by*, paſtei or paſteye *paſtie &c.*

E *eſpecially the ſhort before* B, KK, NK, X, *into* I *and* A *e. g.* lekken *to licke*, ſtekken *to ſticke*, denken *to thinke*, bedenken *to bethinke*, beſprenkeln *to beſtrinkle*, reht *right*, melken *to milke*, niſten *to neſte*, leben *to live*, geben *to give*, ſex or ſehſe *ſix*, peh pich, ſtern *ſtarr*, hellebarte *halbert*, ferne farr, faſt *faſt*, meſſe *maſs*, eſel *aſs*, ſtandfeſt ſtedfaſt. *but the finall* E *into* OW *or* EW *e. g.* der ſne *the ſnow*, kroeen *to crowe*, kue cow, ſæen *to ſowe*, eine reye *or* reie *row*, kiæe *a crow*, dreen *or* werfen *to throwe*, bleen blæen or blaſen *to blowe*; nun *(of old*

nue) naw , wi (elſe wie) how or why , ſene
ſinew,trewe true and truth.

I long commonly into EE and ſometimes into E,
EA or IE , e.g. hir hier here or heer ; bir bier or
beer , kni knee , di the , dif deep , ſiden to ſeethe,
ein rim or rimen (ſeiſe i. ſope) a ream (of paper
i: ris papir,) ſigeln to ſeale, ſigelring ſealring,
ſibene ſeven , eilfe now elſe eleven, ſhild ſhield.
wit we, nitlih neatly, dir to thee &c.

F in the midſt or end of a word into P, the
which is omitted , if an other P precede , e. g.
ein ſhaf a ſheep , ein ſhif a ſhip , ſeite ſope ;
hoffen to hope , rauſen to reape , eine pſeiſe
a pipe , ein aff an ape , ein pfaff (excellently
and eminently) a pope , der pfad the path ,
ein tropf or tropfen a drop , ſlupfen or ſluppen to ſlippe , ſlipferih ſlippery, pſoften poſts ,
pfund pound, fusftapf footſtep , pfennig penny,
trumpf trumpcard, apfel apple, helfen to helpe,
verpfanden to pawne , ein pfand a pawn , di
hulfe the help , pflafter plaiſter and plaſter,
eine pflanze a plant , pflanzen to plante, ein
dorf a dorp , waffen weapon , pfeffer pepper,
reif ripe , kupfer copper , ein kufer or boettiger a cooper , offen open , gaffen to gape ,
eine ſleife a ſleev , hopfen hop or hoppes , gras
-hupfer grashopper , knitten or knupfen to
knutte , phpfen or pipen als ein vogel to peepe
as a bird , rumpf or rumf rump , ſhaffen or
ſhoepfen to ſhape , ſtampfen to ſtampe , ſtopfen to ſtoppe or ſtuffe , ſtrumpf ſtrump , harſe
harpe , krampf the kramp or cramp ; knopf
knop , pfalz-grav palz-grave, pflug plough ,
ſharf ſharp , eine ſnepſe a ſnip , der zapen

the tap, wein-zæpfer *wine-tapʼler*, flafen *to
fleepe*, pflokken *to plucke*, ein pfil *a pillow*,
pfau *peacock. fee the letter* V.

G in the beginning of the preformativ fyll.
GE is quite taken away with its vowell, and
in the middle it is changed into Y or I e. g.
eine magt *a myd or maid*, gegen-gefagt
gain-fayd or faid, hagel *hailftone*, the Low-fax
-onick brægen or gehirn *brains*, geflagen
flay'n or flain, ein nagel *a nayl*, ein flægel
a flayl or flail, fegel *fayl or fail*, our word ei
or æi and the Nederlandifh ey from the An-
gle-Saxonick æg, Engl. egg. but in the
end or before an E. into Y or IE e. g. honig
bonny, ein aug *an eye*, der weg *the way*,
fagen *ta fay*, tod flagen *to flay*, moegen
may, ligen *to lay*, lügen *to lye*, heilig *holy*,
goettlih *godly*, zwanzig *twentie or twenty*,
and fo forth through all the adjectivs and adverbs
of this termination, notwithftanding it be fpel-
led by fome with an H e. g. koeniglih *kingly*,
herzlih *heartly*, bitterlih *bitterly &c. and
elfewhere efpecially after an L or R into OW
e.g. di forge the forrow, forgen to forrowe,
borgen to borrowe , eine forge or furge a
furrow*, ein vogel *a fowle*, morgen *to morrow*,
tallig *tallow*, folgen *to followe*, fwælgen
to fwallowe, galgen *galiow*, eigen *owne*,
gelbe *yellow*, ellbogen *ellbow*, boegen *to
bowe*, ein bogen *a bow*, ein hargen *a harrow*,
eine fxge *a faw*, magen *maw &c.

H the mute and needlefs afpiration ufed by fome
after an other letter of the fame fyllable is alwayes
fyncopized as well here by us as in Englifh, and

*that often not without mutation of the foregoing
letters e.g.* eine kuhe *now* kue *a cow,* ſtroh
now ſtro ſtraw *;* ein ſhuh *now* ſhu *a ſhoe,* eine
ſchlœhe *or* ſchleh. *now.* flœe *or* flee *a floe,*
næhe. *or* nae. *nigh. or near,* krœhen *now* krœ
-en wi ein han *to crowe like a cock,* rohe
now roe *raw,* gehen *now* geen *to goe,* ſtehen
now ſteen *to ſtand,* ſtehen machen *now* ſteen
mahen *to ſtaye,* wœhe *or* wœh *now* wœe
or woe *woe,* zweihe *now* zweye *or* zwei
twe, fliehen *now* flien *to flie &c. ſee the lett.*

H *the hard aſpiration uſed now by us for* CH,
*in the middle or end of a ſyllable, ſometimes
into* GH *e.g.* leiht *and* das liht *light,* reht
right, gewiht *weight,* naht *night,* lahen *to
laughe,* tohter *daughter,* di maht *the might,*
mæhtig *mightie,* durh *thorough,* rauh *rough,*
hœe *or* hœhte *hight,* gebraht *brought,* dreihte
drought, gedaht *thought,* ahte *eight,* kneht
knight, fehten *to fighte,* hoh *high,* doh *though,*
fluht *flight,* ihtwas *ought,* nihts *nought,*
nahbar *neighbour,* ſlaht-haus *ſlaughter-houſe,*
di pſlihte *the plight,* keihen *or* huſten *to
coughe,* ſleht *flight &c. and ſometimes eſpecialy in the end of a ſyllable into* K *or* CK.
e.g. ein buh *a book,* eine wohe *a week,*
ſik *or* ſih *ſick,* der lauh *the leek,* ſuhen *to
ſeeke,* eine eihe *an oak,* brauhen *to brooke,*
mahen *to make,* weih *weak,* gleih *like,* horh
-en *to hearken,* ſprehen *or* ſpræhen *to ſpeake,*
eine ſahe *a ſake,* eine ſe-lahe *a lake,* ein
koh *a kook,* ein kuhen *a cake,* rehenen
to reckon, rehnung *reckning,* ein werk *(or*

werh) *a work*, eine hehel *a heckle or hit-*
chel, ein ſtorh *a ſtork*, brehen *to breake*,
ein mœnh *a monk*, eine fihel *a ſickle*, ein
kühlein *or junges hûngen a chickin* milh
milk krahen i' m brehen *to cracke*, ein knœh-
el *a knuckle*, eine lærhe *a lark*, eine ſpeihe
des rades *a ſpoke of the wheel*, ſegel ſtreih-
en *to ſtrike ſails*, ein beher *a beaker*, *Belg.*
een beker *or* beecker, *Ital.* un bicchiere;
rûhen *or* rûhen *to reeke or ſmelle*, ein deih
a dike or ditch. ſtreihen *to ſtroke and ſtrike &c.*
but often eſpecialy after an L (the which moſt
commonly is left out in Engliſh) into CH, *to*
which (being pronounced as TSH) the letter T
is often added e.g. di kûrhe *the church*, reih
rich, erſuhen *to beſeeche*, reihen *to reathe*,
predihen *to preache*, ein brûh *a breach*, ſolh
ſuch, welh *which*, ſprahe *ſpeech*, jaht-ſhiff
yatch a ſort of ſhips, krûhen *to crouche*, di
kûhe *the kitchin*, wahen *to watche*, das dah
the datch, ein ſtih *a ſtick*, ſtrekken *to ſtretche*,
krûkken *crutches*, peh *pitch*, panlh *or* pantſh
panch *&c. ſee the letter K.

J conſonant and initiall into Y *e.g.* jar *year*,
joh *yoak*, jung *young*, jugend *youth*, garn
or jarn *yarne*, geſtern *or* jeſtern *yeſter*, gerte
or jerte *garth and yard*, jænen *or* gænen *to
yawne*; ja *yes or* yea *&c.*

K before A, O, U, K, L, R, into C, *e.g.*
eine kanne *a canne*, ih kann *i can*, kommen
en *to come*, klawe *clawe*, kûle *cool*, ein
kalb *a calf*, klokke *clock*, akker *acre*, ankel
el *ancle*, kirſhe *cherrie*, nakken *neck* das
korn *the corn*, di krone *the crown*, krihen

to creepe, klœben *to cleave*, klinge *to clinge*, pakke auf deinen pakk *pack up thy pack*, fprekkel *fpeckle*, kutfhe *coach*, di kofte *coft*, kalk *or* kalh *chalk*, kammer *chamber*, klinim -en *to climme*, ein kukku *a cuckow*, kole *cole*, kol *colwort*, pikken *to pick*, pikkel *pickle &c. but fometimes*, *efpecialy before* E *or* I *into* CH, *e. g.* kind *child*, kinn *chinn*, fink *or* finken *finch*, kifte *cheft*, kirhe *church*, kæs *cheefe*, kæwen *to chewe* kifen *or* kûfen *to chofe*, kaftanien-nufs *chefs-nut*, kaufen *Belg.* koopen *to cheapen*; kœpfen *or* kûppen, *to chop*, *Belg.*kappen *&c.*

KK *into* CK, GG *or* DG *e. g.* wakkeln *or* waggeln *to wagge*, ein flukker *a flug grd*, fhoggeln *or* fhukkeln *to fhogge*, brikke *or* brûkke *brigg or bridge*, hekke *hegg or hedge*, rokken *or* korn *rogge or rye*, rokk *i. tunica*, rugg *i. ftragulum hifhidum*; fakk *fack or bagg*, ftekken *a ftick or to ftick*, fokke *fock &c.*

L *in the midft of a fyllable*, *after the Hollandifh and French fafhion*, *either in writing or at leaft in pronouncing into* U *e. g.* ftolz *i. proud*, ftout *i.* dapfer; wald *wood*, falz *falt*, *Belg. and Gall.* fout; kalb *calf qs. cauf* folte wolte *fhould would qs. fhoud woud &c.*

M *in the beginning*, *but feldome*, *into* W *or* WH *e.g.* wærmut *wormwood*, mit *with*, das menlh (*an unmarried woman*) *the whench. but elfewhere efpecially after an other* M, *into* B *ufed before alfo by us in fome words e. g.* flummern *or* flumbern *to flumbere* grummeln *or* murren *to grumble*, krûmeln *to crumble or* crume, ein kamm *or* kamb *a comb*, kæmmen

to combe , ein lamm *or* lamb *a lamb,* der daum
-en *the thumb* , marmel *marble* , taumeln *to
tumble* , mummeln *or* mumbeln *to mumble,*
ein bramber-ſtrauh *a bramble* , ſtummeln *or*
ſtumbeln *to ſtumble* , ein ſhæmel ſhæmmel *or*
ſhæmbel *i. a low ſtool* , *ſhambles i. places where
meat is ſold upon* ; ſtumm *or* ſtumb *dumb.*

N *finall of the infinit and definit moods is taken
away leaving behind its vowell as the characteristick letter , whereby the better to ſhow as well
Harmony and Derivation as the Difference betwixt a noun and a verbe. ſee the foregoing
chapter.*

O *ſhort into* U *or* OO , *e. g.* torf *turf* ,
koh *cook* , ſommer *ſummer* , wolle *wool* , wolf
wulf , ſonne *ſunne* , blutt *blood* , tonne *tunn,*
mond *moon* , nonne *nunne* , ſtottern *ſtutter.*
œ *and* û *into* A, I , O , U , EE , *or (but
ſeldom)* EO *and* EA *e. g.* wûſte *waſt* , ver-
wûſten *to waſte* , kœnig *king* , ſœne *ſons or
ſonnes* , brœnnen *to burne* , kûn *keen* , rœſten
or roſten *to roſte* . grûſſen *to greete* , über *over* ,
Rœmiſh *Romiſh* , kûſſen *to kiſſe* , ein kûſſen
a cuſhion , fœrdern *or of old* fûrdern *to further,*
frœlih *frolick* , kûl *cool* , plûndern *to plunder,*
hœlle *helle* , hœle *hole* , hœren *to heare* , der
pœbel *the people or rabble* , ſtœren *to ſtirre,*
ſtœrmen *or* ſtûrmen *to ſtorme* , ein ſtûkk lak-
rœzen *a ſtick of liquoris* , imann *or* jemann
yeoman. &c. ſee the lett. U

P *into* B , *as this into* P , *both ſeldom e. g.* rum
-peln *to rumble* , palm-baum *balm-tree* , plapp
-ern *to blabber* , lumpen *lumber* , ſtupfel *ſtub-
ble* , hûppeln *or* hûpfeln *to hobble* , di bangig-

keiten *the pangues*, boren *to bore pore or poare*, eine birn *a pear*, pralen *to brawle*.

KW *into* QU *e.g.* kwitte *quince*, kwitt *quit*, kwellen *to quelle &c.*

both S *and* Z *commonly short and final*, *as also* Z *initiall into* T, *e.g.* was ist das? *what is that?* wasser *water*, hassen *to hate*, lassen *to let*, sezen *to set*, sizen *to sit*, kaze *cat*, stelzen *stilts*, swarz *swart or black*, zweig *twig*, zam *tame*, erzælen *and* zælen *to telle*, das geringste zin *or* bleh *tinn*, zu smelzen *to melte*, filz *filt*, zunge *toung*, zangen *tonges*, herz *heart*, malz *malt*, salz *salt*, milz *milt*, eine zære *a tear*, zerren *to teare*, sweis *sweat*, swizen *to sweate*, essen *to eate*, vergessen *to forgette*, strafe *street*, münze *mint*, der spis *the spit*, eine nuss *a nut*, zwillinge *twinnes*, weis *white*, zunder *tinder*, ein winzer *a vintener*, ein shufs *a shot*, shufsen *to shoote*, heis *hot*, hize *heat*, zan *tooth*, nez *net*, nessel *nettle*, wezen *to whette*, zwinkeln mit den augen *to twincle with the eyes*, beze *bitch*, zigel *tile*, zimmer-holz *timber*, ein ganser *a gander*, der lenz *the lent*, zuzien *to tie*, besser *better*, das los *the lot*, erd-klos *clod of earth*, der zoll *the toll*, beisen *to bite*, zæe *tough*, eine fus-zœe *a foot-toe*, strozen *to strutte*, der ziz *or* di wærze einer brust *the teat or wart of a breast*, zeitung *tiding*, zeit *tide and time*, kessel *kettle*. *but* S *long and finall into* C *or* Z *e.g.* frisen *to freeze*, eis *ice*, reis *rice*, preis *price or prize*, ein zirkel *a circle*, prinz *prince*, plaz *place*, zepter *scepter*, læuse *lice*, unzimlih *unseemly*, glans *or* glanz *glance*

Belg. glants; glæntſen *or* glænzen glæɲzɑrd
glinzern *or* gleiſen *to gliſter.*, *Belg.* glantſen,
Dan. glantzer.

SCH *finall (uſed by others hitherto) alwayes into*
SH *which old ſpelling of the Saxons, ſtill kept up
in Engliſh, we alſo embrace here in this new method of ours* e. g. ein fiſh *a fiſh*, fiſhen *to fiſhe*,
ein biſhoff *a biſhop*, friſh *freſh*, erfriſhen *to
refreſhe*, waſhen *to waſhe &c. but abeximinall
eſpecially before* L, M, N, R, W, *into* S,
e. g. ſleht halten *to ſlighte*, ſlukkiſh *ſluggiſh*,
ſmal *ſmall*, ſmerzen *to ſmarte*, ein ſmitt *a
ſmith*, ſnell *ſnell*, ſnorren *to ſnorte*, ſnuppen
to ſnuffe, ſhrœter *ſcroter*, Swed *Swedlander*,
Sweizer *Swizer*, ſwingen *to ſwinge*, ſmeit-
ig *or* geſmeitig *ſmooth &c. more examples
ſee in the firſt chapt. of the firſt part at the 3. ſect.
and lett.* CH *of this ſect.*

HS *into* X, e. g. ein fuhs *a fox*, der flahs
flax, das wahs *wax*, der ohs *ox*, wahſen *to
waxe*, eine bihſe *a box*, ſehſ *ſix*, ſehzig
ſixty, ſehzen *ſixteen*; di abſel *the axell*;
næhſt *next*; zwiſhen *betwixt*; Sahſen *Saxony*; ein Sahs *a Saxon*, ahſel *or* axel *axle.*

T *of the nouns and particles often, but in the
Imperfects, and in the participle paſſiv alwayes,
into* D, e. g. wittwe *widdow*, ſhatten *ſhaddow*,
überſhatten *overſhaddowe*, brot *bread*, matte
or wiſe meddow, ku-euter *or* utter udder of a
cow, wittwer *widdower* di ſhulter *the ſhoul-
der*, blut *blood*, trummel *drum*, treige *dry*,
garten *garden*, ſattel *ſaddle*, futter *fudder
or food*, dritte *third*, flut *flood*, haupt *head*,
hæt-lang *head-long*, der tod *death*, leiten

to leade, mittag *midday*, wort *word*, di Gott-
heit *the Godhead*, hart *hard*, alt *old*, weit
wide, bitten *i. beseeche*, *to bidde i. commande*;
bett *bed*, mittel *middle*, blat *blad*, blatter
or blafe *bladder*, trinken *to drinke*, toll
dull, teufel *devil*, gut *good*, eine leiter *a
ladder*, ein ræzel or rætfel *riddle*, unter
under. fee the preced. chapt. *and fometimes
into* TH, *both in nouns and particles* e. g. monat
moneth, motte *moth*, ftreng e *ftrength*, vater *father*, mutter *mother*, trad *thread*, latte
lath, wærme or warmte *warmth*, troen or
treyen *to threaten*, wetter *weather*, mit *with*,
fmt or fit *fith &c.* *but in the third prefent
finguler of the reft alwayes into* TH *or* S, *the
which is quite taken away in the fecond plurall of
both the fingle tenfas, whereof fee the foreg. ch.*
TH *ufed by others into* D *e. g.* thuen *to doe*;
eine that *a deed*; theier *dear*, eine thûre
or ein thor *a dore*; rothredd, roethläh *red-
difh*; eine ruthe *a rod*, ein theil *a deal*;
moerterer *murderer*, mort *murder*, ermorthen
or moerthern *to murder*, theilen *to deale*; ein
thal *a dale*, thumb *dome*; herzogthum *dukedome &c.* *our method has either* T *or* D
e. g. das dor *dore*; rot *redd*, tuen *to doe &c.*
U *and* û *into* EE, *or* I, *e. g.* fûlen
to feele; fuhen *to feeke*; bluten *to
bleede*; grün *green*; eine buhe *a beech*; fûfse
fweet Belg. foet; ein kufs *a kiss*; kifsen *to
kifse*; mihr dûnkt *me thinks*, dûrften *and* durft
entoa dhirft, der durft *the thirft*. *but fometimes
th efpecially being long, into* OO *e. g.* eine
blume *a bloom*, ein pful *a pool*, ein flur

floor , buh *book* , blut *blood* , der huf *hoof* ,
beute *booty*, bude *booth* &*c. and when short into*
O *or* OU *e.g.* rond *or* rund *round* , hund
hound , gefund *found* di zunge *tongue*
and (better) toung *or* tung , wundern *to*
wonder , wunde *wound* , durh *through* , du
thou , daube *dove* &*c. but our dialect has*
common'y the same vowel O *e. g.* mofs *or*
mos *mofs* , dorh *thorough* , gold *gould or gold*,
golden *golden* , voll *full* , *fo likewife* konft
art , omfonft *in vain* &*c. elfe* mus , durh,
guld , yull *or* full , kunft , umfunft &*c. fee*
the letter O.

V *into* F , *as that (but feldom) into* V
e. g. vater *father* , vafs *or* fafs *fat*
or vefsel , vor *for* , bevor *before* , voll *full* ,
vire *four* , volk *folk* , vogel *fowl* , funfe
five , ein ofen *an oven* , prüfen *to prove. but*
the fyllable VER *is commonly left out, e. g.*
verlifen *to loofe* , verdammen *to damme* ,
verblenden *to blende* , verhintern *to hinder* ,
verlæubnüfs *or* erlaubnufs *leav* , verloren
loft or forlorne , ein verluft *a lofs* , verlang-
en *to longe* , vermanen *te monifhe* , *and thefe*
are changed thus : verfteen *to underftand* ,
vegefsen *to forgette* , verlafsen *to forfake*, ver-
geben *to forgive*.

W *fometimes into* WH , *which were alfo ufed*
by the Angle Saxons *e. g.* wann *or* wenn
whan or when, wer *who*, was *what*, wirb-
el-wind *whirle-wind* , war (*or* wo) *where* ,
weizen *wheat* , weifen *to whiten* , weder *whe-*
ther , wezen *to whette* , welh *which* , eine
weile *a while* , weinen *to whine* , wifpern

to whisper, ein walfish *a whale*, spinn-wært-
el-wharle *to put on a spindle* , eine radewelle
or rade-bære *a wheel-bare.*

*finaly we can not but know , that as in the
High and Low-countries both of England and
Germany there be diverse provinces and shires,
and consequently severall idioms and manners
in the pronunciation : so tract of time hath
made (and makes still) various alterations not
only in writing and spelling, as we have seen
just now all along ; but also in the very signification , partly by taking sundrie words formerly used for the same things , either in a
limited or in a quite other sense , and partly
by receiving (especially in England) or making
new ones.   whence it comes to pass , that
some of'em (as coined money) are perhaps in
this part of a countrie in continuall use and
wellcome , but in an other less regarded growing
out as of countenance so of fashion ; till we forgette them quite , as for examples fit to our purpose, the words : earle , lord , lady, to bide ,
to write , to spell &c. were in the former times
as well used in Saxony (from whence they came)
as now in England; where as in stead thereof wa
use in Germany other words of the same signification: graf, groser Herr, Fræulein or Fræugen,
warten, shreiben, buhstabiren. thus the High-
dutch word der krig and the Netherlandish
Oorlogh had antiently got in Germanie an
other emphatick name , to wit , wærr werre
or warr, signifying such an action , where upon
followeth commonly * a strange confusion and
disorder called in our toung* eine unordent-*

lihe *verwerrung* or ein *gewerr*, *the which
uſualy is the cauſe*, *ſupport and effect of
any warr.*, *as both Low - and High - Germany* (*the very ſtage of Heroick actions and
the muſterplace of* Mars) *can teſtify it abun-
dantly not only now for its own ſelf*, *but
hath ſhown it alſo unto others and thereby ſo
well given to an everlaſting remembrance its
notition* warre *to the Britains*; guerre *to the
French*, guerra *to the Italian and Spaniſh
&c. nations*; *as brought upon its poſſeſsors
the glorious name* German *or* Guerman *i.
warriour or man of warre*, *which title they
firſt got from their enimies. this aboliſhing
of words we could prove alſo in the Engliſh
(or in any other) toung*; *but it will ſuffice
for the preſent to tell you*, *that we finde in
reading Engliſh books and in diſcourſing
with antient people*, *ſeverall naturalized
words now almoſt unknown to the younger
ones*, *eſpecially in thoſe places as London is
where almoſt all nations under heaven reſort
and by converſing and trading mix their own
with thoſe of the inhabitans*, *and take every
foot a nativ word in a wrong ſenſe and ſignification*, *which then amongſt the rabble gets
the upperhand in ſpite of the dictionaries and
ſometimes againſt all reaſons of the learned,
or their firſt inventors*; *as the words* knab
and bub *i. knave and boy, have here both quite
an other ſignification*, *then they had there*;
for ein knab *is alwayes taken with us in
the beſt ſenſe as the word* Boy *amongſt the
Engliſh*, *on the contrary* ein bub *ſignifyeth*

*usualy in our toung as much as a Knave in
the English, and that is always taken in the
worst meaning for a base fellow or rascal.
our and the Lowdutch word kneht, Eng'i-
shed knight, doeth in all Germanie signify
a mean he-servant, but in England it claim-
res: at the title of no less than a noble man;
the word mag't or maget, in English, maid
or may'd was formerly indifferent and taken
as it was spoken both for a virgin and for a
servant, but now it signifyeth in our toung
nothing else then a poor and vile maid-ser-
vand without any addition; whereas in England it denotes (absolutly taken) a virgin, and
not without a certain suppofition of a byword
it hath the signification of a servant. ein
Tilh in Germany is now as much as a Table
in England; whereas a Dish signifyes here
a little platter, to serve the meat in. der
drekk or trekk the dreggs is in Dutch as
much as muck or dirt, but in English it
signifyeth our word hoefen or the Latin fae-
ces; our word luft, Hollandish lucht, air or
vent, is no more used by the English unless
in to lift up, auflüften or sublevare qs.
in aerem; lofty, lüftig or elatus qs. in aerem or superbus; a-loof or loof, in a-
perto aere or in superiori aura, eine stüde,
Eng. a steed, AS. stodmyra i. equa ad
foetum, is taken now in English for an ex-
cellent brave and gallant horse. krank in
our tounge is used for sick and weak, but in
the English it importes the contrary. of our
word wifsen; Holl. weeten i. to know, in*

English is now used only to wit and the imperfect wote. the *A Saxonick* and the *Frankteutonick* word hereberga and heriberga did of old signify as much as in *Latin* mansio exercitus or castra, according to its composition of Her or Hær i. e. exercitus militum or army, and bergen i. abscondere or to hide; but now both our word hærberge, and the *Lowdutch* herberghe, as also the *Franco - Gallick* auberge hauberge or herberge, the *Ital.* albergo, the *Span.* alvergue coming all from thence, signify a lodging for any stranger, but the *English* word harbour being of the very same pedegree, only for ships, in stead whereof we have the word shiff - haven *Holl.* schip - haven; and in lieu of the other we use now Hær - læger or Kriges - lager i. leaguer &c. whereby everyone may easily see, that never so learned a man whoever, is able fully and radically to understand as any other language (though his own) derived from ours, so especially the *English*, without some knowledge of the *German* toung. for how emphatick and significant be the most part of the best *English* words derived from us e.g. king, *Godfory* or *Godfrid*, *Frederick*, *Richard*, beadle, alderman, husband, woman, quick silver, window &c. would be too long here to describe; therefore we shall bring forth but one example viz. *Gospel* commonly taken abusively for evangelion or good and merrie news, whereas it clearly and properly signifyes both a bad and a glad tiding, as coming from *Gott God*.

and ſpell *biſtory* or *ſermon*, *and that from* ſpell-ian *to* ſtelie, *which in the* ASaxonick *denoted* (*as it does ſtill in the* Belgick) *to interpretate* *explicate &c. and thus* Gottſpel *or* Goſpel, *AS.* Godſpell, *old-Frankiſo* Gotſpel *importeth as much as a divine hiſtorie or an interpretation and explication not only in matter of Chriſt's bleſſed incarnation and birth, happie redemtion of mankind, comfortable ſending of the holy Goſt, grati -us forgivneſs of ſin, life everlaſting and other joi -full things to all penitent ſinners, but alſo of the whole Triunities Eſſence, attributes and works belonging as well to his juſtice as to his mercy; where the former, to wit, the conſuming wrath of the incenſed God, the laſt Judgement, the cruell divel, flaming hell, eternall torment and other fright-full things cannot but κατ' ἀντίϕϱασι be termed* evangelium *or* bonum laetumque nuncium in reſpect to the wicked and damned.

nevertheleſs the inhabitans of the countrie eſpeci -ally of the Northern pirts of England and gene-rally in Scotland retaining better their nativ words (and thoſe of Kent and Suſſex becauſe of their neighbourhood and converſe with the Dutchs) come very nigh to our expreſſions, whereby they have a greater advantage to attain with more facility to our and the Lowdutch language, than any other people in the world. for in ſtead of the words (now commonly uſed in ſuch places, where gentle folks of both ſexes, ſcholars and courtiers live and beare the ſway) e. g. a bridge, cheſt, broom, oats, cough, church; ſalefaced, ſtrong, ſtiff; to cover, to revenge, to dwell &c. they *ſaÿ : a brigge, kiſt, bieſem or beaſom, bævir, buſte, kirke; bleak, ſtark, ſtiſe; decke, wreake, to wone; from the High-german : eine brŭkke or brigge, kŭſte or kiſte, beſen or beſem, haber or haver, huſt or huſten, kirhe; bleih, ſtark, ſteif; dekken, ræhen, wonen; Hollandiſh : een brucke, kiſte, beſem, haver, kerke; bleek, ſterk, ſtyf; dekken, wreecken, woonen*

Sect. 3. of
the Compounded Words.

here we ſhould adde the art of making lawfully new words (called elſe Onomatopoeia) as the third ſort of etymologie ; but that we waite for a better opportunity, we will at the preſent give a hint of our compounded words, the which if anatomiſed and opened from their ground, will give the Learner an accurate and clear underſtanding of them, as having a congruity with his owne toung, and bearing in their ſingle roots diverſe things, that expreſſe in compoſition the nature of one only thing though of various reſpects, as they make one only (compounded) word and name e. g. like as we ſay in High - dutch and Engliſh gold - ſmitt gold - ſmith, ſtokkfiſh ſtock - fiſh, ſhulmeiſter ſchool - maſter, ſhumaher ſhoe-maker, ſhu - læiſt ſhoe - laſt, haus - haltung houſe - holding, bir - bræwer beerbrewer, bræu - haus brew - houſe, ſhafhirt ſheap - heard, bluts- freind blood-freind, feyer - zange fire - tonge, lein - wæber lin - weaver, pomp - waſſer pomp - water,

bofom - freind , *bofom- freind* , augen-lid
eye - lid , buh- binder *book - binder* , lamms-
fufs *lambs-foot* , ftif-vater *ftep-father* , ftif-
mutter *ftep-mother* , halb-bruder *half-bro-
ther* , halb-fwefter *half-fifter*, kwekk-filber
quick-filver, deitungs-mann *tidingman*, fne-
ball *fnow-ball*, fufs-ftapf *foot/tep* , fonn-tag
funne-day, montag *monday*, donners-tag *thurs
-day*, freitag *fryday &c. fo an Englifh-man know-
ing the fingle words, will prefently underftand the
meaning of the compound, when we fay e.g.* eine wol-tat *qs. well-deed, a benefice.* ein fleifh
-hawer *qs. flefh-hewer or one that chops the
meat in pieces , a butcher.* ein zimmer-mann
*qs. timber-man or one that works in timber ,
a carpenter.* alle-zeit *qs. all-tide or all-time ,
alwayes.* eine zeit-vertreibe *qs. driving a
way the time or a paftime.* Gottes - akker
qs: Gods acker , churchyard. maus-
or ratten falle *qs. mouf-or rat-fall,trap.* wol
-luft *qs. well-luft , pleafure.* fonn-abend *qs.
funn-evening i. faturday* ; mitt-woh *qs. the
middle day in the week i. wednesday*; vornam
*qs. forename or the name that ftands before the
firname i. Chriften - name* ; zunam *qs. too-
name or the name added to the Chriften-name
i. firname*; brande-wein *qs. burned wine or
brandy*; kæfe-made *qs. cheefe-moath magot*;
feld-zeihen *Belg.* veld-teken *qs. field-token , a
fcarff of a foldier*; or-feige *qs. earfigg , box
an the ear*; butter-fafs *qs. butter-fat, churn*;
bærenhæuter *qs. one that lyeth alwayes upon a
beares-hide or - fkin (ufed in the times of old by
the German foldiers to fleep upon) i. lafy fellow.*

ein rehen-pfennig *qs. a reckon-penny or a counter*. ein arm-band *qs. arm-band or bracelet*. ein fuſs-eiſen *qs. foot-iron, a fetter or ſhackle*. ein hoſen-band *qs. hoſe-band or a garter*. ein zigel-ſtreiher *qs. a tile-ſtriker or a brickmaker*. mon-ſhein *qs. moon-ſhine or moon-light*.

ein {irr-wiſh / irr-liht} *qs.* {*irr-wiſk / irr-light*} *will of the wiſp*

pfeffer-kuhen *qs. pepper-cake, ginger-bread*. eſel-treiber *qs. aſs-driver, one that lookes and goes after the aſses*. ſeifen-ſider *qs. ſope-ſeether, one that makes ſope and candles, a chandeler*. ein par hand-ſhue *qs. a pair hand-ſhoes i. a pair of gloves*. ein laub-froſh *qs. a leaf-frog, a green frog feeding on leaves*. gros-vater *qs. great-father, grand-father*. groſe-mutter *qs. great-mother, grand-mother*. ein ſtraſen-ræuber *qs. ſtreet-robber, highway-man*. tod-feind *qs. death-feind, implacable enimy*. hornu-man *qs. horn-man, cuckold*. wein-haus *qs. wine-houſe, taverne*. buh-hændler *qs. book-handler, book-ſeller*. fiſh-hændler *qs. fiſhhandler, fiſh-monger*. abend-mal *qs. evening-meal, ſupper*. mittag-mal *qs. midday-meal, dinner*. ein landsmann *qs. a man of the ſame land, countrieman*. zukker-bækker *qs. ſugar-baker, confeſtioner*. ſing-vogel *qs. ſinging fowl, a bird that whiſtles*. ein dib-hænker *qs. thief-hanger, a hang-man*. hut-maher *qs. hat-maker, ein hüter a hatter*. finger-hut *qs. finger-hat, a thimble*. ein zan-breher *qs. tooth-breaker, a tooth-drawer*.

{hæi- / wein- / herbſt} monat *qs.* {*hay- / wine- / harveſt*} month *i.e.* {*Julius / Oſtober / September &c*}

Orthologia

OR

The Third Part of Words in their Conſtruction.

Chap. I. of the *Syntaxis.*

though our conſtruction be commonly knowne not onely by either the Greek or Latin Grammar, but alſo by the Engliſh it ſelf, wherin our man -ner of expreſſion frequently prevailes ; never- theleſs we cannot but touche at leaſt thoſe neces- ſary obſervations, that acquainte the learner with our generall proprieties and idiomes, leaving the ſpeciall particularities for the next and laſt Chapters.

Sect. 1. of the Conſtruction of Nouns.

R. 1. *the adjectivs goe alwayes before their Subſtantives and the articles before them both* e. g. etlihe meiner freinde *ſome of my friends* not etlihe freunde *meiner ſome friends of mine &c.* ein halbes pfund, ein halb- es jar *&c. a half pound, a half year, not* halb ein pfund, halb ein jar, *half a pound, half a year.* yet *we ſay* der zwitter iſt halb ein mann und halb ein weib *the her- maphrodite is half a man and half a woman,* das ſe-wunder war halb eine jungfrawe und halb ein fiſh *the ſea-monſter was half a maid and half a fiſh* ; ein ſolher mann *and* ſolh ein mann *such a man*, eine folhe tohter *and* folh eine tohter *such a daughter*, ein folhes buh *such a book*; welh *(and* was vor*)* ein mann ift das *! what a man is this!* alle di kinder, alle kinder *and* di kinder alle *all the children*; all das volk *all the people*; all di ftatt *or* welt *all the town or world*.

R. 2. *the adjectivs after a verbe keepe alwayes their abfolute termination without any change either in refpect of the fubftantives gender or number, as in Englifh e.g.* der mann, di fraw, das kind ift alt *the husband, wife and child is old*; di mænner, di frawen, di kinder find alt *the husbands, wives and children are old &c. unlefs they be preceded by either of the articles e g.* dife waren di weifen aus morgen-lande *they were the wife men out of the East*, fi waren di elenden *they were the miferable ones*, er ift grœfser *or* der grœfs -ere *he is bigger or the bigger*, fi ift fetter *or* di fettere *fhe is fatter or the fatter*, fi find di fettelten *they are the fatteft &c. the fame is to be obferved, when the fubftantiv immediatly precedes the adjectiv; for then this fuffers its finall alteration both in the fingular and plurall number through all gendres and cafes e.g.* er ift ein erliher *(* der erlihe *)* mann *he is an (the) honeft man*, fi ift eine *(* di *)* erlihe frawe *fhe is an (the) honeft woman*, es ift ein erlihes *or* das erlihe kind *it is an (the) honeft child*, fi find alle erlihe leute *they are all honeft people*, wir find alle elendige menfhen *we are all miferable men &c.*

R. 3. *when we couns or number, the lefs ad-*

jectiv of the compound both cardinall and ordinall number, being over twentie and under an
hundred, goes before the greater one, coupled
with the particle und and, e.g. ein und zwan
-zig *one* and *twentie*, der-di-das ein und
zwanzigste *the one and twentieth*,siben und seh
-zig *seven and sixtie*, der-di-das siben und
sehzigste *the seven and-sixtieth &c. not* zwan
-zig ein *twentie one*, zwanzig erste *twentie
first*, sehzig siben, sehzig sibende, *sixtie seven
sixtie seventh*.   but *the rest both of the compound and single number, as well under twentie
as over an hundred, are construed as in English*
e. g. neine, zwœlfe, drei-zeen, hundert
und ein, hundert und zwei &c. *nine, twelve,
thirtien, an hundred and one, an hundred and
two*; der-di-das neinte, zwœlfte, drei-
zeende, hundert-und erste, andere &c.
*the nineth, twelfth, thirtienth, hundred and
first, second.*   *we observe nature most exactly, when we will expresse the time . making
first of all mention of the day, then of the month,
and at last of the year; as for the present we write
and say* den fünften tag des winter-mc-
nats i'm sehzeén hundert nein und siben-
zigsten Hæil-jare *December the fifth* 1679.
*a speciall and usuall manner of speaking is, when
we say* halben weg vire or auf vire qs. *half
way four or upon four*, halben weg eins or auf
eins q. d. *half way one or upon one &c. where
-as the English say: half an hour past three
or before four, half an hour after twelf or before one*; ein tag oder sehse (qs. *one day or
six) about six dayes one less or more*; binnen

aht tagen *qs. within eight dayes,* binnen virzen tagen *qs. fortien dayes* , binnen drei virtel jar *qs. three quarter year &c. inſtead whereof they ſay in Engliſh: within a ſennight or ſeven -night , a fort-night , nine months or three quarters of a year.*

Sect. 2. of

the Conſtruction of Verbes.

R. 1. *the Verbes* befreyen *to free* , benem -en *or* berauben *to ſtrippe or robbe* , bezůht -igen *to blame* , entledigen *or* entnemen *to unloade,* erinnern *to putte in mind or to remember* , entſezen *to depoſe* , gedenken *to mention* , gewæren *to grante* , harren *or* warten *to ſtay for* , loszælen *or* losſprehen *to quitte or forgive* , verſihern *to aſsure* , ůberweiſen *or* ůberzeugen *to convince with arguments or witneſses* , wůrdigen *to count worthy* , zeyen *to accuſe* , miſsen *to miſse; fæilen to faile , and all the Reciprocks doe alwayes receive the fourth caſe of the perſon and the ſecond of the thing , which later is done , whether the verbe be active , paſſiv or Reciprocall ; but the former only , when it is activ and neutrall ; for the paſſiv verbe recciveth then the firſt caſe of the perſon e. g.* ih verſihere euh deſsen *i aſsure you of this* , er iſt deſsen verſihert *he is ſure of this* , er ſhæmet ſih einer ſolhen tat *he is aſhamed of ſuch a deed. of the ſame conſtruction is the ſubſtantiv verbe* ſein *to be , added to a verball noun or particle of the ſaid or the like verbs e.g.* er iſt diſes mordes giltig *or* ſhuldig *he is guilty of this murther &c.*

hither are to be brought the following expres-
sions, having some affinitie with the second case
and signify commonly the state or disposition of a
thing e. g. dreiges fusses *with dry foot*, nüht-
ernes mundes *with a fasting mouth*, bloses
angesihtes *with a bare face or bare-faced*, des
tages *by day*, des nahtes *by night*, des erst-
en *or* andern *&c.* tages *the first or second &c.*
day, des morgens *in the morning*, des somm-
ers *in the summer*, des winters *in the win-*
ter, einsmals des jares *once a year*, zwei-
mals des monats *twice a month*, er ginge
seines weges *he went (on) his way &c.*

R. 2. *when the verbe stands betwixt two nouns,*
the worthiest (that is either the first or the second)
goes before it and the third followes, *e. g.* ih
bin es *qs. i am it*, du bist es *qs. thou art*
it &c. not es ist ih, es ist du; *it is i, it is*
thou; ir seid es niht, di da reden, sond-
ern ewers vaters geist ist es, der durh euh
redet *it is not ye, that speake, but the spirit of*
your father, *Matth.* 10, 20.

R. 3. *the adverbes doe commonly precede the*
oblique cases, which promiscuously followe after
the auxiliar verbe or, for want of that, after
the principall e. g. geet geswinde mit der
arzeneye zu den kranken goe *quickly with*
the physick to the sick body, ih bin heute in
der kirhen gewest *i have been to day in the*
church, er war gestern mit mir bei dem
buhbinder *he was yesterday with me with the*
bookbinder. *but when the verbe is prece-*
ded by an indefinit particle, the oblique cases
precede also, and the auxiliar is put after the

principall verbe or its participle , which (prin-
cipall verbe and auxiliar) both must else be kept
to the end of the proposition , especially in its
(being composed)former part , and in the later
the verbe either auxiliar (if it be present) or
principall goes ordinarly before the first case
e. g. nahdeme Judas seinem meister heïl
gewünschet hatte, küssete er in *when Judas*
had wished hail to his master , he did kisse him.
Io bald als nur der vater seinen son erseen
wird, so wird er in um den hals fallen,
as soon as the father shall see his son , he will
embrace him. wann ih euh inn dem garten
gehœret hætte , so wolte ih mit freuden
hinnein gegangen sein und mit euh von
unserer sahe geredet haben, *if i had heard*
you in the garden , i would have gone thither
to speake with you about our busines. wer
mih wird vor den menschen verlæugnen,
den will ih auh vor meinem himmlischen
vater verlæugnen , *whosoever shall deny me*
before men , him will i also deny before my
father , which is in heaven, Matth. 8, 38. -
R. 4. *to shewe a different respect to different*
persons spoken or writen to ; necessity or at least
civility requires , to make use of diverse ex-
pressions also , seing there is a notable diffe-
rence between a rationall creature and irratio-
nal beast as dog or cat ; between a mad or claws-
-ish fellow, and a civil man ; or betwixt this
(though civil and honest , yet mean and vulgar
man) and a person of learning and quality ; to
say nothing of Demigods , as Heroes , great
Princes and crowned Heads. whence it comes

to pa*s* , that the *Germans* (*confidering this* better than any people in the world el*s*e , and not
regarding either the *Latin* , the *Greek* or the
Orientall to*ng*ues differing herein *q*vite from ours
*sp*o*k*en now a dayes in Eu*r*ope , nor mattering the
Grammaticifme , much le*s*s the *Fanaticifme*)
doe *sp*eake and write to one that has no rea*s*on
as bea*s*ts and other *s*en*s*ele*s*s creatures, or has
not the u*s*e of rea*s*on and his own liberty as mad
people , children and our own *s*ervants *&c.*
in the *s*econd per*s*on *s*ingular , and to *s*ervants
of others or to the common *s*ort of people as
pea*s*ants and trade*s*men are , in the *s*econd per*s*on
plurall ; but to a Gentleman or Gentlewoman and
upwards , in the third per*s*on *s*ingular , and to
a magi*s*trat of authority (though a *s*ingle per*s*on)
in the third per*s*on plurall , now in the concrete
and then in the ab*s*tract , which is often done
with *s*ome title added. when we have turned
our face towards that per*s*on whome we would
*sp*eake to , we *s*ay e. g. to a labourer or a jur-
nieman of a handicraft , which does not work
for him *s*elf nor has made his ma*s*terpiece, Heinrih! wa *s*eid ir gewe*s*en oder wa wollet ir
hinngeen ? but to a trade*s*man , that has made
his ma*s*terpiece, we add the word mei*s*ter, as meis
-ter Heinrih ma*s*ter *Henry* ; the wife of this
we doe call jungefrawe mi*s*tre*s*s , but that of
the other is called only by her *Chri*s*tenname* ;
to a Gentleman der Herr gee herein , or
mein geneigter Herr beere mih doh mit
einem zu*s*pruhe ; to a married Gentlewoman
di Frawe or meine vilgeerete Frawe belibe
zu *s*izen ; to an unmarried di Jungfer or meine

geerete (ſhœnſte) Junꝫfer laſſe ſih doh erbitten ; *to a knight* der geſtrenge Herr *or*
ewer geſtrengten hat hir einen guten hond;
to his noble Lady di geſtrenge Frawe *or* ire
adlihe (hohadlihe) Tugenden, *the later word
we uſe alſo*, *when ſhe is yet unmarried*; *to a
Baron and Earle* der gnædige Herr *or* ewer (Herrlihe *or* Græflihe) Genaden hat *or*
haben hir einen luſtigen garten; *to a great
Prince* ewere Fûrſtlihe Durhlæuhtigkeit hat
or haben eine ſtattlihe rûſtkammer; *to a
King or an Emperour* ewere (Kœniglihe *or*)
kæuſerlihe groſsmæhtigkeit (*or* Majeſtæt *)*
hat (*or* haben)einen groſen ſig erhalten. *and
thus in as well Eccleſiaſtick as Politick and Civil
State*, *e.g. to an Archbiſhop* der hohwûrdige
Herr *or* ewer hoherwûrden; *to a Biſhop and
antient Deacon* der wolerwûrdige Herr *or*
ewer wol-erwûrden; *to a Parſon* der er-
wûrdige Herr *or* ewer erwûrden; *to a Vice
-chancheor* der groſtætige Herr *or* ewere
groſtætigkeit *or* magnificenz; *to a Doctor*
ewere vortreffligkeit *or* excellenz &c. *the
ſame doe alſo ſome of the Lowdutch*, *which particularly take it as a piece of a phantaſtick
ſullenneſs and enthuſiaſtick humor to addreſs
themſelves to God in their prayers. and other
holy ſervices with a leſs reſpectfull language,
than they uſe in common converſation with civil
men*, *and therefore they write and ſay e.g. in
the Lords prayer* onſe vader, di daer zyt in
de hemelen ; geheylight werde uwe name;
uwe ryck kome; uwe will &c.   *or   Pſ.*
119. *v.* 158. Herr !   ik onderhoude

uwe beveelen en uwe getuygenisfen :
want alle myne weghen zyn voor u &c. *word
for word: our father, which are in the heavens;
hallowed be your name; your kingdome come;
your &c. and, Lord! i keep your precepts and
your teftimonies: for all my wayes are before you.*

Sect. 3. of
the Conftruction of Particles.

R. 1. *the particles denoting quality or quantity doe immediately precede the infinit mood, as
alfo the oblique, except when we befeech or
command. for here and in the reft mood they
followe either after the principal verbe or, if
there be any, the auxiliar; which is to be
obferved alfo of fome other particles , efpecially
that fignify the time* e. g. wol zu duen ver-
gefset niht , *to doe good, forget not, Ebr.* 13,
16. ringet darnah, dafs ir erbarlih wandelt ftudie , *ye may behave your felves honeftly*
1. *Thefs.* 4, 12. bætet ftæts *pray allwayes.
Eph.* 6, 18. wandelt weislih *walke wifely.
Col.* 4, 5. fhæmet euh niht , di warheit
frei und künlih zu bekennen *be not afha-
med , to confefs the truth freely and boldly.*
R. 2. *when as before verbes there comes an
adverbe either mediatly or immediatly; then
the verbes come before the pronouns in the later
part of the fentence , as we have feen in the*
3. R. *of the preced. Sect.* e. g. fo bald ih
eweren brif empfangen hatte , fhikkete
ih eine antwort zurükke *as foon as i had
received your letter , i returned an anfwer;*
nah verrihtetem gefhæfte kerete ih um

after i had done my busines , i returned; hir taten wir es *and* wir daten es hir *here we did it* , geste.n waren wir lustig und heute find wir traurig *yesterday we were merry and to day we are melancholy &c.*

R. 3. *the negativ particle* niht *(expressing the Latin word* non *and the English Not , or No standing before a comparativ adverbe e.g.* niht mer *no more or non ampli\\s) is of the same construction with the other indefinit particles, but the other parts of speech doe sometimes followe it and sometimes goe before it. the Latin adjectiv* nullus , a , um , *or the English* none *or* no *before a Substantiv is rendred in our toung* keiner , e , es , *but the negativ adverbe or denying particle* no *of the Spaniards , Italiens and Englishmen is in Lowdutch* neen *and in Highdutch* nein , *after which we repeate sometimes in the answer almost the whole question to confirme the better our negation e. g.* habet ir niht ein messer bei euh? nein , ih habe kein s bei mir *have you no knife about you?* no , *not i, or i have none* ; habet ir auh einzigen mangel gehabt? ni keinen, *lacked ye any thing? nothing. Luc.* 22, 35. Herr ! füre uns niht inn versuhung, *Lord! leade us not into temtation;* es hat kein aug gesehen, und kein or gehöret, ist auh inn keines menshen herz kommen , was Gott bereitet hat denen, so in liben, *no eye hath seen , and no ear hath heard , neither came into mans heart, which God hath prepared for them, that love him,* 1. Cor. 2, 9. ewere rede sei ja ja , nein nein *let your commu-*

nication be yea yea , nay nay. Mat. 5, 37.

R. 4. *after the particles* wiwol , ob , obwol, oblhon , ob-auh , *ſtanding in the forepart of a propoſition , followeth one of theſe* dennoh , idoh , doh , ſodoh , *in the hinderpart , e. g.* ob er gleih reih iſt , ſo lebet er doh armſelig *though he be rich , yet be lives very miſerably.*

R. 5. zwar or zward (*ſtanding ſeldome in the beginning of a ſentence*) *requires in the later part* doh , idoh , aber , *e. g.* der geizhals hat zwar vil geld inn ſeiner kiſten, der teufel aber hat (or doh hat der teufel) den ſlüſsel darzu *the covetous hath much money in his cheſt , but the devil hath the key to it.*

R. 6. diweil , weil , demnah , ſintemal , nahdem , *of the firſt part are followed in the later by* als , ſo ; darum , derowegen *e. g.* weilen ir ſolhes getan habet , ſo ſoltet ir geſtrafet werden, *ſince ye have done ſuch a thing , ye ought to be puniſhed.*

R. 7. *the prepoſitiv particles conſtrued with the relativ pronouns* dar *or* da *there* , wa *or* war *where* , hir *or* hi *here* ; *likewiſe* wegen , halber *or* halben , gegenüber *conſtrued with other nouns , become poſtpoſitions and follow their nouns alwayes ; except* wegen *and* gegenüber *ſtand alſo before them e. g.* wamit *or* warmit *wherewith* , waraus *not* waaus *whereout* , hizu *or* hitzu *hereto* , hirauf *not* hi auf *hereupon* &c. des bruders wegen *or* wegen des bruders *for* (or *in behalf of*) *the brother* , unſerm hauſe gegen ber *or* gegenüber unſerm hauſe *overagainſt our houſe* ,

meinet (deinet , feinet , iret , unferet ,
eweret, iret) wegen, halben halb *or* halber,
willen *in my* (*thy , his , her , our , your,
their*) *behalf. see the* 3. *Sect.of the* 3.*chapt.
in the II. part. note here by the way , that
the pronouns here mentioned , being in lieu of*
welher, e, es *&c. are fit for any number,
cafe , gendre and perfon without any change of
their finall termination , as in Englifh, e. g.* feid
ir mit difen bedingungen (difem vorflage,
difer antwort *&c.*) zu friden ? ja wir find
damit zu friden *are you content with (thefe
conditions , this propofal) this anfwer &c. yes
we are contented therewith.*

R. 8. *the prepofitions are of as many forts
and diverfe conftruction, as we have oblique
cafes. for fome of them govern the fecond ,
as* auserhalb *without or out of* , innerhalb
within , hinterhalb *there abouts behind,* unt-
erhalb *thereabouts below* , disfeit *on this fide,*
jenfeit *on the other fide* , feit *or* fint *fith* ,
mitten *or* zu mitten *in the midft* , von - her
becaufe , lang *time. e. g.* aufserhalb der ftatt
out of the citie ; mein lebens lang *or* lebe-
lang *as long as i live or my life time &c. the
words* wegen *or* von wegen , halben, halb
or halben , willen *or* um-willen , vermittelft , vermœge , kraft , laut , innhalts,
befage , angefeen , unang feen , unverhin
-dert *&c. are ufed as prepofitions with the
fame cafe ; but (to fpeake accuratly) thefe are
nouns , as in Latin* caufa , gratia , medio *or
fuch like e. g.* um Gottes willen *for Gods
fake* ; vermittelft goldes und filbers *by the*

help of gold and silver &c.

some of them require the third case, as aus *out*, beſeit or beſeits *beſide or beſides*, binn-en *within*, gegenüber *overagainſt*, mit *with*, nah *after*, nae *nigh*, næhſt *nighſt*, ob *over*, von of *from by*, zu *at*, *e.g.* nah mir *after me*, ſi .reden von euh *they ſpeake of you*, ſi entfinge es von mir *ſhe received it from me;* er wird von ſeinem meiſter geſlagen *he is beaten by his maſter &c.* binnen *and* innerhalb *ſeem to govern alſo the ſecond caſe e.g.* binnen (innerhalb) zweyen jaren *and* zweyer jare *within two years &c. where we may underſtand the word* friſt *or* zeit, *thus* innerhalb zweyer jare zeit *within two years time.*

ſome of them require the fourth caſe, as durh *thorough,* *für *for*, gen *towards*, one *or* ſonder *without*, um *for*, wider *againſt*, *e. g.* durh di luft fligen *to fly through the air*, durh das waſſer ſwimmen *to ſwimme thorough the water*, durh di ſünde iſt der tod inn di welt kommen *by ſin came death into the world*, one mih *or* ſonder dih *without me or thee*, ſi trauren um ir kind *they mourn for their child &c.*

but ſome of them govern both the third and fourth caſes as, an *on*, auf *up or upon*, auſer *without*, bei *by or with*, gegen *againſt or towards*, hinter *behind*, inn *or* in *into*, neben nebeſt nebſt *or* nebenſt *near*, über *over*, unter *under*, * vor *before*, zwiſh-en *betwixt or between*; *all theſe particles ſtand before the third caſe, when they ſignify*

at - *and* *from* *a* *place*, *or* (*as the Latins say*)
in *and* *de* *loco* *e. g.* ih lige inn dem bette.
i lay in the bed, ih fize auf dem ftule *i fit
upon the ftool*, er ftande vor *or* zwifhen
mir und ir *he ftood betwixt me and her &c.*
but denoting ad locum that is to - *or into a
place*, *they alwayes will have the fourth cafe
e. g.* er gabe mir's in's maul *he gave it me
into my mouth*, fezet euh auf den ftul *fet
you down upon the chair*, er legte fih vor *or*
zwifhen mih und den bruder *he did lay
himfelf before or between me and the brother
&c.* * für *and* vor *both fingle and in com-
pofition are often taken one for an other e. g.*
fürwar *or* vorwar *truly*, fürspreher *or* vor-
fpreher *advocate*, fürwenden *or* vorwend-
en *to pretend*, vorlegen *or* fürlegen *to lay
before or for &c.*

*when our difcourfe is of a thing, that is or
that hapneth in a city, town or village; we
commonly ufe the particle* zu *anfwering the Englifh At; but before the names of the countries
and the appellativs is only ufed the particle*
inn *v. g.* es gefhae zu *or* inn Venetig inn
(*not* zu) wälthlantle *it did happne at or in
Venice in Italy;* getrukkt zu (inn) Braun-
sweig, zu (inn) Paris, zu (inn) Dublin &c. inn Teutfhlande, inn Frankreihe,
inn Irrlande &c. *printed at* (*in*) *Brunfwig,
Paris, Dublin; in Germany, France, Ire-
land &c.* er iffet in der kühen *he is eating
in the kitckin;* fi wartet ewer (*or* auf
euh) inn der kammer *fhe ftaith for you in
the chamber.*

Chap. II. and III. of

the Highdutch and English Idioms.

as these Idiomes and manners of saying (the harder to understand , the more naturall they are to each tounges Genius) doe not all at once meet in our discourses, bearing or reading now and then only one and an other of them, the which requires a good deal of trouble and time , before a stranger gets them together : so we would not bringe' em into nice dialogues either by force , or by other common talk knowne already to everyone before, as well by his own language , as by the common grammar-rules and dictionaries ; but we are sure , that , if only these chiefest and sometimes uncouth phrases, were unfolded open to every-ones view , be well observed ; the beginner will certenly by this help be better and sooner instructed in the knowledge of either of our tounges , than by any other books made for that purpose.

Germanismes. Anglicismes.

ein vornemer Rat's-herr , ein geringer (slehter) mann.	*an Alder-man of great account, a man of small account.*
ein nihts würdiger mensh.	*a man of noaccount at all.*
er hilte grose stükke (or vil)auf si or von ir.	*be made great account (or much) of her.*
ih frage niht vil dar-	*i make no great account*

nah, *or* ih ahte es *(not much) of it; i doe*
niht so gar gros. *not care much for it.*
warum niht ? *why do not you?*
ih vermeinte zu ver- *i made account to*
harren; ih gedahte zu verwarten. *stay.*
smæet mih niht; nam *doe not abuse me; do*
-et mih niht zu, *not call me names.*
berihtet mih ja alles *be very carefull to*
auf das fleisigste; tu- *acquaint me, (or to*
et mir alles auf's ge- *make me acquainted)*
naweste zu wissen. *with all.*
einer von meinen *one of my acquain-*
freunden; meiner be *tance; an acquaintance*
-kanden (freinde) einer. *of mine.*
was vor ein spil ist da! *what ado is there!*
ih könte mih kaum *i had much ado to for*
des lahens erweren *-bear (hold from)*
or enthalten. *laughing.*
lezlihen so vername *at last with much ado*
ih es mit groser mûe. *i perceived it.*
sehzeen jarè alt, *or* *at sixteen years of age;*
als er sehzeen jar alt *when he was sixteen*
war. *years of age.*
vor disem; eedessen; *long agoe; in the time*
vor zeiten ; vor alters. *of old.g*
shon vorlængsten ; *a good (or reat)*
vor einer gute weile. *while agoe.*
wi lange ist es? vòr *how long a goe? how*
wi vil jaren, tagen *many years, dayes or*
er stunden ? *hours agoe ?*
vor etlihen jaren, tag *some years , dayes*
-en &c. *&c. agoe.*
Bifs an den lihten *till broad day-*
hellen tag. *light.*

er ift nur neulih ge-　*it is but a while a-*
ftorben; es ift niht　　　*goe since he*
gar lange, dafs er geftorben.　*died.*

mein vater-land.　　*my nativ countrie.*

fi willigen alle dar-　*all are agreed upon*
ein; fi ftimmen alle-　　*it ; this all agree*
mit-einander einmüt-　　*upon ; it is a-*
-ig(einhellig)darein;　　*greed upon by all,*
alle kommen hirinn-　　　*with one mouth,*
en über-ein.　　　　　*voice , mind.*

di zeit ift gefezet *or*　*the time is agreed*
beftimmet *or* beflofsē.　　*upon.*

fi find des tages eins　*the day is agreed*
worden.　　　　　　*on.*

er ift noh a'm (*or*　*he is ftill alive or*
bei'm) leben.　　　　*living.*

es haben es andere　*you are not allone*
auh getan.　　　　*in it.*

lafset mih zu friden.　*let me allone.*

lafset mih dafür forg　*let me allone for that;*
-en; ih will fhon rat　　*leave me to*
darzu fhaffen.　　　　*that.*

es ift mir alles eins ;　*it is all one to*
es gilt mir alles gleih.　　*me.*

wenn wir ihtwas (*or*　*if we have done any*
etwas verfeen habō.　　*thing amifs.*

er zœrnet mit euh;　*he is angry at you or*
er ift bœfe aufeuh.　　*with you.*

ih verftee niht das ge　*i underftand not*
-ringfte (*or* niht ein　　*any one*
einziges) wort.　　　*word.*

ir werdet mih fwer-　*you are never like to*
lih imals wider feen.　*fee me more or any more.*

nemet inn obaht ,　　*mind what you*

℘

was ir vorhabet. *are about.*

ſi ſind unter ein-an- *they are at*
der urieias. *odds.*

fraget er nah mir? *does he ask for me?*

heiſet di amme (wær *bid the wetnurſe (dry-*
-terin) herkommen. *nurſe) come away.*

er merkete, daſs ir *he perceived, you ſtood*
euh vor im fœrhtet. *in aw of him.*

ſein pferd abrihten *to put his horſe to be*
laſsen. *back'd.*

der hengſt liſe ſih *the ſtonehorſe ſuffered*
reiten *or* liſe auf- *one to back him, or,*
ſizen. *himſelf to be backed.*

er hælt übel haus; er *he takes bad cour-*
füret ein bœſes leben. *ſes.*

ir wiſset di leute niht *you know not, how*
zu kœrnen *or* niht *to lay baits for*
reht an-zu lokken. *men.*

er verſwige ime niht *he balked him not a*
das geringſte. *whit.*

ih will ewer haus *i will not balke your*
niht meiden. *houſe.*

den getroffenen vergleih *to ſtand to ones*
(*or* aufgerihten vertrag) halten. *bargain.*

vor gerihte zu tuen *to plead at the*
haben; i'm rehte ligē. *bar,*

verrigelt di dore. *bar up the dores.*

er iſt aus dem ganzen *he is barred out of*
kœnigreihe verwiſen. *all the kingdome.*

er gabe ime niht ein *be bated him not*
har nah. *an ace.*

er name kein blatt *he bated him not*
vor das maul, ſon- *an ace, but*
dern hilte ime alles für. *told him of all.*

dem pferde di fporn   *to clap ſpurs to the*
geben; das pferd anſpornen.   *horſe.*

er hat di Franzoſen   *he has a clap or*
or di Venus - krank-   *the French*
heit.   *pocks.*

eine ſlaht lifern; eine   *to give bat-*
felt-flaht halten *or* duen.   *tel.*

er befloſse des næhft-   *he reſolved the*
en tages mit inen (zu   *next day to*
flagen *or*) ein treffen   *give them*
zu duen.   *battel.*

unſere nahbarinne   *our neighbour is*
iſt inn di wohen kommen. *brought to bed.*

es wære beſser gewe   *you had better*
-ſen *or* ir hettet vil   *not kept a*
beſser getan, (dafs)   *bawling here.*
ir hættet hir kein geblærr gemahet.

der hund balle treff- *the dogg kept a huge*
lih.   *bawling.*

der preis ſei ſo hoh   *be the price never*
(*or* gros) als er immer   *ſo great, it*
wolle, es iſt ein guter kauf. *is well bought.*

damit ih niht ver-   *not to be te-*
drûſslih falle.   *dious.*

ir ſelbeſt ſollet mir   *you your ſelf ſhall*
zeugniſs geben *or*   *beare me*
mein zeuge ſein.   *witneſs.*

er bereitete ſeinen   *he was making*
weg-zug; er mahte   *ready to be*
ſih reiſe-færtig.   *gone.*

was gelten hir di *what prices bear ſwine*
ſweine?   *here?*

ſi find tewer *or* gelt-   *they beare a*
en vil.   *price.*

das Sizilifhe honig	Sicilian honey bea-
ift unter allen das befte.	res the bell away.
mit reht or unreht.	by hook or by crook.
er hælt inen di wage;	he beares up with
er duet es inen gleih.	them.
er geet wi ein bawer	he goes like a bear to
inn das hunds-loh.	a ftake.
ein alter ausgedint-	an old beaten
er landes-kneht.	foldier.
ih will dir den kopf	i will beat out your
einflagen or drethen.	braines.
wære es fahe gewe-	had it been fo , that
fen, dafs u. f. w.	&c.
der herr verpflihtet	i am mighty behold-
ime mih all zu fere or	ing to you ,
all zu hoh.	Sir.
ih will (tuen or) mih	i will make , as if
ftellen , als ob. ih da	i had been
gewelt wære.	there.
es ift mir niht entfall	i knowe what
-en , was mir zu hand	hath befallen
-en geftofen.	me.
er behälfet fih mit	he gets his living by
den bettel-ftikken.	begging.
er leget fih auf's	he feeks his living by
betteln.	begging.
Gott behüte (or be-	God be with
ware) euh !	you !
er hatte es feinem	he was beholden to
fwerde zu danken ,	his fword for his not
dafs er niht wurde	being taken prifo-
gefangen genommen.	ner.
es wird überall vor	it is believed at e-
war gehalten.	very hand.

wenn mir zu glauben | if i may be believ-
fteet ; wenn mir ein- | ed ; if there is a-
ziger glauben mag | ny believe in
beigemæfsen werden. | me.
ir follet mih das (or | you fhall never make
defsen) ni überreden. | me believe this.
was geet mih difes | what is that to me ?
an ? was hab' ih doh | what doeth that
damit zu duen. or zu | belong to
fhaffen? | me ?
aH fein dihten und | he bends all his
trahten ift dahinn (or | wits about
darauf) gerihtet. | this.
er leget fih ganz und | he bends himfelf wholy
gar darauf. | to this.
ift er fo erbiht | is he fo bend on
darauf ? | it ?
was meinet ir , dafs | what think you , had
wir nun gutes an- | we beft doe
greifen (or anfangen) | müfsen ? now?
wenn euh zu raten , | you had even beft
fo tuet , wi ih euh ge- | doe , as i had
heifen. | you.
ir kœntet niht befser | it were the beft courfe
verfaren dann fo. | you could take.
ein weib inn iren beft | a woman of her beft
-en jaren. | life.
meines behaltes ; fo | to the beft of my remem-
vil ih mih erinnern kann. | -brance
ih fluge fluhs das haf- | i prefently betook
e n-bannir auf; ih ga- | me to my
be ftraks verfen -gelt. | keel.
wider alles reht und | contrary to law
alle billigkeit. | and right.

fi ergriffen gefwinde	*they quickly betook them.*
ire waffen.	*to their weapons.*
was gilt es? was foll	*name your bet? fay*
es gelten? was woll-	*what bet you will lay*
et ir legen? was woll	*on it? what will*
-et ir mit mir wetten?	*you bet on it?*
ih mag niht wetten;	*i will bet nothing. i*
ih will nihts auf di	*will lay no bets (or*
wette fezen; ih will	*wager) with you. i will*
niht um einen pfenn-	*not bet a penny with*
ig mit euh wetten.	*you, no not i.*
was hülfet es mir?	*what am i (the) better*
was bin ih defsen gebefsert?	*for this?*
wer gewinnet? wer	*who has the better of*
træget das befte davon?	*it?*
fi wollen nimande	*they will give the*
das geringfte nah-	*better of it to*
geben.	*none.*
geet auf di feite.	*give way or ftand by.*
noh einmal (or noh	*as big again and*
eins) fo dikke und	*drüber.* *better.*
er fiet efsig-fawer	*he looks as big as*
aus.	*bull-bief.*
er fneidet tapfer auf.	*he talkes big.*
fi ift hoes leibes; fi ift	*fhe has a great bellie;*
fwanger.	*fhe is with child.*
eine wunde ver-	*to bind up a*
binden.	*wound.*
er ift einer von adel	*he is a nobleman or no-*
or ein geborner ædelmann.	*ble by birth.*
mann darf ime fih-	*you may (credit or) give*
eren glauben geben	*credit to him; he may*
or) wol trawen; es ift	*be credited.*
ime wol zu glauben or wol zu trawen.	

ir kœnnet ganz *you can not ſay , black*
nihts auf (*or* wider) in ſagen. *is his ey.*
ei! wi wird es euh *blak's your*
geen ! *day !*
ſnæuze dih du garſtig *blow your noſe ,*
-er ſakk ! *or* puze di *you ſlut*
naſe du unflat ! *you !*
heye! iſt nimand dar! *ho! is any body there ?*
nein , nimand ; niht *no , no body at*
eine *or* keine leibſele. *all.*
er tate einen fæil- *he miſsed his*
ſlag ; er ſluge fæil. *blow.*
ſi wurde zunder- *ſhe bluſhed as red*
(*or* feyer-)rot. *as fire.*
ein ding oben-hinn *to get a bluſh of a*
angaffen *or* erſnappen. *thing.*
war laſset ir euh *where doe you*
ſpeiſen ? *or* wa geet ir zu diſhe ? *board?*
ſi gingen (ſprangen) *they boarded their e-*
inn des feindes ſhiffe *nemies ſhips , by the*
vermittelſt eines bretes. *help of a board.*
ih erkünete mih ſi zu *i made bold to aſk*
fragen. *her.*
ih darf wol (*or* kün- *i dare be bold to*
lih) ſagen. *ſay.*
ih hab' ime eines *i have given him a*
gegeben *or* ange- *bone to*
hænget. *picke.*
er mahete im gar *he made no*
kein gewiſsen darüber. *bones on it.*
ih hætte wollen mit *i would have been con-*
dem geringſten (*or* *tented with any ,*
kleinſten) winkel zu *though never ſo*
friden ſein. *little a corner.*

auswendig lernen.	*to get without book.*
etwas inn ein buh tragen.	*to book a thing down.*
wa wollet ir hinn reifen ?	*wither are you bound?*
ffh i'm zaume (*or* inn den fhranken)halten.	*to keep within their own bounds.*
du fnæpperling ! du gelb-fnabel ! du rozlæffel !	*you faucebox! you puppy !*
einen hinter di oren flagen; einem eine orfeige geben.	*to box one ; to give one a box on the ear.*
er hat di kinderfhue ausgetreten *or* vertreten.	*he is paft a child or a boy.*
bei anbrehung des tages.	*at (the) break of day.*
einen fherz mahen.	*to break a jeft.*
ein pferd bændigen.	*to break a horfe.*
frü - ftäkken ; das morgen-brot effen.	*to break his faft ; to eate the break-faft.*
aufhœren zu arbeiten.	*to break off (or to leave) work.*
er kann keinen adem holen *or* fhœpfen; niht zu aden kommen.	*he is out of breath.*
ih kann mih niht darzu gewœnen, und folte es auh mein leb -en gelten *or* koften.	*i can not bring (or ufe) my felf to it for my life.*
di fah- ift nun dahin (gedren, kommen *or*) gelanget, dafs &c.	*the matter is now brought to that pafs, that &c.*
er braht mir zu'r antwort.	*he brought me word.*
heutiges tages; iziger zeit.	*now a days.*

laſset mih wiſsen;	*ſend me*
duet mir zu wiſsen.	*word.*
wol-an.' mahet euh	*come! clear up*
wakker luſtig.	*your brow and look*
friih- auf ! erzeiget	*merrily on*
euh ſein frœlih ! ſeid	gutes nuts ! *lt.*
ſih zum krige rûſten.	*to buckle for war.*
ſih geben (als über-	*to buckle to one*
wunden;) *or* den	*i. to yeeld or*
kûrzern zien.	*to ſubmitte.*
ih hatte zu duen *or*	*i had buſineſs. in*
zu verrihten; ih ware beſhæftiget.	*hand.*
ein mäſames leben.	*a life full of buſineſs.*
ih habe meine hænde	*i am full of bu-*
voll zu duen; ih habe	*ſineſs; i am very*
zu ſhikken und zu	ſhaffen. *buſie.*
einem zu ſhaffen	*to finde one*
mahen.	*buſineſs.*
kommet zu der (unt-	*come to the bu-*
er handen habenden)	*ſineſs in*
ſahe ſelbſt.	*hand.*
bei hellem ſonnen-	*to burne day-*
ſheine liht brennen.	*light.*
ir habet keine weit-	*you have not gone*
læufigkeit gebrauhet.	*about the buſh.*
es iſt beſser etwas	*one bird in the hand is*
denn gar nihts;	*worth two in the buſh.*
der hab' ih iſt gewiſser denn der hætt' ih.
unverſeens ; ungefær.	*by the by.*
beihalben;beilæuſig.	*by the way.*
inn kurzem ; alſo-	*by and by ;*
bald; inn dem; von ſtund an.	*anon.*
es wird ime ein rum	*it will be for*
(*or* eine ere) ſein.	*his credit.*

wi nennet ir dis? wi	*what doe you call this?*
wird difes bei euh	geheifen ?
wi heifet er ? wi	*what doe you call*
wird er genennet?	*him? what is his*
wi heifet fein nam ?	*name ?*
feine fhulden einfo-	*to call for (or to call in)*
dern.	*his debts.*
lafset das efsen auftragen.	*call for meat.*
lafset zu trinken herbringen.	*call for drink.*
fraget nah der zeh-	*call for the account*
en. was haben wir	*or the fcore. what is*
zu bezalen?	*(or have we) to pay?*
lafset in rehnung	*call him to ac-*
duen.	*compt.*
befinnet (or bedenk	*call it to mind or re-*
-et) euh darauf.	*membrance.*
nun fællet mir's ein;	*now i call it to mind.*
izo befinn ih mih darauf	*or ih gedenke dran.*
kœnnet ir euh dar-	*can you call it to*
auf befinnen ?	*mind ?*
ruffet bei mir an;	*give me a*
ruft mih.	*call.*
zu'm aufzuge or zu	*to found a*
felde blafen.	*call.*
es heifet ein efel	*the pot calls the pan*
den andern einen	*burnt-(black-)*
fakk-træger.	*arfe.*
fi bitten vor ir leb-	*they call for*
en or um gut wetter;	*quarter.*
fi krühen zum kreuze.	
fi hife in kurz und	*fhe did call him all the*
lang wi fi dazu kame.	*nought , fhe could.*
warumm namet ir fi	*what doe you call her*
denn zu ?	*names for ?*

fi flugen uns aus dem felde. — *they took our camp.*

es kann euh niht (bergen, umbewuſt or) verborgen ſein. — *you can not but knowe, or* verborgen ſein.

es wil inen gar niht inn den kopf or kropf; es ſnuppet inen (or fi) inn di naſe; fi kœnnen's niht vertragen. — *they can ill (or not) away with it; they take ſnuff at it.*

gedenket er, daſs ih ime zu fuſe fallen (or in vil hofiren) wolle? — *does be think, i will come with cap in hand to him?*

er weis di karte zu ſeinem vorteil zu legen. — *be can pack the cards.*

ih muſs zuſeen or mih vorſeen. — *i muſt have a care (for.)*

nemet euh damit inn aht. — *bave a care of this; take beed!*

was frage ih darnah? — *what care i?*

was bekümmere ih mih darumn? — *what doe i care (for.)*

mann muſs aht haben or ahtung geben. — *care muſt be taken.*

es ſoll inen niht geſhienket ſein. — *they ſhall not carry it ſo.*

eine reht-ſahe verliren. — *to be caſt in ones ſuit.*

di naht überfile in. — *night catched him.*

fi lœſeten das kleine und grobe geſhüz. — *they did discharge their ſmall and great gunnes.*

meine ſhuldigkeit bei dem (or gegen den) Herren ab-zu ſtatten or ab-zu legen. — *to discharge my dutie to you, Sir!*

habe ih euh niht — *did i not charge*

tewer genung einge   *you , you should*
-bunden , dafs ir es   *not doe*
niht duen foltet?   *it ?*
einen anfall auf des   *to charge the enemi-*
feindes reiterei duen.   *es horse.*
das getrætig ift   *corne is dog - cheap*
fhande wolfeil *or*   *or beares no*
gilt ein fpot-gelt.   *price.*
es flæget auf; es   *it rifes in*
fteiget.   *price.*
das korn flæget ab;   *corne hath flackened;*
es fællet.   *it is fetled of price.*
wir wurden fürftlih   *we had royall (or good*
(*or* hérrlig)gefpeifet.   *and great) chear.*
wir wurden fleht (*or*   *we had fmall (or flen-*
elende) bewûrdet.   *der) chear.*

oben an { fizen *or* gefez-   { *hold* }
{ et werden.   *to* { } *the chief*
{ fezen *or* fizen   { *give* } *place.*
{ lafsen.

difes ift di haupt-   *this is the chief*
fah'e.   *point.*
er ware der aller-   *he was in chief com-*
vor nemfte obrifter.   *mand.*
von kindheit auf; von   *from a (very)*
kindes beinen an.   *child.*
er erkande fein weib   *he lay with his wife*
und zeigete ein kind   *and got her with*
mit ir.   *child.*
fi wurde von ime   *she is with child*
fwanger.   *by him.*
ir habet das (menfh   *you have gotten*
or) weibes-bild ge   *the wench with*
-fwæhet *or* zu'm fall gebraht ;   *child;*

ift es niht (alſo or) war? *have you not ?*

ſi kriget kein kind mer *ſhe is paſt child-bea-*
or es geet ir niht mer *ring or bearing of*
nah der weiber weiſe. *children.*

es ſteet bei uns ; di *we may be at our*
wal iſt unſer ; es iſt *choice.*
(liget , ſteet) inn unſerer maht or willkûre.

leſet-euh aus (or wælet *take your choice.*
euh heraus) was ir wollet or begeret.
der ausſhuſs von bûrg- *the moſt choice men*
ern. *of the citie.*

ausſhuſs-papir. *out-ſide paper.*

ir habet ſi euh ſelber *ſhe is of your own*
(auserkoren , auserle- *chuſing .*
ſen, auserſeen, ausgekernet or) auserwælet.

ih kann mih des wein- *i can not chuſe but*
ens niht (enthalten or) ent- *weepe.*
brehen; ih mus weinen or trænen vergiſen.

ſi iſt engelrein or ſond- *ſhe is (without all*
er allen tadel. *blame or) innocent.*

ſi ſind ganz ûber und *they are as clean as a*
ûber rein. *clock, or as a penny.*

ih gefalle mir ganz *i am (clean, quite or)*
niht mer. *clear out* *of love with my ſelf.*

wi ril hat es geſlagen? *what is it a-clock ?*
um welhe zeit iſt es? *what a-clock is it ?*
di glokke ſlæget vire. *the clock ſtrikes four.*
es iſt bald um fûnfe. *it is almoſt five.*
der zeiger weiſet auf *it is half an hour paſt*
halben weg dreye. *two.*

wir rihten uns nah uns- *we goe by our*
erem zeiger or nah unſerer klokken. *clock.*
ih erſtaunete ; ih ver- *i was at my wits*
narrete ganz. *end.*

U

eine halbe ſtunde vor	*half an bour befare*
zwœlfen *or* nah. elfe;	*twelve a clock ; a*
eine virtel ſtunde	*quarter of an bour af*
nah eins.	*-ter one a clock.*
er iſt ein rehter haſen-	*he is the very cocks-*
kopf *or* has ; er iſt	*comb or cock*
ein erz - narr.	*-fool.*
wi ſolte ih's (wiſsen *or*)	*bow ſhould i come*
erfaren , *or* zu wiſsen	*to knowe*
bekommen ?	*it ?*
ih komme ; ih bin auf	*i am coming ; i am*
dem wege.	*a - coming.*
es wird auf di lezte	*it will come to no-*
nihtes daraus werden.	*thing at laſt.*
wann es um und um	*when all comes to*
kommet.	*all.*
zukünftige dinge vor-	*to fore-ſee things to*
ſeen.	*come.*
er gibet nimande i'm	*he comes ſhort of (or*
geringſten etwas nah	*behind) none for*
a'm prahte.	*brauery.*
wol bezæhet; berauſh-	*well come on in*
et ; beſoffen.	*drink.*
wa will diſes hinaus?	*what will come on it?*
was will daraus werden?	*or - of it ?*
grüſset beſter maſen	*have me beartily*
alle meine freinde von	*commended to all my*
mein t wegen.	*freinds.*
es læſet ſih trefflih wol	*he is excellent*
mit ime umgeen.	*company.*
man mſaget i'm gemei-	*it is a common ſay-*
nen ſprih-worte; mann	*ing.*
ſpriht in's gemein ; mann pfleget zu ſagen.	
haltet eine maſe.	*keep within compaſs.*

es geet mih niht gros — *it does not concerne*
an; es hülfet und hind — *me much; i am not*
-ert mih niht gar vil. — *much concerned in it.*
ih bin mit fhaden dar- — *i have learned it*
innen klug worden. — *to my coft.*
es koftet nihts we- — *notking ftands in lefs*
niger; nihts ift wolfeiler. — *coft.*
er hat hopfen und — *he hath loft both his*
malz daran verloren. — *labour and coft.*
wir wollen es anders — *we will take an other*
angreifen *or* anfangen. — *courfe.*
ih pflege es alfo zu — *this is my (courfe*
maken; difes ift mein — *or) common*
gebrauh. — *courfe.*

um di wette { laufen. — *to run { a courfe.*
{ rennen. — *{ a race.*

es wird der andere — *the fecond courfe is*
gang aufgetragen *or* — *brought in or*
aufgefezet. — *fet on.*
es wird i'm andern — *it is brought up (or*
gange mit einge- — *in) at the fecond*
ihoben. — *courfe.*
maht es, wi ir wollet. — *take your courfe.*
hafen (*or* woelfe) jagen; — *to courfe hares or*
eine hafen-(*or* wolfs-) jaht halten. — *wulves.*
es flæfet einer (um den — *they fleep by cour*
or) nah dem andern; fi — *-fes or by*
flafen wehfels-weife. — *turnes.*
grobe fpeife; grobe — *courfe fare; courfe*
wolle; grobes papir. — *wooll; courfe paper.*
ein friden-ftoerer. — *an enemy to peace.*
einem mit weltaten (*or* — *to be-before hand*
hoefligkeit) zuvor — *with one in benefits*
kommen. — *or courtefie.*

das frawen - zimmer	the *Ladies made a*
neigete. sih.	*courtesie.*
er ist kein grofer	*he is not much given*
praler *or* aufsneider.	*to crack.*
es steet (hæfslih *or*)	*it is an ugly thing,*
garstig , wenn ein	*to crack of a mans*
menfh (sih selber rûmet *or*) aufsneidet.	*felf.*
er wird euh den shetel	*he will crack your*
(*or* kopf) einslagen.	*crown.*
ih jauhzete fast vor	*i. did almost cry out*
freuden.	*for joy.*
er bate si um verzey-	*he cryed her*
ung.	*mercy.*
jderman shilt darûber,	*every body cryes*
er fluhet darauf.	*shame on it.*
er war ausgefhryen wi	*he was cryed up*
fawer bir.	*mightily.*
difes mahet , dafs er	*that makes him cry*
fo erbærmlih shreyet;	*out fo.*
das ift's warûber er fo hæftig fih beklaget.	
wenn kame ir das ge-	*when did she cry*
bæren *or* di wœe an ?	*out?*
wenn lage si inn den kindes - nœten ?	
wir fhryen ûber-laut.	*we did cry out.*
si kann iren kindern	*she can not crofs her*
niht zuwider fein.	*children.*
ei ! feid mir doh niht	*pray! doe not crofs*
fo entgegen *or* zuwider.	*me fo.*
fi færet iren emann an,	*she is crofs to her*
wi di fawe den bettelfakk.	*husband.*
wir hatten (bœfes , û-	*we had crofs wea-*
beles , garftiges *or)* ftûrmiges wetter.	*ther.*
mer dann (genug) *or*	*enough and enough*
zu vil ; ûbrig genung.	*again.*

das wort liget mir auf	the word is at my
der zungen or es lauf-	tounges end.
et mir inn dem maule	(or munde) herum.
di kreuz - weise ge-	the cross keyes are
fhrænkten flûfsel find	the Popes two
des Pabſtes zwei fwerter.	fwords.
es iſt aus mit ime; es	he is paſt cure, or
iſt um in (or mit ime)	géfheen. remedy.
hœbet di karte ab.	cutte the cards.
es duet mir inn der fel-	it cuts me to the
en (or i'm herzen) wœ;	(very) heart.
es verdreuſt mih (von herzen or) herzlih.
hir geet ir am næeſten; this is the neareſt (or
da kommet ir a'm eeſt	the ſhorteſt) cut.
-en; dis iſt der næeſte (or kurzeſte) weg.
einen zu'm kampf (or to challenge (or dare)
ſtreit) heraus forderen.	one to fight.
ih habe fi ni als heute	i never ſaw her be-
gefeen.	fore to day.
àber-morgen.	after to morrow.
eegeſtern or vorgeſtern.	the other day.
den dritten tag nah	three dayes after he
feiner ankunft.	came.
biſs es hoh a'm tage	till it was far of the
wær.	day.
ih habe meine fpringe	my good dayes ar:
(or dænze) getan.	done.
tag vor tag.	day by day.
zu mitter-naht or mitt	in the dead time of
-en inn der naht.	the night.
mifhet (or menget) di	ſouffle the cards and
karte und gebet fi	deal them
wider.	again.
ih bin fer wol mit ime	i have got a

(dran or) bekant; ih ftee — a great deal of acquain
fer wol bei (or mit)ime. -tance with him.
handelt ir alfo mit mir? doe you deal fo
or geet ir fo mit mir um? with me ?
ein weit meres or vil a great deal
mer, vil weniger, vil more, lefs,
befser. better.
ih will nihts mit euh i will have no
zu duen (or zu fhaffen) dealing with
haben. you.
fi haben mir leihtfertig i am bafely dealt
mitgefpilet or mitgefar withall.
-en; es ift mir gewalt und unrecht gefheen.
er mahet ein grofes be keeps a deal
(fpil or) wefen. of ftirr.
geet aufrihtig mit mir deal truly (or honeft-
um ; handelt fein (er- ly) with me ;
lih or redlih) mit mir. ufe me well.
ih habe mit dem bûrg- i deal in the
erlihen rehte zu duen. Ciuill law.
ein unter-handler; ein one that deals berwixt
fhid'smann. men and man.
mein libftes herz! mein my dear ! my
allerlibfter fhaz ! mein libgen ! dear love !
fi hatten (or fi hilten) be was dear to e-
in alle lib und wert. very-one.
es ift noh ein mal fo it is dearer by half.
tewer; or es koftet noh ein mal fo vil.
es ift bei leibs und leb- it is death to doe it.
ens ftrafe verboten; es koftet einem das
leben (den hals or den kopf) der es tuet.
wann foll der arme when is the pri-
fünder abgetan foner to be put to
werden ? death?

es læſſet ſih noh dar-   *it falls under*
über ſtreiten; *or* mann   *debate.*
hat ſih noh. darüber zu beratſlagen.
feine ſhulden ein-   *to demand payment of*
manen.   *his debts.*
di aſhe auf dem herde *he is deeply (or over*
iſt niht ſein; er ſtekket   *head and ears) in*
inn ſulden bifs über di oren.   *debt.*
inn dem härteſten (*or*   *in the deep of*
ärgeſten) winter.   *winter.*
als feine güter inn das *when his estate was*
abnemen geräten.   *gone to decay.*
ih mus ſi (one verzug *i must be married to*
or) ſonder aufſhub hei-   *her without*
raten *or* elihen.   *delay.*
ir mahetet niht vil fed- *you made no delay*
er-lefens *or* aufzüge.   *et all.*
ih date es (unverzüg- *i delayed not the*
lih *or*) ſonder einziges   *doing of it*
zauden *or* aufſhiben.   *at all.*
ih kann mih niht ge- *i can never be ſtalled*
nug damit erluſtiren.   *with that delight.*
wenn kame ſi inn di *when was ſhe deli-*
wohen? wenn gelage   *vered?*
ſi? wenn genafe ſi des kindes?
es foll euh eure bitte   *you ſhall not be*
gewæret werden; ir   *denyed.*
foilet keine abſlæglihe antwort bekommen.
er krigte einen korb.   *he got the ſlip.*
er lebet inn den tag *he makes even at the*
hinnein wi eine wilde gans.   *years end.*
dorn- (*or* ſtahel-) bere.   *goos-berries.*
bevor ih ſterbe; ee ih *before i depart*
aus diſem leben ſheide   *this (-world*

or dise welt gesegne;   *or) life.*
noh vor meinem tode *or* absterben.
das amt (*or* di obrig-   *to depart aut*
keitlihe gewalt) ab-   *of office.*
legen *or* abtreten ; abdanken.
ræumet mir mein haus! *depart my house!*
nah dem ih von euh ge- *after i departed from*
shiden (*or* gegangen) ware.   *you.*
warnah mih hœhlih *what i have a great*
verlanget ; warnah ih   *desire to.*
mih herzlih sœne; warnah mih ser gelüstet.
si liget inn den lezten *she is like to die ;*
zûgen ; si will gleih *she is just adying.*
izo iren geist aufgeben; der tod sizet ir shon
auf der zungen ; si ringet mit dem tode.
erd-bere sind izo new- *straw - berries are*
es von jare.   *now novelty.*
wir sind'ein wenig an *there is a little small*
ein ander geraten *or* *difference be-*
meins worden ; wir   *twixt us.*
haben uns veruneiniget *or* zerzweyet.
das krigs-volk ab- *to disband the*
danken.   *army.*
er warf'es ime vor (*or* *be laid it in his dish*
er rükkete es ime auf, *as a foul crime.*
or er ribe es ime inn di nase) als ein
shændlihes laster *or* als eine grobe missetat.
von ferne *or* von weitem. *at a distance.*
wi geet's dem herren, *how doe you,*
der frawen *or* jung- *Sir? Mistress?*
frawen?   *Madam?*
grosen dank (*or* ih be- *i thanke you ; how*
danke mih) der nahfrage. *doe you doe ?*
wi geet's des herren *Sir! how does your*

libſten ? *or* was mahet   *Lady ? how does your*
ewere jungfrawe gutes ?   *wife , Sir !*
es geet für-war niht   *it will not do indeed;*
an ; gewiſlih es ſhikket   *to be ſure it does not.*
ſih niht ; traun es læſſet   ſih gar niht duen.
er hat immer etwas   *he is alwayes a-doing*
für , *or* zu duen.   *ſome thing or other.*
hætte ih di mittel   *had i wherewithall*
darzu.   *to doe it.*
es wird darüber (ge-   *it is now a-*
arbeitet *or*) gemahet.   *doing.*
ſeid ir fertig ?   *have you done? yes*
ja *or* ih bin fertig.   *i have.*
habt ir geſpeiſet *or* ge-   *have you done with*
malzeitet ?   *your dinner , ſupper ?*
wol bekomme den   *Gentlemen and Ladi*
herren und dem fraw-   *-es! much good may it*
en-zimmer di malzeit !   *doe you , or : much good*
may doe you , your dinner   *or your ſupper !*
trinket der herr ta-   *doe you take (Tobac-*
bak ? rauhet (*or* ſmœg-   *co or). a pipe ? doe*
et) der herr ?   *you ſmoak , Sir ?*
an der türe; für der dœre.   *at the dore.*
ih habe euh eine ab-   *i have ſent you a*
ſhrift des lezten will-   *draught of*
ens zugeſand.   *the will.*
duet einen guten zug;   *drinke a good*
trinket einen wakkeren drunk.   *draught.*
rote Johannes-bere.   *redd currants.*
einen fluſs ableiten.   *to draw away a river.*
er brahte ſi auf ſeine   *he drew them to take*
ſeite.   *his part.*
ſi zogen vo'm leder ; ſi   *they drew their*
zükketen ire tegen *or* ir gewer.   *ſwords.*

der winter naet (her- *winter drawes near*
zu , herbei-, or) heran. *or drawes on-*
er mahte graben kwær *he drew trenches a-*
über (or kwær-graben *cross the*
über) di wege. *wayes.*
weil ſih ſein weib (an- *whil'ſt his wife is*
leget, antuet, ſmükket, *getting herſelf dres-*
ziret , puzet, aufpuzet *ſed; or- is dreſsing*
or) zu rehte mahet. *her ſelf.*
ſi geen ſtattlih einher *they are dreſs'd in*
or præhtig gekleidet ; *print ; they are gott*
ſi halten ſih koſtbár (or *-en into a rich*
herrlih) inn kleidung , *(or into a moſt pre-*
auf di neweſte att or *tious) dreſs , after*
nah der beſten (or zir- *the neweſt (neateſt*
ligſten) traht. *or beſt) faſhion.*
rihtet di fiſhe zu. *dreſs the fiſh.*
rihtet den garten an. *dreſs the garden.*
mih doerſtet; ih bin *i am dry or adry; i am*
doerftig ; ih habe dorſt. *thirſty or a - thirſt.*
ih will ime eins zutrink *i will drink once to*
en or zubringen. *him.*
er brahte mir's ; er *he did drinke to*
tranke mir's zu; *me.*
trinket es alles aus. *drinke it all (out, up or) off.*
gebet ime zu (or laſset *make him drinke;*
in) trinken. *give him ſome drink.*
er gedenket mih zu bo- *he has a mind to*
den (or darnider) zu *drinke me*
ſaufen. *down.*
kutſher! da hab't ir ein *Coachman! there is*
trank- (or trink-) *ſome thing for you to*
geld . *drinke.*
geſodene (erbs-)ſhoten. *hot peas - cods.*

wamit geet doh der
mann um ? was hat
der mann für ? warnah ringet er ?
einen mit geſhreie ü-
bertæuben or tumm
und taub ſhreyen.
das geld iſt noh niht
gefællig.
er iſt toll , niht aber
dumm , vil weniger
ſtumm.
ſi hœrete niht gar (or
all zu) wol ; ſi ware
etwas daub; das gehœr legete ir ab.
es lindert di kwal.
ih will euh (wakker
abſmiren or) mit ein-
em prügel empfangen.
knæufelt ewere oren
auf; ſpizet ewere oren.
er iſt inn libe erſoffen;
er hat ſih ganz und gar verlibet.
nimand iſt , der gehor-
he; nimand hœret zu or mærket drauf.
ih hab' eine bitte bei
euh ein-zu legen vor N.
ih hab' eine groſe bitte
an euh , daſs u. ſ. f. a.
er gabe ſeiner libſten
etwas auf di libe; er
gab' ir einen braut-ſhaz or einen mal-ſhaz.
ſi gabe irer newen
magd einen mid-
groſhen.

what does the
man driue
er ? at ?
to drown one
with a
cry.
the monney is not
yet due.
he, is mad and not
dull; much leſs
dumb.
ſhe was ſomewhat
dull of bearing.
it dulles the pain.
i will duſt your
coat for
you.
prick up your
ears.
he is over head and
ears in love.
no body gives ear.
i haue a ſuit to you
for N.
i make earneſt ſuit
to you for &c.
he gaue his ſweet-
heart an earnſt-penny.
ſhe gaue her new ſer-
vant an earneſt-
penny.

gebet mir etwas drauf. *give me earneſt.*

i'm winter leget deſto *in winter -time ſet*

weniger eyer unter ; *the fewer eggs.*

des winters ſezet deſto weniger eyer an.

er reizete mih da zu ; *be egged me on;*

er hezete mih an. *be ſet me on.*

der ſommer ware bald *ſummer was almoſt*

vorbei geſtrihen , hin- *at an end.*

weg gegangen , faſt ganz vergangen.

er ſpilete mit dem gut- *be made an end of the*

en alten das gar-aus; *old man.*

er brahte den alten mann um, *or* um's leben.

ſih mit einander ver- *to make an end be-*

tragen *or* vergleihen. *twixt themſelves.*

es kůmmert in niht,ob *be does not care. or*

es drunter oder drůber *be cares not , which*

gee ; er (læſset ſih's *end goes fore-*

niht anfehten *or*) be- *ward.*

kůmmert ſih gar wenig , es mag gleih

zu hinterſt oder zu fœderſt geen.

es wære (um ſi geſhe *there had been an*

-en geweſen, *or*) aus *end of them ,*

mit inen geweſt, wa niht *&c.* *but that &c.*

faret fort ! weiter ! *on an end ! go an end!*

vergebens ; umſonſt. *to no end or purpoſe.*

es iſt ganz vergebens *it is to no end in*

und umſonſt. *the world.*

er iſt gemeiniglih (*or* *be is there moſt an*

meiſtenteils) dar. *end.*

eilet geſwinde , daſs ir *get you an end*

fertig werdet. *quickly.*

kommet eilens her! *come an end.*

zu ende (*or* zu'm ende) *to make an end*

bringen. *of.*

meine hare ſtanden *my hair ſtood an end.*
mir gen berge; das har ſtonde mir zu berge.
er plaudert alles was *he talks any thing ,*
ime einfællet ; wi es *that comes next to his*
ime auf di zunge kommet. *tounges end.*
es iſt unter das volk *folks have got it*
kommen ; es iſt aus- *by the end.*
kommen ; di leute tragen ſih überal damit.
nah dreyen tagen ; nah *by three dayes*
verflüſung dreyer tage. *end.*
ſtreitigkeiten entſheit- *to end differences*
en ; zwiſligkeiten unt- *or quarrels.*
ernemen ; zweiſpaltungen (zank) autheben.
unſer künftiger *our ſon in law*
tohter-mann. *that ſhall be.*
er will durhaus niht *he can not endure*
heiraten. *to marry.*
eine mannbare dirne *a girle or maid at*
or jungfrawe. *marriageable eſtate.*
alles (or alle ſahen) nur *to give a flight touch*
obenhinn beriren. *upon every thing.*
von angeſite zu angeſiht. *face to face.*
ih will euh eines in's *i will lay you*
geſiht or inn di freſſe geben. *on the face.*
ih habe kein herz (or *i have not a face*
keinen mut) es zu du- *to doe it ; with what*
en ; wi darf (or ſolte) *face can (could) i*
ih diſes tuen ? *doe this ?*
di kriges-here ſtunden *the armies ſtood*
ein ander reht i'm *facing one an*
geſihte. *other.*
wi iſt mir doh mein an- *how am i. fail-*
ſlag (or meine hoffnung) *ed in my ex-*
zu waſser worden! *pellation !*

V

ir feid ewerem ver- *you have failed of*
fprehen niht nah- *your word; you have*
kommen; ir habt ewer *not been as good as*
wort niht gehalten. *your word.*
ir follet euh allezeit auf *i will not faile you*
mih zu verlafsen habē. *in any thing.*
wenn ih fi nur folte zu *if i could get a fight*
gefihte bekommen ; *of her , or fet my*
wann ih irer nur kœn- *fight (mine eye)*
te anfihtig werden ; *on her.*
kœnte (folte) ih fi nur erægugen *or* erblikkē.
und ob ih noh fo *if i would never*
gerne wolte. *fo fain.*
wenn es nah unferem *if things fall out*
wunfhe ergeet. *to our minds.*
geet mir vo'm leibe. *ftand off !*
fi haben fih verzœrnet. *they are fallen out.*
ir werdet ewere angft *you will fall in*
(or not) mit difem *hand with that*
kerl krigen. *fellow.*
zu lahen (zu flafen , fih *to fall a-laughing,*
zu flagen und zu balg *a-fleep , a - figh-*
-en u. f. f.) anfangen. *ting &c.*
lafset uns zu was and- *let us fall in hand*
ers fhreiten *or* greifen. *with fomewhat elfe.*
krank werden. *to fall fick.*
wenn ir gebætet habt, *when ye have faid*
fo greifet(*or* langet)zu. *graces , fall too.*
er lebet (erbærmlih. e- *be fares hard-*
lendiglih *or*) armfelig. *ly or pittifully.*
ob es gleih krig ift, fo *we will fare well for*
wollen wir doh luftig *all the warr.*
und guter dinge (*or* frœliges gemūtes) fein.
habet ir euh mit ew- *did you bid fare-*

eren ·freinden gelezet? *well to your freinds?*
hab't ir abfhid von ew- *have you fhaken*
eren freinden ge- *hands with your*
nommen ? *freinds ?*
lebet wol ! Gott be- *fare well ! God be*
folen ! *with you !*
fi fae mih ftarr (*or* ftar- *fhe faftened her eyes*
gleih) an; fi verwande *upon me.*
niht ein aug (*or* einen blikk) von mir.
er flæget feinem vat- *hs takes after his*
er nah. *father.*
wir geben (legen *or* *we father our fault*
wælzen) di fhuld auf fi. *upon them.*
fi fagt, dafs ein ander- *fhe fathers the child*
er mann vater zu'm *upon an other*
kinde fei. *man.*
fi halten ime difes vor *they find fault*
übel ; fi legen's ime *with him for*
niht wol aus. *that.*
er hat fhuld dar- *be is in fault or*
an. *to blame.*
di fhuld war niht fein; *it was not (or none*
er·war unfhuldig daran. *of) his fault.*
was wird mir (fhuld ge *what fault am i char-*
geben *or*) aufgebürdet? *ged with ?*
einem eine gonft er- *to beftowe a favour*
weifen. *upon one.*
mit urlaub *or* vergœnft *under favour or by*
-igung ; mit gonft zu-u. f. w. *your favour.*
einem eine forht einjagen. *to put one in fear.*
es hat keine not (gefar) niht. *no fear on it.*
ih fae es vor gut an, zu *i thought good to*
fülen, ob ime auh di zæne *feele his mind.*
feft fteen , *or* zu feen was er i'm fhildefüret.

er will nur wenig hab-
en; er ist mit wenigen zu friden.
be is for having but a few.

ein so breiter weg, dafs
vire darauf neben ein
ander geen kœnnen.
a way enough for four to walk a-breast.

als das unglükklihe
treffen gehalten ward.
when that fatall field was fought.

er will (genug bulen
or) sih satt liben.
be will bave bu fill of love.

ih bin alles dinges
überdrüfsig.
i bave bad (or got) my fill of all.

er ernæret und ver-
forget das ganze haus
alleine.
be finds all the boufe by bim-self.

kurz davon zu reden,
es ist fein, wenn ein-
er seinen feind mit geld
abstrafen kann.
in fine, it is a fine thing, when a man can fet a fine on bis enemies bead.

wi wolte ih doh mit
ime umgeen! (wi wol-
bow would i finger bim!
te ih in (zerzaufen, absmiren or) zurihten!
gar leihtlih; one be-
fwerde; fonder grofe mühe.
with a wet fing -er.

einem einen roten han
auf's haus fezen; ein
haus (anstekken or) inn den brand stekken.
to fire ones boufe; to fet ones boufe on fire.

er fiet es niht vor gut
(ratfam or genem) an.
be thinks it not fit.

es wird einen streit fez
-en; es wird an ein zanken geen.
we shall bave a scol-ding fit.

ein mann inn alle fätt
-el gereht.
a man fit for all men.

er weis fih inn alle pofs
-en zu fhikken.
be is fit for any thing.

hab't ir eweren raufh   *is your drunken fit*
ausgeflafen ?   *over.*
warzu ein igliher (fih *what every man will*
wird fhikken or)gefhikt fein wird. *be fit for.*
feine fhue find ime (or   *his fhoes fit his*
feinen fûfsen) gereht.   *feet.*
er ift reife-færtig.   *he is fit for going.*
inn der hize ; vor eine weile. *for a fit.*
feet zu, dafs alles zu- *get all (or every*
bereit (or zugefhikket) fei. *thing) fit.*
ift das geltaufgezælet? *is the money fit ?*
wol-an ! ftreihet uns *come now , ftrike*
eins auf; mahet et-   *up and give us*
was luftiges.   *a fit.*
gefaft auf alles.   *fitted at all points.*
er hat alle jare einen ge *he hath every year*
-færlihen anftos der krankheit. *an ill fit.*
fi ertappete mih inn   *fhe took me in a*
einer œffentlihen lûgen. *flat lye.*
es treibet fi auf enge *it drives them a-*
und feihte œrter. *mongft the flats and fands.*
als ih difen brif zu- *as i was folding up*
fammen legete.   *this letter.*
fhafe (einftallen or)inn *to fold fheep ; to get*
den ftall tuen. *fheep up into their folds.*
er lage den rehten ob; *he followed the law*
er legte fih auf's reht. *i. was a lawyer.*
er will (euh verklagen *he will follow the law*
or) fih mit euh in's reht legen. *on you.*
mann kann inen zu *there is no coming*
fufse niht beikommen. *at them on foot.*
di fufs-knehte ereilet- *the foot overtook the*
en (or ûberlifen) di reiterei. *horfe.*
gleihwol aber ; idenn- *for all that ;*

noh; nihts deſto weniger. *neverthelesſ.*
das ſei ferne! da ſei Gott fâr! *God forbid!*
ſi verliſen ire fanen *they forſook their*
or ſaen ſi mit den rûkken an. *colours.*
einen ausfall duen. *to ſally forth.*
laſſet ewer ſhænden *leave your giving of*
und ſmæyen unter-wegen. *foul language.*
es wird auskommen; *it will be found*
es wird (kund or) ruh- *out.*
bar werden; mann wird dahinter kommen.
warnah ſeet ir euh um? *what do you look for?*
di ſpeiſe war ein wen- *the meat was ſome-*
ig zu gelinde geſalzen. *what to freſh.*
laſſet euh's niht ver- *doe not fret your ſelf,*
drûſen, wenn ir verſpilet. *when you looſe.*
ein neuling. *a freſhman.*
über dem fluſſe; auf *on the further ſide of*
der anderer ſeiten des fluſſes. *the river.*
pakket euh (weg or) *get you gone ; be*
von hinnen ; ſhæret *gone ; get you*
euh fort; geet hinnweg. *hence.*
hœret auf; laſſet nah. *have done; give over.*
diſe dinge (gelten gelr, *they are things ,*
bringen pfennige ein *that will give*
or , tragen gelt. *money.*
ſi gelten ganz und gar *they give nothing*
nihts. *at all.*
ih will es euh zu- *i will give you my*
ſagen or verſprehen. *word.*
es (ſwanete or) anete *my heart mûgave*
mir ; es ginge mir i'm *it me ; or , it*
gemâte vor; mein herz *gave me in*
ſagte es mir. *my mind.*
i zu weilen; zu zeiten. *ever now and then.*

gelib't's Gott; wenn Gott will. *God willing.*
ih bin durhaus frœlih.　　　*i am full glad.*
des herren (wolſtand,　　*Sir ! i am very*
wolweſen *or)* geſund-　　*glad , to ſee you*
heit iſt mir von herz-　　　　　　*well.*
en lib , *or* erfrewet mih ſere *or* herzlih.
er iſt verreiſet.　　*be is gone out of (the) town.*
wa wollet ir hinn-　　*whither are you*
geen ?　　　　　　　　　　　*going ?*
wi wird geſpilet ?　　*how goeth the game?*
mahet fort; faret fort; weiter. *goe on ; goe to!*
iſt *(or* geet) ſi ſwanger? *goeth (is or proves)*
iſt ſi hoes leibes ?　　　*ſhe with child ?*
er wird heute *(*Doctor　*be goes out Doctor*
or) zu einen Doctor gemaht.　　　*to day.*
ih bin bald vir und ah-　*i am going on my*
zig jar alt; ih gee inn　*four ſcore and four.*
das vir und ahzigſte jar; ih bin faſt ein
vir - und ahzig jæriger mann ; *or* ih bin
faſt vir - und ahzig jare meines alters.
ih wolte es euh gleih　*i was juſt a - going to*
izo geben.　　　　　　　　　*give it you.*
bei jaren; ſer alt; betaget. *far gone in years.*
er gabe alles *(*verſpilet　*be gave all for*
or) verloren .　　　　　　　　　*gone.*
es iſt um mih geſheen;　　*i am a gone*
es iſt aus mit mir.　　　　　　　*man.*
es ſei denn , daſs ir *i ſhall be gone bey ond*
mir (helfet *or)* beiſteet　*unleſs you help me.*
ſonſt werde ih hinter's liht geführet werde.
mih friret.　　*i am cold ; i have cold.*
was wolte ih doh　　*what was i going*
ſagen ?　　　　　　　　　　*to ſay ?*
warzu *(*dinet *or)* nuz- *what is it good (for*

et es? warzu ift es *or)* *to?* *what good*
gut ? *does it?*
koennet ir es (erweis- *can you make it*
en, beweifen, darduen *or)* *ausfüren?* *good?*
nemet es niht übel auf. *take it in good part.*
ih will vor allen fhad- *i will make good all*
en (gut fein *or)* fteen; *dammage.*
ih will allen fhaden gut mahen *or* erfezen.
warhaftig ; warlih ; *in good faith ; truth;*
gewislih ; bei mein- *earneft ;*
er trewe. *fadnefs.*
ein gefhikter *(or* rüft- *a man good at*
iger)* mann. *any thing.*
ein gelærter mann. *a good fcholar.*
mit dem früeften. *good and early.*
es hat niht gros auf fih; *it is no great matter.*
es hat niht vil zu bedeuten; es ift wenig
daran gelegen ; es ift keine reihs - fahe.
ih will fi ausforfhen, fi *i will find her out,*
mag auh ftekken wa fi *if fhe be above*
immer will *or* wolle. *ground.*
di zu pferde begaben *the horfemen gave*
fih zurükke; di reitereye wihe. *ground.*
der morgen briht an ; *it growes towards*
es beginnet morgen zu werden. *morning.*
der tag briht an; der *it growes near day ,*
tag , di naht, der frü- *night, fpring, harveft.*
ling, der herbft koemmet herbei *or* heran.
wære ih nun (ein narr, *had i been ought but*
tummer fhoeps , ein- *a block-head.*
fæltiger tropf *or* alberer toelpel geweft.
fo vil mir (bewuft *or)* *for ought i know; to*
wiffend ift. *my knowledge.*
ih koenne feine weife *i underftand his bu-*

(or ih weis feinen ge-   *mour to a hair.*
brauh) hares-klein *or* inn -und auswendig.
gee an den galgen *! goe and be hanged.*
der hanker hole dih! dafs dih (der galgen
hole *or*) das rad erfmeife , erfllage *!*
dife rede (trift niht û- *this tale hangeth not*
berein *or*) ftimmet niht zufammen. *together.*
fi bleiben niht auf ein- *their tales hang not*
erlei worte *or* auf einer rede. *together.*
es ift (nae bei , niht *it is hard (or near) at*
weit *or*) niht ferne. *hand; hard by; next by.*
unreht von einem *to take wrong at*
leiden. *ones hand.*
aus dem ftege · reife ; alfobalden. *out of hand.*
überhinn ; unbedahtfamlih. *hand over head.*
er ift der han i'm kor- *he has the chief*
be ; er ift der (mei *hand in it.*
fter *or*) vornemfte i'm fpile *or* handel.
eine vir - fhrœtige *a two - handed*
frawe. *woman.*
fi wird bald (inn di *fhe is hard at down-*
wohen kommen *or*) einkommen. *lying.*
einem auf dem fufse *to be hard at ones*
folgen; ftraks hinter einem her fein. *heeles.*
es hilte hart; es ginge *it was a hard*
fwer zu. *(great) matter.*
einer fo tag und naht *a hard ftudent ;*
über den bühern liget. *belluo librorum.*
er arbeitet fleifig. *he workes hard.*
ir komt mir zu ftark *or you are too hard (or*
zu grob; ir feid mir überlegë. *too many) for me.*
ein ftrenger *or* fæwerliher wein. *a hard wine.*
ein dummer kopf zu *one hard to*
lernen. *learne.*

ein huf-eifen.	*an horfe-fhoe.*
ih bin eilfertig.	*i am in great bafte.*
ir liben leutigen efset	*good people feed*
wakker drauf und lafs	*beartily , for you*
-et euh's wol fmækken,	*are all very*
denn ir feid mir alle	*wellcome to it.*
fer angeneme (*or* willkommene) gæfte.	
wir feen es wol.	*we find it fo.*
da hab't ir eins!	*have at you!*
nah feinem kopfe *or* finne.	*of his own head.*
fi daten uns dapferen	*they made head a-*
widerftand.	*gainft us ftoutly.*
das herz war mir inn	*my heart was at my*
di (hofen *or*) knikele gefallen.	*heels.*
aufewendig her-	*to fay (by heart, or)*
fagen.	*without book.*
das (land *or*) feld ift	*the (land or) field is*
unfruhtbar.	*out of heart.*
feid (gutes muts *or*)	*come , take a good*
unverzaget ?	*heart !*
mein (gehûlf *or*) gefell	*my partner is quite*
ift ganz verzaget.	*out of heart.*
von herzen gerne ; mit	*with all my*
allem willen; fer gerne.	*heart.*
als ih a'm meiften zu	*in the heat of my*
(duen *or*) verrihten hatte.	*bufinefs.*
einem den kopf warm	*to put one into*
(*or* heis) mahen.	*a heat.*
leget euh felber vor ;	*help your felves.*
nemet euh felbften hinnaus; greifet felbft zu!	
es will mir niht ein-	*i can not hit on it ; i*
fallen ; ih kann gar	*can not call it to*
niht drauf kommen ; ih	*mind.*
kann mih niht darauf befinnen *or* bedenken.	

ih kann meinen brud-	*i can not hit on my*
er nirgens antreffen.	*brother any where.*
ſtoſet euh niht an (den	*doe not hit your*
kopf *or)* das haupt.	*head.*
ſi ſind (unterſhidliher	*they doe not hit*
meinungen *or)* verſhidener gedanken.	*it.*
ſweiget ſtille ; gebet	*hold your peace; hold*
euh zu friden ; haltet ewer maul.	*your toung.*
ir bleibet *(bei or)* auf	*you hold on your old*
ewerer alten weiſe *or* gewonheit.	*wont.*
er leget hand an ſi.	*he layes hold on her.*
di gelegenheit inn aht	*to lay hold of the*
nemen *or* ergreifen.	*opportunity.*
wollet ir mih niht geen	*will you not hold off*
(*or* zu friden) laſsen?	*your hands ?*
das hemd iſt mir næer	*charity beginnes at*
dann der rokk.	*home.*
ein rehter bûtermann ;	*a downright honeſt*
ein alter Teutſher.	*man.*
er iſt (eine gute erlihe	*he is a good honeſt*
haut *or)* ein aufrihtiger kærl *or* tropf. *fellow.*	
mein weib iſt (ganz i'm	*my wife is quite off*
harniſhe *or)* durhaus bœſe.	*the books.*
er iſt gewiſs genug (ein	*he is bookt in , as*
-gelappet *or)*gefangen.	*ſure as can be.*
ih zweifelte (*or* ver-	*i was out of hope*
zweifelte) an dem fride.	*of peace.*
er iſt ganz verzaget ;	*he is paſt hope.*
es iſt um in geſheen ;da iſt kein retten.	
du hurenſon *!*	*you ſon of a whore!*
ih bringe es dem herr-	*here is to you , Sir*
en! der jungefrawen!	*or Miſtreſs.*
auf diſes herren (*or* auf	*to this Gentlemans*
diſer frawen , jung-	*(or Gentlewomans)*

frawen) gute gefundheit!	*good health!*
Gott gefegne es dem	*with all my heart!*
herren! der frawen!	*der jungfrawen!*
komm' ih über den	*i will win the horfe,*
hund, fo komm' ih ü-	*or loofe the faddle.*
ber den fwanz; entweder	alles oder gar nihts.
fi find fer ftark.	*they are of huge force.*
ein ftein-reiher mann.	*a huge rich man.*
ir hættet ime follen	*you fhould have hu-*
durh di finger feen.	*mour'd him.*
einen übertœbern *or*	*to runne one*
übertœlpeln.	*down.*
ih wære (bald umge-	*i had like to be*
braht worden *or*) umkommen.	*killed.*
mih hongert; ih bin	*i am (an hungred)*
hongerih; ih habe honger.	*or hungrie.*
über dritthalb ftund-	*two hours and an*
en. vor anderhalb	*half hence. an hour*
ftunden.	*and an half agoe.*
übel haushalten; übel	*to be an ill husband; to*
haufen; ein (bœfer	*play the bad husband.*
haushalter, verfwænder *or*) faulenzer fein.
ir müfset (fparfam,	*you muft husband it*
genawe *or*) beratfam damit umgeen.	*well.*
einen (pofsen *or*) fherz	*to put a thing off*
daraus mahen.	*with a jeft.*
er ift heftig krank	*he is fallen very*
worden.	*ill.*
er ift (*or* liget) krank	*he is ill of the*
a'm fteine, zippergen.	*ftone, gout.*
es ift mir niht wol;	*i am not well; i am*
es ift mir reht übel.	*very ill.*
Gott lob und dank! ih	*i am indifferently*
bin noh zimlih wol auf.	*well, i thank God.*

innwendig, innerlih .   on the inſide.
als exempels weiſe ;   as for inſtance i. e.
zu'm beiſpile.   for examples ſake.
auf ewer anhalten, an-   at your inſtance.
regen, antreiben, anmanen, anſuhe, geheiſ-
in bitte euh hoehlih; I'intreat you of all
ih will euh freundlih erſuht haben.   love.
er iſt niht (zu erbitt-   there is no intreat-
en or) m't bitten zu   ing of him ; be
bewoegen ; es hülfet   is not to be in-
kein bitten von ihren   treated at
bey ime.   all.

ſi laſſen ſih (gar leiht-   little intreating ſervu-
lih erbitten, or) ire   eth (or will ſerve) to
kappen niht zerreiſen   ſtay them.
um zu verbleiben or zu verwarten.
der henker hole ſeinen   hang his journieman
(werk-) geſellen or arbeiten   or workman?
ſi gabe es mir auf-zu   ſhe gave it me to keep
heben or zu verwaren.   or to lay it by.
der himmel henget in-   they keep Chriſt-
en allezeit voller geig-   mas all the
en ; ſi leben immer-   year long.
fort i'm vollen ſauſe und ſmauſe ; es
iſt immer (hohzeit or) kirmeſse mit inen.
ſi hzlt niht farbe.   ſhe does not keep touch.
was vor ein ſhiff iſt   what kind of ſhip
das ewere?   is yours ?
er ſtellet ſih freundlih   he is kind to
gegen mih.   me.
er iſt ein leutſeliger   he is a kind (Gen-
(or freundliher mann.   tleman or) man.
ſi ſind inen nihts (boe-   they know nothing
ſes) bewuſt.   by them ſelves.

wenn ih ſi ſee , ſo ken-   *i know her by*
ne ih ſi ; ih kenne ſi von geſite.   *ſight.*
ih will euh (dih) læren,   *i will make you know,*
was es ſei , ſeinen herr   *what it is to couſin*
-en (meiſter) betrügen.   *your maſter.*
er wird euh (zu bodem   *he will knock you*
or) darnider ſlagen *or* ſmeiſen,   *down.*
er tribe mit ir unzuht.   *he knocked her.*
es iſt der mũe wert ; es   *it is worth the (while*
verlonet di mũe.   *or) labour.*
er verwũſtete alles, wa   *he lay'd all waſte ,*
er nur hinn kame; er   *where he came.*
verherete und verzere was er nur antrafe.

ſtif-*or* halb- ſweſter. ſwægerin.	*ſiſter*	
ſtif-*or* halb- bruder. -ſwager.	*brother*	*in law.*
ſtif- vater. ſwiger - vater.	*father*	
ſtif-mutter. ſwiger - mutter.	*mother*	

ir ſollet (vortanzen ,   *you ſhall lead the*
or) den vorreyen haben.   *dance.*
ih lernete es von wort   *i learnt it every word*
zu worte auswendig.   *without book.*
der text lautet von   *the text runnes word*
wort zu wort alſo.   *by (or for) word thus.*
ih weis zuvor wol ,   *i am not to learne,*
was vor ein leihtfert-   *what a ſad rogue*
iger vogel (*or* ihelm)   *(baſe knave, villain,*
ir ſeid ; *or* was du vor   *or raſcal) you are.*
ein (galgenſwengel *or*) galgen- vogel biſt.
wenn ir derweile (*or*   *if you be at leaſure.*
zeit) habet : i'm falle daſs ir mũſig ſeid.

wenn es meine geſhæſte (verrihtungen) werden (or wollen) zulaſsen	if my occaſions will give me leave, or vergœnnen.
feyeret eine zeit-lang;	leave work for awhile.
henget di arbeit eine weile an den nagel.	
er iſset alles rein auf;	he leaves not manners in the diſh.
er friſset alles hinnein.	
greifet (or langet) ein wenig zu.	lend me your hand a little.
helfet mir ein wenig.	lend me your help a little.
endlihen, nahdeme es lange gewæret hatte;	at length. or nah viler zeit.
er liget alleine.	he lyes by himſelf.
einem auf den dinſt warten; auf einen lauren.	to lye in wait for one.
wann ih (lebe or) das leben habe; wa mir Gott das leben gœnnet, gibet, verleyet.	if God ſend life, health.
wenn ih auh ſterben (or ob ih ſhon mein leben verliren) ſolte.	if my life ſhould ly on it.
ih ſeze mein leben zu'm pfande; ih will mein leben verloren haben.	i lay my life on it.
er ſtige von dem wagen.	he lighted from the charriot.
von dem pferde ſteigen.	to light off from his horſe.
er koſtete es ein klein wenig; er ſmakkerte nur daran.	he took a light taſte of it.
er læſſet di hænde klæben.	he is a light-fingered fellow.
inn den wind ſlagen;	to think light of--
zu einem ore ein-und zu'm anderen widerum	or to ſet light by; to make light of;

lassen aus-geen; vor — *light reckoning (or account) of.*

nihts ahten.

ir gabet es ime unter den fuß; ir halfet im' auf di bane; ir brahtet in auf di sprünge. — *you lighted him the way to*

wi gefællet euh dises? — *low doe you like that?*

es gefæll't mir gar wol. — *i like it very well.*

ih habe mih unterhalt-en lassen. — *i have listed my self for a soldier.*

inn der kürze; inn kurzem; inn kurzer zeit. — *ere long; a little while after.*

zupfet euh bei ewer-er nasen; greifet inn eweren bosem; keret vor ewerer düre. — *look to your self; look to your own home,*

mann siet sih ser nah euh um; si warten ew·erer mit verlangen. — *there is much look; for of you.*

so war ih lebe; so ge-wiß als ih das leben habe; ih will niht gesund von der stelle geen; ih will niht erlih sein. — *as i live; ih will niht leben, would i might never live if &c.*

Gott spare in gesund! Gott lasse in lange leb·en! Gott erhalten in bei langem leben! Gott gebe, daß er lange lebe? — *God send he live long! God send him long to live?*

si müsen sih von dem blösen honige erhalt-en; si haben sonst nihts als honig zu essen, wol verwaret und ver-flosen sein. — *they are fain to live all upon honey. to be under lock and key.*

was isset di jungfer gerne? — *what meat doe you love, Madam?*

will fi einen flûgel   *are you for a*
haben ?   *wing ?*
ih habe weder ftern *i have no luck at*
noh glûkk ?   *all.*
er flæget fein wafser   *he makes water ; he*
ab ; er pifset; er feihet; er brunfet.   *pifseth.*
ih zweifele niht; ih   *i make no queſtion*
trage keinen zweifel.   *or doubt.*
er bildet ime etwas ein;   *he makes much of*
er dûnket fih was zu fein.   *him ſelf.*
er lœfete gelt daraus.   *he made money at it.*
ir habet heute wakker   *you have made a*
darauf gearheitet ; ir   *good dayes - work*
hab't euh's difen tag   *on it .*
inn euerer arbeit lafsen fawer werden.
er rihtete (*or* ftellete) • *he made a funerall*
ir ein leih-begxng-   *for her.*
nifs an ; er life fi zu'r erden beftattern.
er hat fein hab und   *he haib made away*
gut (durh di gurgel   *his eſtate.*
gejaget , verflukket , verprafset , ver-
flampampet , verfaulenzet *or*) durhgebraht.
er halfe ime felbft vo'm   *he made away him*
brote ; er name ime   *ſelf.*
felbft das leben ; er brahte fih felber um.
hofmeifter ! lafset ime   *ſteward !* *make*
etwas zu efsen und zu   *him eate and*
trinken geben.   *drinke.*
ih will mih bei euh   *i will make you*
fhon bezalet mahen.   *pay me.*
was mein mund redet, *my toung and heart*
das meinet das herz.   *are twins.*
es ift aufer allem   *it hath no manner*
zweifel.   *of doubt.*

idwede tugend beſteet	*all vertue in a man-*
gewiſſ ·r maſſen inn	*ner ſtandeth in*
drei flůkken.	*three points.*
es iſt um mein leben	*my life is in a man-*
faſt geſheen.	*ner done.*
ein ſolher mann (*or*	*this is the manner*
menſh / iſt er.	*of the man.*
was vor ein mann	*what manner of*
war er?	*man was he ?*
ſi hat freyers- gedank-	*ſhe hath a mind to*
en ; ſi geet mit heiraten um.	*marrie.*
ih will dir fort helfen ;	*i will make you (thee)*
ih will dir beine (fůſse)mahen.	*runne.*
er verjagete (*or* jagte)	*he made them all*
ſi alle.	*runne.*
es kůmmert mih nihts;	*i make it all a matter,*
es geet mih nihts an ;	*it matters me not.*
ih frage nihts darnah.	*i doe not matter it.*
ungefær ſehs (ſex)	*a matter of ſix*
meilen ; ungefær hund-	*miles ; a matter of*
ert reihstaler ,	*five and twentie*
u. ſ. f. a.	*pound ſterling &c.*
bei mannes gedenk-	*ſince man could*
en.	*mean.*
ei freilih ! gar gewiſs.	*by all means.*
bei leibe niht.	*by no means.*
vermittelſt deſsen ; hidurh.	*by that means.*
durh mih ; durh meine hůlfe.	*by my means.*
arme (*or* geringe , un-	*men of ſmall*
vermœgende)leutgen.	*means.*
wadurh ? wamit? auf	*by what means?*
was weiſe *or* wege ? welher geſtalt ?	
eine maſe halten.	*to keep a mean.*
innzwiſhen; unterdeſs-	*in the mean time ,*

en ; unter wærender zeit ; mittler weile.	*while , space , season.*
ein kriges-shiff (von si- benzig stükken *or*) si- sibenzig geshüze fürend.	*a man of warr moun- ted with three score gunnes and ten .*
über (di mase *or*) alle mase aufwenden.	*to spend beyond (all) measure.*
über alle di mase (*or* aufer masen) zornig.	*angry oub; of all measure .*
mittelmæsig ; mit masen.	*is measure.*
einziger (*or* etliher) masen.	*in a (or, in some) measure.*
guten teils ; fast alle ; gemeiniglih ; meistens.	*in a very great measure.*
menget euh niht unt- er si.	*doe not you meddle with them.*
habe ih (des eweren *or*) von dem eweren etwas angeriret *or* angegriffen?	*have i meddled with any thing of yours ?*
es ist billih und reht.	*it is meet.*
es steet Fürsten niht an *or* zu.	*it is not meet-for Princes.*
ih werde in shon ein- mal dafür bekommen *or* bezalen.	*i shall meet with him one time or other.*
nemet ewere gesund- heit inn aht.	*mind your health,*
hœret ir drauf? ge- bet ir ahtung darauf ?	*doe you mind?* merket ir auf ?
ih bin diser (*or* ew- erer) meinung.	*i am of that (or of your) mind.*
seine gedanken offen- baren ; seine meinung	*to speake his mind.* entdekken *or* sagen .
er hat seines herzens	*he hath*

wunſh *or* verlangen.

er iſt (anders geſinnet, *or*) anderer meinung.

er hatte einen narren an diſem weibe gefreſsen.

es iſt feiner tohter unrihtig gangen,

laſset uns ein wenig friſhe luft ſhœpfen.

ih habe ulkda nihts verloren *or* nihts zu ſuhen.

mǎndlih *or* mǎndlihen.

was ir einbrokket, das mǎſset ir auseſsen.

er ſtrekket alle ſeine makt und kraft (*or* ſtærke) dran, er arbeitet

mann trawet euh nirgends *or* auf keiner ſeiten.

er legete (*or* zalete) ime (das pare gelt *or*) das gelt par auf den

eingeſalzen ründ-fleiſh.

ein jüngling (*or* jung er kærl) mit namen

gegen (*or* auf den) abend; auf di naht ſoll es færtig ſein.

nahtliher weile; des nahts.

geſtern waren es aht tage, als das kind getaufet wurde.

bis minds

be is of an oiher mind.

be bad a very great mind to thit wife.

bis daughter bath miscartied.

let us take a mouthfall of freſh aire.

they neither ſow nor mowe for me there.

by word of mouth.

what you ſow, that you muſt mow.

he laboures tooth and naik.

mit hænde u fuſen. you are truſted on neither ſide.

he paid the money down upon the nail.

tilh *or* inn di hand. poudred beef.

a youngman William. Willhelm. by name.

i will get it done by night.

by night; in the night ime.

yeſterday it was a ſennight, when the child was chriſtened.

vor virzeen tagen.	*a fortnight agoe.*
morgen über aht tage;	*to morrow cum-se'n-*
über virzeen tage.	*night; — cum fortnight.*
vorsezlih; von freyem,	*for the nonce; on*
fleiße; mit fleiße.	*purpose.*
er will euh niht haben;	*he will have none*
er begeret ewer niht.	*of you.*
di shuld ist niht mein.	*it is none of my fault.*
was newes? nihts	*what newes? none*
niht.	*at all.*
umsonst; frei; für	*for nothing; at*
nihts.	*free cost.*
ir sollet keinen narren	*you shall not make a*
(aus mir mahen or) an	*fool of me for*
mir haben für nihts und umsonst.	*nought.*
es ist nihts gutes an dem	*the ringleader is*
rædgens-fürer.	*naught.*
ih brauhe; (bedarf or	*i have occasion for*
habe nœtig) mein gelt.	*my money.*
das alter or altertum.	*the old age.*
vor langen jaren.	*in old time.*
ih rihte mih nah der	*i am for the old*
alten welt.	*way.*
zu fusse oder zu	*on foot or on horse-*
pferde.	*back.*
mit einem; auf ein-	*all under one;*
mal; or zugleih,	*at once.*
ih will euh wider (ver-	*i will set you at one*
tragen, vereinigen or) einsmahen.	*again.*
ih erzogesi (kleine or	*i brought her up of a*
da si noh (klein or) jung ware.	*little one.*
ih konte niht überall	*i could not be here*
auf ein mal (or zu	*and there and all*
gleih) sein.	*at once.*

ih will es fo deutlih für -ftellen, dafs ir gedenk -en follet; als ob ir duet(*or* nemet)das ftah -el-fwein und den zaun -kœnig vor meinen augen hinn weg.	*i will lay it open, as if you faw it.* es felbften fæet. *take away the bedge -hogg and the bedge -fparrow from before my eyss.*
ih will feine tükkgen (fhelmerei *or* fhelm- ftükkgen) offenbaren,	*i will lay open his villany.*
or offenbar mahen.	*to take an oath.*
ein eid (duen, fwœer- en *or*) ablegen.	
er mufte fwœeren.	*be was put to bis oath.*
etwas eidlih zufagen; einen mit einem eide	*to give one fecurity by*
verfihern.	*oatb.*
wollet ir ein geiftliher werden? nein, ih wer -de keiner werden.	*will you goe into orders? no, i fhall not.*
ir irret; ir fæilet; ir verirret euh.	*you are out or out of the ftory; that is your miftake.*
weit gefæilet; hin- ten-aus tragen di bauren di fpife.	*you are quite out or quite from the market.*
einen i'm laufen *or* ren -nen, mit dem ver- ftande *or* wize u. f.f. übertreffen.	*to outgoe or out- runne one, to out- wit one &c.*
pakket euh von hinnen *or* geet weg; fhæret euh fort.	*pack hence and be gone.*
eine treppe, eine kar- te, eine orgel, eine fhære, ein blafe-balg, ein kræufel-eifen, eine zange, u. f. f. a.	*a pair of* { *ftairs, cards, organs, fcis- fars, bellowes, curling-irons, tonges &c.*

ih wolte liber in's gras beiſen. *i had rather die.*
ih will liber ſtérben *or* *i will part with my*
mih laſsen umbringen. *life firſt.*
iſt diſes erlih (aufrih- *is this an honeſt mans*
tig *or* redlih) gehand- *part , to abuſe an*
elt, wenn mann einem *innocent ſtranger ?*
unſhuldigen fremdlinge gewalt und unreht
duet ? *this is no honeſt mans*
das tuet kein(rehtſhaff- *part; ſure none but a*
ener *or*)erliber mann; *villain would do this.*
dis, kommet einem redlihen manne niht
zu; diſes ſteet keinem erlihen kærl an.
ein neid-hæmmel. *an envious dog.*
Gott verleye ir eine *God's peace be with*
ſanfte rue *or* einen ſel *her! God reſt her ſoul!*
-igen ſlaf ! Gott troeſte ſi *or* ire ſele !
mer dann zu oft; zu vil malen. *over often.*
ein (ſtükk *or*) werk, *a ſtudied piece.*
darauf vil müe und fleis gewand iſt worden.
ruffet Gott den all- *call upon God all-*
mæhtigen an, ſo wird *mighty , and he will*
ér ſih ewer erbarm- *(take or) have pitty*
en. *on you , or pitty you.*
laſset uns der karten *let us play at*
ſpilen. *cards.*
wer (ſlæget aus *or*) *who playes*
ſpilet aus ? *firſt ?*
was ſoll ein ſpil gelten? *what will you (or*
um was wollen wir *ſhall we) play*
ſpilen ? was wollen *for?*
wir auffezen ? was ſoll auf dem ſpile ſteen ?
was für (ſprünge *or*) *what pranks would*
aufzüge und poſsen *we have play'd*
würde er mir gemaht haben ? *me !*

er ſtilet als ein rab *be playes the thief*
or naht-rab. *moſt ſlïly.*

ir narret euh (*or* ir *you play the fool*
ſherzet) mit mir; ir *with me.*
treibet (ſherz *or*) narren-poſsen mit mir.
es gefællet mir ; ih *i am pleaſed with*
habe (meine luſt *or*) ge- *it ; it pleaſeth*
fallen daran *or* damit. *me.*

was belibt dem herren? *Sir , your pleaſure?*
der herr ſage was ime *what is it you want,*
belibe . *Sir ?*

ih will dem Muſen-flei- *i will ply my*
ſe (*or* dem ſtudiren) nahfolgen. *book.*

rudert wakker drauf! *ply your ores !*

einem mit dem (drun- *to ply one with*
ke *or*) drinken zuſezen. *cups.*

wir müſsen fortmahen *we muſt ply us ; we*
or ellen. *muſt make haſte.*

ermannet (*or* ermand- *pluck up your*
ert) euh ! *ſpirits!*

reiſet *or* dnet) di ſih *pluck aſunder the*
mit einander belſend- *fighting*
en hæne ronſammen. *cooks.*

laſset mih doh euh er- *let me prevail with*
bitten ; laſset meine bitte ſtatt finden. *you .*

mein pferd iſt verna- *a nail doeth prick*
gelt. *my horſe.*

es iſt ein vortrefliher *be prevail an ex-*
mann aus im worden. *cellent man.*

vor izo ; izo gegen- *at preſent , at this*
wærtig ; zu gegenwær *preſent , for the*
-tiger zeit; vor diſes mal. *preſent.*

er hat wakker geræiſt *be is a great travel-*
und ſih wol verſuhet. *ler indeed.*

er zoge feinen hals ein.	he pull'd in his neck,
er (es) fhikket fih inn	he (it) is for your
eweren kram ; er (es	purpofe.
ift) or dinet vor euh or	vor eweren kram.
es ræumet fih niht ;	it is to no purpofe.
es fhikket fih wi eine	fault auf's auge.
es ift auf das (æuferfte	it is come to the
or) hœhfte kommen.	laft pufh.
weifet fi ab; lafset fi laufen.	put her off.
nemet den mantel um.	put on the cloak.
er kleidet fi von dem	he puts her into filk
fufse auf (or vo'm haup-	from the top to
te bifs zu'n fufsen) inn feide.	the bottome.
puzet das liht aus,	put out the candle ,
wann ir euh habet	when you have put
ausgezogen.	off your garments.
etwas aufzeihenen or	to put a thing in
aufhreiben.	writing.
ein buh ausgeen lafsen.	to put forth a book.
di fhiffe laufen inn di	the fhips put to
fee; di fhiffe geen zu'r	fee.
	fea.
ir wurdet ubergangen	you were put
or aufen - gelafsen.	by.
bringet fi um.	put them to death.
burgen ftellen; verfih-	to put in fureties
erung tuen.	or fecuritie.
gelt auf zinfe legen	to put money
or , ausleyen.	to ufe.
er ftekket fein fwert	he puts up his
ein or inn di fheide.	fword.
ih begere difes niht	i fhall not put you
von euh.	to that.
œffentlih vor aller	in the open face of
welt.	the whole world.

X

einen gleihfam auf den hænden tragen, d. i. herz - inniglih liben. *to put one (as if it were) in his bofom i. e. to love moſt affectionately.*

ih. weis weder aus noh ein; ih binn inn der groeſten not or hœhſten gefar; ih ſtekke zwifhen dûre und angel; ih habe den wolf bei den oren. *i am in a quandary.*

es iſt inem das leben gefhenket, worden. *they have quarter given them.*

wa liget ir zu'r herber-ge? war haltet ir euh auf? wa wonet ir? *where is your quarter?*

nun fo find wir einander gleih or nihts fhuldig. *now then we are even or quit.*

fi wihen zurûkke; fi hilten niht fufs or grund. *they did quit their ground.*

gedenket ir frei (aus-zu geen or)los zukommen? *doe you think, you ſhall be quit?*

ih will es euh eindringen or gedenken. *i ſhall cry quit with you.*

bevor ih ganz ausge-redet hatte. *before i had done quite ſpeaking.*

wi, hoh haltet ir es? wi tewer wollet ir's geben? *what rate fet you on it?*

fi halten es hoh; vor (or ,um) einen grofen preis. *they hold it at a huge rate.*

einen mit fharfen wort abfheweren. *to rate one found-ly.*

einen bogen fhufs weit. *within reach of dart.*

filefen alles (heimlih or) fahte; fi lefen kein wort laut. *they read all to themfelves.*

er mœhte vor dorſt ver-fmahten or vergeen. *he is readie to die for thirſt.*

fplitter-nakket; mutter-nakket. *ſtark naked,*

ih wolte difes noh ein   *i would doe this ra-*
mal fo lib *(or* gerne)   duen. *ther by half.*
ih ahte es wenig.   *i reckon little of it.*
ih frage nihts nah ir;   *i make no reckoning*
ih verahte fi.   *of her.*
ir werdet niht *(*wider *you will not recover*
-um gefund werden *or) fcil. your health.*
zu voriger gefundheit gelangen *or* gerat n.
wird es auh wol einer   *will any refufe*
abflagen *or* fih defsen   *wæigern? it.*
ih will euh nihts ver-   *i will refufe you*
fagen *or* abflagen.   *nothing.*
ih will es mit euh an-   *i will refufe you at*
nemen auf was weife ir begeret.   *nothing.*
ei liber! grüfset fi von *pray! remember me*
wegen meiner eren- *to her; prefent my*
dinftlih; vermeldet ir *fervice to her.*
(meinen eren-grufs *or)* meine eren linfe
es (ift *or)* fteet ime we- *he (or it) is paft re-*
der zu raten noh zu *medie; there is no*
helfen; es ift damit gefheen.   *remedie.*
hab't ir es bei euh   *are you refolved*
beflofsen?   *on it?*
benemet mir difen   *refolve me this*
zweifel; befreyet mih difes zweifels. *doubt.*
wir konten weder raft *we could take no reft*
-en noh ruen inn der *all the reft of*
übrigen zeit der naht. *the night.*
erftlih (erftens, zu'm *at firft they make a*
erften, i'm anfange, *ftand, then they*
anfænglih)fteen fi, dar *retreat.*
nah fo begeben fi fih widerum zurükke.
zu'm abzuge blafen. *to found a retreat.*
antworten. *to returne an anfwer.*

ih kann feiner niht los *i can not be rid of*
werden; ih kann mih *him.*
feiner niht entflagen, entæufern, entbrehen.
er fure auf einer *he did ride in a*
kutfhen. *coatch.*
er lage vor anker. *he rode at anchor.*
ein koftbarer ring. *a rich ring.*
fi ftanden alle inn ein *they ftood all in a*
-em kræife. *ring.*
meine oren (gellen *or*) *my ears ring with*
klingen mir. *noife.*
das glokken-geltut. *the ringing of the bells.*
gleih wenn di vœgel *juft when the birds*
aufflügen wollen *are going to rife.*
mit der fonnen aufgange. *by fun-rife.*
der wind beganne fih *the wind beganne*
zu erhœben. *to rife.*
ir herfhet ganz alleine. *you rule all by your felf.*
folget meinem rate. *be ruled by me.*
wi es pfleget her-zu ge *as the world rules.*
-en; der welt lauf und gewonheit nah.
er wird nærrifh darü- *that makes him run*
ber; das mahet in (toll *or*, tœriht. *mad.*
ih frage niht ein fnipp *i care not a rufh*
-gen *or* einen ftro-halm nah ir. *for her.*
es ift niht einen kwark *it is not worth a*
(pfifferling *or* drekk) wert. *(pinn) rufh.*
eine ftatt plünd- *to fack (or ranfack)*
ern. *a town.*
dem fekke ift kein *no wine to*
wein gleih. *fack.*
wi (*or* warum) feid ir *why are you (or*
fo traurig? betrübt? *what makes you) fo*
beftürzt? *(melancholy or) fad?*

es ift ein jammer und *it is a fad thing,*
eleñd ; es ift ein erbærmlih - elendes ding.
ir kinder! wenn ir fatt *children , when you*
feid ; (or genung ge- *have dined , rife from*
gefsē habt;) fo ftetet auf vo'm tilhe. *the table.*
ih will euh difer mũe *i will fave you*
ũberhœben. *that labour.*
bifs auf den winter auf *to fave till win-*
-hœben. *ter.*
wa ih nur niht fhaden *fo i can but fave*
(damit *or)* dabei leide! *by it.*
der lezte one einen , *the laft but (fave or*
one zweye u. f. f. a. *except) one, two &c.*
es ware nimann (*or there was no crea-*
weder hund noh kaze) *ture with me fave*
bei mir, als ein klein *one little old*
altes *(mũttergen or)* weihgen. *woman.*
fih mit der fluht rett- *to fave him felf*
en. *by flight.*
bleibet *or* wartet, fag' ih. *ftay , i fay.*
fo ginge di gemeine *fo it was fay'd or*
rede ; das gefhrei ware. *reported.*
ei ! ift es war ? *fay you fo ?*
es ift niht anders, als *yes in deed doe i*
wi ih fage. *fay fo.*
alle di fhiffe ftœen fe- *all the fhips are*
gel-fœrtig. *under fayl.*
wir haben folher bũrg- *we are very fcarce*
er wenig *or* niht vil. *of fuch Citizens.*
waran *(or* warauf*)* er *which he fcarce*
kaum gedahte; welhes *thought of.*
er ime fwerlih einbildete *or* trœumen life.
er brœnnet vor zorn. *he is fire and tow.*
ir waret kaum(gegang *you were fcarce gone*

-en or) hinnweg , so   *but (i. e. before)*
kame ih.   *i came.*
fhreibet es mir an;   *put it upon my*
fezet es an meine reh-   *ſcore or account.*
nunge *or* zehe; rehnet es mir an *or* zu.
auf ewer er verantwort *upon your ſcore or*
-ung.   *account.*
di zehe *or* rehnung   *to clear (or , to pay*
bezalen.   *off) the ſcore.*
ir feid zu'm wenig-   *you are four ſcore*
ſten drei und neinzig   *and thirteen years*
jar alt *or* ein drei-und neinziger. *old at leaſt.*
unſer er freundſhaft *up on the ſcore of*
halber; von wegen uns   *our freind-*
-erer freindſhaft.   *ſhip.*
fiben jare nahdeme er *ſeven years after his*
das bürger · meiſter-   *ſecond Conſulſhip.*
amt zu dem andern male gefüret hatte.
er weihet nimanne an *he is ſecond to none*
wiſsenſhaft ; er gibet   *for learning.*
keinem menſhen etwas an gelærigkeit nah.
wenn not vor handen   *to ſecond me , if*
or vorfællet , daſs ir   *need be.*
mir (beiſteet, beiſtand leiſtet *or*) beiſpringet.
er vertrawete ir alle *he truſted her with*
heimligkeiten.   *all ſecrets.*
er kann nihts verſwei- *he can keep no ſe-*
gen *or* heimlih und ver *cret; he is not able*
-borgen halten.   *to keep a ſecret.*
er iſt ſein geheimer *he is one of the ſe-*
rat; er weis alle ſei- *cret Cabal; he is privy*
ne heimligkeiten.   *to all his ſecrets.*
es konte niht ſo gar *it could not be ſmo-*
verſwigen bleiben.   *thered up in ſecret.*

der herr fize an feinem *fit ftill or keep your*
orte ftill! er bleibe fizend. *feat, Sir!*
di frawe fprehe uns *pr.ry come and fee*
doh einmal zu. *us, Madam.*
ih werde es einmal du- *that i fhall one of*
en, ee ir euh defs- *thefe dayes,*
en vorfeet. *unawares.*
wi koemm't es, *or* was *what is the matter,*
ift di urfahe, dafs ir *that you can not fee*
weder heute noh mor- *us to day nor to mor*
gen uns befuhen koennet? *-row neither?*
hülfe fuhen; fih nah bei *to feek for aid, help,*
-ftand umfeen *or* umtuen. *afsistance.*
wi dewer geb't ir dis? *how fell you this?*
was wollet (*or* wi vil *what doe you*
wollet) ir dafür haben? *fell that?*
es hülfet (ime *or*) in *it fignifyes nothing to*
nihts; er ift defsen *him; he is never the*
nihtes gebefsert. *better for that.*
das geringfte ding *any thing, never fo*
ift genug für *fmall a matter, will*
mih. *ferve me.*
er dinet dem koenige *he ferves the King*
zu fufse. *on foot.*
wollet ir mir aufwart- *will you ferve*
en (*or* auf-) dinen? *me?*
traget efsen auf. *ferve up meat.*
es dinet (es ift dinlih *or it ferveth for many*
gut) zu viler arznei. *medicines.*
er hat ein gutes (*or* ge- *he hath enough to*
nugfames) auskommen. *ferve his turn.*
fo vil als von noet- *as much as will ferve*
en ift (*or* noetig) fein wird. *the turn.*
fhenke mir zu trinken ein! *fill me fome drink!*

ih habe an einem wenigen genug.	*a little will serve me.*
eines ftelle vertreten.	*to ferve in ones turn.*
es ift euh gar reht gefheen *or* widerfaren ;	*you are right enough ferved.*
mann hat euh (reht getan *or*) wol bezalet.	
meine augen legen mir ab *or* ih hab' ein blœdes gefiht.	*my fight ferves me not.*
gebet euh zu friden.	*fet your heart at reft.*
der wind war gut.	*the wind ferved.*
fpilet ir mir fo mit ?	*doe you ferve me fo ?*
ih hilte defto mer auf fi.	*i fet the more by her or by them.*
er bildet ime zu vil ein;	*he fets too much by him felf.*
er traget di nafe zu hoh.	
fi hezen uns (an *or*) zufammen.	*they fet us together by the ears.*
gering fhrzen.	*to fet light by.*
es ift mir leid, dafs ir euh einen folhen mann zu'm feinde gemaht habet.	*i am forry, you have fet fuch a man againft you:*
wer reizet euh an ?	*who fets you on ?*
oben auf der treppen.	*at the ftairs head.*
vor fih felbften arbeiten *or* eine handirung anfangen.	*to fet up a trade for himfelf.*
er fluge einen lah (*or* ein gelæhter) auf.	*he fet up a laughter.*
ein gefhrei (anrihten, anfangen *or*) erwekken.	*to fet up a cry.*
er befleifiget fih allen zu gefallen.	*he fets him felf to pleafe all.*
feil (*or* zu verkaufen) fein.	*to be fet to fale.*
fi brüftet fih auf; fi puzet fih heraus.	*fhe fets her felf out.*

einem arbeit geben ;	*to set one to work.*
einen (inn di *or*) zu'r arbeit ſtellen	*or* ſezen.
eine vorbedahte rede.	*a set speech.*
einen frei (mahen *or*) ſtellen.	*to set one free or at liberty.*
mahet (*or* duet) das fenſter-gükkergen auf!	*set open the window or the casement!*
ſi rihten korn-hæuſer auf *or* an.	*they set up magazines.*
wenn geet ire reiſe fort? wenn wollen ſi auf ſein? wenn werden ſi ſih aufmahen?	*when are they setting out or forward?*
laſſet imann nahfragē.	*set one body to enquire.*
ſih bemůen einen andern zu verderben.	*to set him self to ruin one.*
hunde auf einen hezen;	*to set dogges on one.*
einen mit hunden hezen *or* jagen.	
ſih zu dinſte begeben.	*to put himself to service.*
ſi lahte, daſſ ir der ganze leib wakkelte.	*she shaked her sides and laughed.*
habt ir denn ganz und gar keine ſham bei euh?	*have you no shame at all in you?*
er ſhewet und ſhæmet ſih vor nihts; er hat das ſham-hütgen abgezogen.	*he never shames for any thing; he has swallowed the shame and drunk after it.*
es ſheinet (*or* es læſſet ſih anſeen,) als ob es (eine lnſuß *or*) ein eiland wære.	*it shewes like an isle or iland.*
dem anſeen nah eine ſtattlihe ſhifs-rüſtung.	*a gallant navy in shew.*
er bulete um ſi.	*he shewed love to her.*
nah der larven (*or* unbedahtſamlih) beten.	*to say prayers by rote.*

wûtet (*or* tobet) liber *ſhew your ſpleen ra-*
wider mih, dann u. ſ.f. *ther upon me, than &c*
God ſhûze (beware *God ſhield you from*
or behûte) euh vor aller gefar! *all danger !*
da hûlfet nihts dafûr; *there is no ſhift for*
es wird nihts anders *it ; there is no ſhift to*
daraus; es kann niht *be made; i can no way*
anders ſein; ih kan's niht ændern. *ſhift it.*
es iſt nur ein einzig- *there is but one*
es mittel wider u. ſ. f. *ſhift for &c.*
ir ſeid verdorben *or* es *you are undone, ex-*
iſt aus mit euh, es ſei *cept you can find*
denn, daſs ir euh auf *out ſome*
ein mittel beſinnet *or* bedenket. *ſhi, t.*
ih will mih ſelbſt vor- *i will now goe ſhift*
ſorgen *or* hinbringen. *for my ſelf.*
ziet euh anderſt an. *ſhift your cloths.*
ziet euh weis an. *ſhift your linnen.*
er behalfe ſih armſel- *he made a poor (or*
ig; er brahte ſih elend- *hard) ſhift to*
iglih (hinn *or*) durh. *live.*
weil mann ſi nimanne *becauſe they can ſhift*
(aufbûrden, auftring- *her off to no body elſe*
en, aufhængen *or*) an- *they come to*
hengen kann, ſo kommen ſi zu mir. *me.*
eine ſahe, di er erbar- *a buſineſs, which*
keit halber niht (wol *or*) *he can with no*
fûglih (abſlagen, aus- *credit ſhift*
ſlagen *or*) verſagen kann. *off.*
teilet (*or* deilet) es. *ſhift (i. e. divide) it.*
er ſpriht di wœrter *he ſpeakes ſhort.*
nur halb aus; er mahet nur halbe worte.
er hælt es mit mir; er *he ſideth with me;*
iſt auf meiner ſeiten. *he is on my ſide.*

an (*or* neben) dem wege.   *by the wayes fide.*
an dem ufer des flufses.   *by the rivers fide.*
auf (*or* an) beiden feit   *on both fides ;*
-en.   *on either fide.*
er entwifhete (*or* ent-   *he gave the watch-*
kame) den wæhtern.   *men the flip.*
er flife ein an dem ran-   *he fell a-fleep by*
de des wafsers.   *the bank.*
er bemſet fih, fo vil   *he does what he can,*
ime mœglih, das hals   *to flip his collar.*
-band (*or* hals-eifen) herunter zu krigen.
klein gelt; nah-bir; ein   *fmall money ; fmall*
geringes ding *or* eine   *beer ; a fmall*
flehte fahe.   *matter.*
fi merket (*or* kœmt   *fhe fmelleth out the*
hinter) den pofsen.   *plot.*
ih rohe den braten   *i quickly fmelt*
bald.   *it out.*
es betrûbet mih,   *i am forry to hear*
wenn ih es hœre.   *it.*
es jammert mih ewer.   *i am forry for you.*
es ift mir leid.   *i am forry for it.*
er hat di hœrner (ver-   *his wild oats are*
ftofsen, abgeftofsen *or*) abgelaufen.   *fown.*
ftreit erwekken; zank   *to fow ftrifes or*
anrihten; uneinigkeit mahen.   *difsenfions.*
unter (*or* binnen) zwan   *by the fhace of twen*
-zig jaren ; inn an-   *-ty years ; or , of an*
derthalb ftunden.   *hour and a half.*
pfize-nafs ; fo nafs als   *as wet as muck , or as*
eine gebadete maus.   *a drowned moufe.*
ûberflûfig genug.   *enough and to fpare.*
fhonet ewer ein wenig.   *fpare your felf a little.*
unten an der treppen.   *at the ftairs foot.*

ih kann es niht(entber- *i can not ſpare (or, be*
en, miſsen *or*)entraten. *without) it.*
es geet uns wol von *it ſpeeds well under*
der hand *or* von ſtatten. *our hand.*
redet laut ; duet das *ſpeak out; ſpeak loud.*
maul auf; duet den brei aus dem munde.
ir habt (ir genung an- *you ſpent a good*
gehænget *or*) auf ſi ge- *deal on*
wand ; ſi koſtet euh genug. *her.*
ſi brahten di zeit mit *they ſpan out the time*
zaudern zu. *with lingering.*
euh allen zu'm poſsen *in ſpite (ſpight)*
or zu wider. *of you all.*
wann diſes niht ge- *if this be not ſpite,*
ſhƚmpfet iſt (*or* heiſt) *i know not*
ſo weis ih's niht. *what is.*
wider iren willen und *in ſpite of her*
dank. *(their) teeth.*
es mahet unſere zæne *it ſets our teeth on*
ſtumpf. *(an) edge.*
einen beklekken *or* be *to drop a ſpot*
-tropfen ; einem ein *upon one.*
klæppgen anhængen *or* poſsen beweiſen.
diſes unglükk wird ü- *this mischief will*
berhand nemen. *ſpread farther.*
über hals u.kopf eilen. *to be upon the ſpur.*
wi ſteen wir zu *how goeth the*
ſammen? *ſquare?*
was ſind wir ein and- *how goes the ſquare*
er ſhuldig ? *with you and me?*
mahet es vir-ekkig. *bring it into ſquare.*
nahdem ih von ime *underſtanding by him,*
verſtande , wi es herginge *how the ſquares*
or wi vil di glokke geſlagen hatte. *went.*

ih gebrauhe es not-   *i stand in need*
wendig.   *of it.*

was habt ir (vor ein ge   *how stands your mind*
·mût *or)* vor einen finn hirzu?   *to it?*

feinem verfprehen nah   *to stand to what one*
-kommen; feine (zufa-   *hath promifed*
ge *or)* worte halten.   *or faid.*

wegere dih niht (*or* be   *doe not stand upon*
-finne dih niht lang)   *it i. e. think much to*
folhes zu duen.   *doe it.*

es ift feiner eren niht   *it stands not with*
gemæs *or* anftændig;   *his dignity or*
feine würde læfset es niht zu.   *honeur.*

wartet (meiner *or)* auf   *stay for me with*
mih bei ir.   *her.*

er læfset fih nirgend   *he never stayes in*
niht authalten.   *any place.*

feine luft ift gebüfset;   *his stomach is*
er hat feine begirden geftillet.   *ftaid.*

er ziet gelindere fæit- *his stomach is come*
en auf.   *down.*

wenn fi nah mir fenden   *when i am fent for,*
or fhikken, fo haltet   *doe not make*
mih niht auf.   *me ftay.*

er befanne (*or* bedahte)   *he ftood a good*
fih eine gute weile   *while at a*
hinn und her.   *ftay.*

ih warte darauf.   *i ftay for it.*

es wird euh zutræg-   *it will ftand you in*
lih fein.   *fome ftead.*

er ift i'm œffentlihen *he is taken ftealing.*
dibftale (ertappet *or)* ergriffen worden.
mahet euh ja keine ge   *never ftick at*
-danken (*or* kein gewifsen) darüber.   *it.*

𝔓

er ſtekket inn gleiher not. di hænde inn den ſhos legen ; maulaffen feil haben; warten	*he ſicks in the ſame mire.* *to ſit ſtill and doe nothing.*
eine gebratene taube bifs in's maul flûget.	
ih will euh das maul ſtopfen.	*i will ſtill your din i.* *make you hold your tourg.*
ih kame (*or* ginge) mit keinem fuſse aus dem hauſe.	*i did not ſtir a-broad.*
ſi hilten euh nur vor einen narren *or* jekken.	*they made a laugh -ing-ſtock of you.*
ih habe (niht groſen hunger *or*) keine luſt zu eſsen.	*i have no great ſtomach.*
es war an allem ein (guter *or*) groſer vorrat da.	*there was a (good) ſtore of all things.*
ſnur - gleih nider *or* - auf.	*ſtraight down (or up) by a line.*
ih verwundere mih hœhlih darûber ; es nimmet mih groses wunder ; es verwundert mih ſer.	*i ſtrange it.*
er iſt ein (poſsirliher, læherliher , ſnakiſher *or*) wonderliher menſh, kauz, kærl, geſell.	*he is a ſtrange fellow.*
o wunder!	*o ſtrange!*
ein groſer ſhritt.	*a huge ſtride.*
ſih überſhreiten ; all-zu -weite ſhritte tuen (*or*) mahen.	*to take over - wide ſtrides.*
es ginge mir ſer nae *or* zu herzen *or* zu gemûte.	*it ſtruck me to the very heart.*
mitten (inn dem *or*) i'm Teutſh -lande.	*in the very heart (or in the midſt) of Germany.*
nah dem (kopfe *or*) haupte ſlagen *or* zielen.	*to ſtrike at (or to aime at) the head.*

einen (bund *or*) ver- | *to strike a league*
trag mit einem mahen | *(or a bargain)*
or engeen. | *with one.*
ein grofes *or* hoes alt- | *to be stricken*
er (*or* vil jare) auf sih haben. | *in years.*
hebe di beine auf! | *stir your stumps!*

	heilige shrift.		*Divinity.*
er	Rehte.		*the Law.*
leget	arznei - konst.	*he*	*Physick.*
sih	welt · weisheit.	*stu-*	*Philosophy.*
auf	rede-konst.	*dies*	*Oratory.*
di	rehen-konst.		*Arithmetick.*
	singe - konst. u. s. f.		*Musick &c.*

um ein amt (*or* einen | *to sue for an office.*
dinst) anhalten; sih um ein amt bewerben.
einen verklagen *or* mit | *to sue one at*
rehte belangen. | *law.*
er war mein bul ; ih | *he was a suitor or a*
war feine libste; er | *servant to me.*
(bulete, loefelte) *or* freyete um mih; er
kame zu mir auf di bulshaft *or* freyereye.
si (namen *or*) litten | *they suffered*
shiff-bruh. | *shipwrack.*
es ist inen niht (zuge- | *they are not suffer-*
lafsen, vergœnnet *or*) verstattet. | *ed.*
si kœnnen niht mit uns | *they suit not with our*
(*or* wir kœnnen | *(or we doe not suit*
niht mit inen) | *with their) temper,*
stallen *or* über- | *humour , nature,*
einkommen. | *disposition.*
seid ir defsen (versih- | *are you sure of*
ert *or*) gewifs ? | *it ?*
er sae nihts denn | *he saw nothing but*
sæge-spæne. | *saw - dust.*

er ginge bifsweilen *his gate was some-*
(fnell *or*) gefwinde, zu *times fwift and fome*
-zeiten aber langfam *or fahte. -times flow.*
lafset fi (iren mut *or*) *let them (her) take*
ir mûtgen bûfen. *their (her) fwing.*
einem den degen ab- *to take ones fword*
nemen ; einen wer- *from him ; to*
los·mahen. *disarme one.*
wollet ir ime glauben *will you (or doe you)*
geben *or* zuftellen? *or* *take him at*
wollet ir feinen worten trawen? *his word?*
unreht von einem *to take wrong*
leiden. *at one.*
nemet es von mir weg. *take it at me.*
er flæget feinem vater *he takes after his fa-*
nah ; er ift geartet wi fein vater. *ther.*
fih vor einen gelærten *to take upon him to*
ausgeben. *be a fcholar.*
fih an andere fpigeln *to take example on*
or keren. *others.*
einem eines hinter di *to take one a box*
oren verfezen *or* geben. *on the ear.*
einen gefallen an et- *to be taken with*
was haben *or* tragen. *a thing.*
folhe fahen gefallen *thefe things take with*
dem volke. *the people.*
was habet ir zu verrih *what are you taken*
-ten *or* zu fhaffen? *up withall?*
ih habe keine herberge *my lodging is*
mer; ih kann nimann mer *taken up.*
beherbergen; mein haus ift ganz vermûtet.
feet ir mih vor fo alber *doe you take me for*
(*or* einfæltig) an? *fuch a fool?*
ein wort ein mann. *take my word.*

für wen (haltet ir *whom doe you take*
mih? *or*) feet ir mih an? *me for ?*
haltet mih von folhen *take me off from*
dingen ab. *fuch doings.*
er fprange über di neze *he took over the*
or garne. *nets i. leapt clear or quite over.*
er kerete da ein; er *he took up his lod-*
flluge allda fein lager auf. *ging there.*
zufluht bei einem nemen. *to take fanctuary.*
er geet *or* fizet(oben an *he takes the upper-*
or) auf der rehten feit- *hand or the wall.*
en, hand ; er nimmet di eren - ftelle ein.
mann konte di erflag- *the number of the*
enen kaum zælen. *flain could hardly be taken.*
fih etwas zum fhümpfe *to take a thing as*
anzien. *done in defpite to him felf.*
wi ih dafür halte; wi *as i take it.*
mih bedünket; wi mir es vorkœmmet.
lafset uns luftwandeln. *let us take a walk.*
zu pferde (zu wagen *or* *to take horfe, coatch*
zu kutfhe) geen. *or wagon.*
es ift ein blofes (ge- *it is a very tale; mere*
wæfh, gefwæz *or*) geplauder. *tales all.*
er kann niht fagen , *he can not tell which*
welher von den beiden *is which or whether*
(*or* unter den zweyen) es fei. *of thefe two.*
als das gelt aufgezælet *as the money was*
wurde. *a-telling.*
es wurde mir von *i was told (or it*
ime gefaget *or* *was told me) by*
erzælet. *or of him.*
bei zeiten ; zu rehter *in time ; in very*
zeit ; eben zu ge- *good time ; in pud*
wünfhter zeit. *-ding time.*

ir kommet zu spæte	*you come out of time*
or zu langfam.	*or too late.*
fi hatte niht lange mer	*fhe was near her*
zu geen *or* zu warten.	*time.*
als ire zeit kame , fo	*fhe went to her*
gelage fi.	*time.*
vor undenklihen jaren,	*time out of*
zeiten.	*mind.*
dazumal; zu der zeit.	*at that time.*
ir wuftet euh inn di	*you knew how to*
zeit zu fhikken.	*make ufe of your time.*
zwei jûnglinge faft ein	*two youngmen much*
-es alters.	*of one time.*
es fei dann *(or* i'm falle)	*without you be told*
dafs mann es euh hund-	*it an hundred times*
ert mal fûrfaget *or* fûrkænet.	*over.*
fi fteinigten mih; fi	*they threw ftones*
warfen mih mit ftein-	*at me.*
en; fi warfen fteine auf mih	*or* nah mir.
er wirfet *(or* wirft) uns	*he throwes (us in*
des Keufers tod fûr;	*the teeth with Cæ-*
er rûkket *(or* muzet*)*	*fars death , or)* Cæ-
uns des Keifers	*fars death in*
tod auf.	*our tee.h.*
ih mufs von etwas an-	*i muft turn my toung*
'ders reden.	*i. e. talk of fomewhat elfe.*
es enthle ime di fprah	*his toung faild*
-e ; er blibe inn der rede ftekken.	*him.*
ih wolte , dafs er fih	*i would have him*
ein wenig i'm rehte	*have a little touch*
umfæe.	*of the law.*
ih will ime einen wakk	*i will ferve him*
·cren pofsen beweifen.	*a cunning trick.*
mihleiden mit einem tragen.	*to pity one.*

ih handelte ja als ein *it were but the trick*
lcihtfærtiger vogel *or of a bafe knave in*
erenvergefsener fhelm *me, if i fhould*
, wenn ih es dæte. *doe it.*
er life fih's ganz niht *he was not a whit*
anfehten. *troubled at it.*
gerewet in nun (di *is he now troubled*
dat? *or)* dafser's getan? *at what he has done?*
es verdreuft (*or* krænk- *it (vexes or) troubles*
et) mih von herzen *me; i am very much*
or heftig. (*vexed or) troubled at it.*
es plaget in di zan- *he is troubled with*
wœe; di wœtagen der *the tooth - ache.*
zæne plagen in;er ift mit den zænĕ geplaget.
es **ift** di lautere war- *it is (moft or) very*
heit;es ift all-zu-war. *true; 't is too true.*
lafset uns Gott dem *let us give God*
Herren danken *or* dankfagen. *thanks.*
es wird entweder zu *it turnes either to*
regen oder zu winde; *rayn or to wind.*
es wird entweder regen oder wind daraus.
ein buh aus dem Grih *to turn a book out*
-ifhen in's Iatein ü- *of Greek into*
berfezen *or* überbringen. *Latin.*
er hat alles verkeret; *he has turned all*
er hat das unterfte zu *things upfide down*
œberft gekeret. *or topfie turvy.*
wehfelweife; einer um den andern. *by turns.*
einem bœfes mit gut- *to doe a good turn*
em vergelten. *for an evil one.*
fi verlifen meine freind *they turn'd their*
-fhaft. (*back or)* tail on *my freindfhip*
ftofet in zum haufe hin- *kick (or turn) him*
aus; flaget im' di dîrĕ vor'n ars. *out of dores.*

zwei oder drei male (auf-und ab *or*) auf- und nider-geen. — *to take two or three turns.*

haltet den dib auf. — *turn (ſtop) the thief.*

auf di hinter-beine treten *i.* læugnen was mann geſaget. — *to turn cat in the pan, or to ſay and unſay.*

ih habe i vil (*or* zu ider zeit groſe ſtükken) auf euh gehalten. — *i have ever ſet a great value upon you.*

was gedenket ir, (daſs ih wol darnah frage? *or*) wi hoh ih es halte *or* ſhætze? — *what doe you thinke i value it at?*

etwas inn di ſhanze ſlagen *or* auf das glükke wagen. — *to put things to a venture.*

auf das ungewiſse. — *at a venture.*

er wird ſeinen vater (verderben *or*) an den bettel-ſtab bringen. — *he will undoe his father or bring him to beggary.*

eine gelübte duen. — *to make a vow.*

warzu? — *for what uſe?*

wi er pfleget. — *as he uſes.*

ih dærfte bald (wett- en, eine wette legen *or*) etwas verwetten. — *i durſt lay a wager.*

ih will mit euh wett- en was ir wollet. — *i will lay you (or with you) any wager.*

einen bekrigen; mit einem krig anfangen. — *to make (or to wage) war upon (a- gainſt or with) one.*

ih hærme mih ganz ab; ih bekümmere mih ſo, daſs ih ganz verfalle *or* abneme. — *i waſte or pine (i. am waſted or pi- ned) away with grief.*

wahinnaus? weihet — *which way? out of*

mir aus! mahet raum! *my way! give way!*
aus'm wege! *turn away!*
das leder gibet nah. *the leather gives way.*
ein wüftes (*or* œdes) land. *a wafte ground.*
befmuztes papir *or* maculatur. *wafte paper.*
er nimmet fi bei der *he takes her about*
mitte. *the wafte.*
er life es an gutem will *he wanted no good*
-en niht ermangeln. *will.*
fi haben fhon di anker *they have already*
aufgezogen *or* aufgehoben. *weighed anchor.*
ewere brife gelten *your letters weigh*
mæhtig *(or* rihten vil *very much with*
aus) bei mir. *me.*
er ift niht (wol *or*) *he is not well in*
reht bei finnen. *his wits.*
ih habe euh zu lib *i love you too too*
or zu wert. *(or but too) well.*
er will euh wol; er ift *he wifhes you*
euh gœntlig *or* geneigt. *well.*
willkommen von der *wellcome home or to*
reife! ewere ankunft ift mir lib! *the town.*
er (bewirtete, empfin- *he made me very well*
ge *or*) bewillkommete mih ftattlih. *-come.*
wenn es nah meinem *if i might have*
kopfe (*or* finne) geen folte. *my will.*
fi fin] ganz von der *they are (quite down*
hitfhen kommen; fi *the wind, or) be-*
nagen an dem hong- *hind hand in*
er - tuhe. *the world.*
ih verwondere mih *i make no wonder*
ganz und gar niht *at all (of it,*
darüber. *or} at it.*
ih weis niht was ih doh *i know not what in*

imm:rmer mahen foll.   *the world to doe.*
glůkk auf (di reife!   *i wiſh you(well bome!*
or)den weg! *a good voyage! or) a good journey!*
ih belanke mih freind *i thanke you (bear-*
-lih or zu'm fhœnſten.   *tily or) kindly.*
ih befare (mih,) wir *i am afraid, we ſhall*
werden (den kůrzern *(come by the worſt*
zien, or) zu kurz *of it) be worſted or*
kommen.   *be put to the worſt.*
næmlih; namentlih.   *to wit ; viz.*
di land-(or hær-) ſtrafe.   *the highway.*
was wollet ir bei mir *what would you*
haben?   *with me?*
ih will meinen zorn (or *i will wreak my*
grimm) ůber ſi ausſhitten. *teen on them.*
er will alles eingeen; *he is willing to yield*
er will mit allem zu friden fein. *to any thing.*
er wolte fih niht geben. *he would not yield.*
was hůlfet es euh, dafs *what are you the(bet-*
ir glůkkfelig, niht a- *ter or) nearer for be*
ber weife feid?   *-ing fortunate and not wife ?*
er hat mit einem fih *he has fought a*
(auf den tegen) geſlagen.   *duell.*
es iſt vergebens, dafs *there is no keeping*
mann ein flofs wolle *(of) a lock for that*
vor der dire ligend *dore, which everyone*
haben, warzu ein id-   *has a key (to)*
weder einen flůfsel (or ditrig) hat. *for.*
er gedahte, er wůr- *he thought, he ſhould*
de (ſterben můfsen (or)drauf geen. *have died.*
er iſt mir unbekand. *he is a ſtranger to me.*
ih bin der fahen   *i am a ſtranger*
ein kind.   *of it.*
ih wolte, dafs ir euh *i would have you*

vor einen folhen aus-gæbet. *owne your felf to be fuch a one.*

fi date einen fæil-tritt; fi trate fæil. *fhe mifsed her ftep.*

er hat des jares hundert ducaten ein-zu kommen. *he is worth a year fifty pound,*

di fhuld ift ewer. *it is long of you.*

es foll an mir niht mangeln or ermangeln. *it fhall not be long of me.*

es werden allerhand vorbereitung zu feiner hohzeit gemahet. *feverall preparations are making for his marriage.*

er weis feine füfse fein (wol or artig) zu fezen. *he makes a handfome leg.*

di milh krihet alle in's brot. *the bread drinks (or fucks) all up the milk.*

eine zuvor getragene müze. *a cap at fecond hand.*

der (fharf or) nah-riht ·er name ir di (flor-) kappe (or haube) ab. *the head - (or hang-) man took her the hood off.*

fi ift (zu'm tode) verurteilet ; das reht ift über fi gefprohen; der ftab ift über fi gebrohen. *the law is pafsed upon her.*

ee di breiten hûte aufkamen. *before broad hats came into fafhion.*

ein fas (inn das andere) abzyen. *to cut one vefsel off into an other.*

der ftifelfhaft reihet weiter niht dann bifs an feine wade. *then* *the top of the boot reaches no farther the calf of his leg.*

wilft du das jenige (mir ausreden or) verlæugnen , was ih doh (felb- *will you (face me down or) outface me of that, which*

selbft *or*) mit meinen   *my felf fawe juft now?*
eigenen augen gleih izo angefeen habe ?
er ift der aller befte   *he is the beft ring-*
glokken·fpiler inn der   *er in all the town.*
ganzen ftatt.   ein ringer.   *a wraftler.*
er redet one allen   *he fpeakes no fenfe*
verftand.   *at all.*
es hat faft und kraft   *he writes a very good*
(or hænde und füfse) was er fhreibet. *fenfe.*
es hat (einerlei ver-   *it comes to one*
ftand *or)* eben dife meinung.   *fenfe.*
es erbitterte *(or* ver-   *it did galle me to the*
drofse) mih i'm herzen drinne.   *heart.*
vollenziet meinen(will   *put my will in*
-en *or)* befel.   *act.*
ewer geheis ift gefheen.   *you are obeyed.*
das wetter erfluge   *lightning blafted*
fi alle.   *them all.*
fie dih nah einem kwer   *look for a fide-*
-fattel um. lafs einen *faddle !*   *call for a*
fænften-træger herkomnıen!   *chearman!*
will er *(or* fi) fih *(or will you be pleafed*
ir) beliben lafsen auf   *to mounte the*
das bei pferd zu fteigen?   *leadhorfe?*
difer flufs (ergeufet *this river is very*
fih bald *or*) dritt gar   *apt to overflowe*
leihtlih aus feinem ufer.   *its banks.*
warum faret ir mih fo   *why doe you fly out*
græfslih an? wi farz- *into fuch - a pafsion*
et ir fo auf ?   *againft me ?*
immer und ewig ; *for ever and ever;*
   von ewigkeit zu   *world without*
     ewigkeit.   *end.*

er weis fih gar vil (*or*   *he is proud of his*
pranget) mit feinem mifthaufen.   *dunghill.*
ih werde meinen diner   *i fhall turne off my*
abfhaffen *or* enturlauben.   *man.*
ir mann ift um's (*or* um   *her husband is taller*
eines) kopfes länger.   *by the head.*
er hat (ein *or*) fein   *he hath a house of*
eigen haus.   *his own.*
er redet in's gelag   *he fpeakes at*
hinnein.   *randome.*
di bæume flagen aus.   *the trees fpring forth.*
wer da eer kœmt, der   *he , that comes firft,*
mælet eer ; der erfte geet vor.   *is ferved firft.*
difer grobe gEfell und   *that rude and clown-*
ungehœbelte flegel   *ifh fellow has not fo*
hat keinen erlihen   *much as the fmall*
blutstropfen (*or* keine   *-eft aire of an ho*
redlihe ader)inn feinen   *-neft man with*
ganzem leibe.   *-in him.*
er ift eine feihe mæm-   *he has not the fmalleft*
me ; er hat kein herz   *aire of (a) man*
i'm leibe.   *within him.*
wann er feine fnauze   *when he is in (drink*
(mit bire) begofsen   *or) beer , all muft*
hat , fo læfset er den   *out of the fool , and*
hafen mit dem narren-   *the drunken fot picks*
fæile laufen und briht   *a quarrell at never fo*
einen zank von idwedem zaune.   *fmall a trifle.*
ih will(niht einen fhritt   *i will not ftirre.*
fort geen *or*) weder weihen noh wanken.
fo du wirft nur einen   *if you ftirre but an*
fufs fort fezen ; fo will   *inch , i will flea you*
ih dih bei'm lebendigen leibe fhinden. *alive.*
ih will euh anhelfen.   *i will preferre you.*

Z

ir feet (fer) fein aus.	you look (very) well.
duet andern was ir von	doe as you would
inen begeret.	be done by others.
mit verleyung goett-	by the grace of
liher genaden.	God.
wir von Gottes gnaden.	we by the grace of God.
verzeyet mir, dafs ih	pardon my interrup-
euh inn (ewere rede or)	tion; pray! give me
di rede falle.	leav to speake.
es hat uns imann be-	we are overheard
horhet or zu gehœret.	by some.
so bald als — —	no sooner than —
es ift (ganz und gar	the trade is dead.
keine narung or) weder	handel noh wandel.
ih ftelle es inen ver-	i leave it to them
nünftig bei fih zu be-	in cold blood to
trahten anheim.	confider.
unter hundert vætern	what father of an
ift niht einer, der —	hundred is there that
ih habe mih erkæltet;	i have (got or) caught
di kælte ift mir inn den	leib geflagen. cold.
ih will mih fhon felbft	i will be my own
bezalet mahen.	paymaster.
ir laufet fo gefwinde,	you walk at fuch a
dafs ih euh niht (ein-	rate, i can not o-
holen or) ereilen kann.	vertake you.
ir follet eine weile	you shall be farr
warten.	enough.
ir habt euh niht ge-	you are not
wafhen darzu.	like.
er lekkete di finger	his chaps watered
nah mir.	at 'me.
ir fwizet (über und	you are all
über or) als ein braten.	of a sweat.

ir feid ganz über und *you are all of a beat.*
über heis; ir brœnnet an eurem ganzen leibe.
wann ih mit euh rede, *when i speake to you,*
fo ift es eben fo vil, als *you doe not minde me*
ob euh eine gans anzifhete. *at all.*
warauf finnet ir? wa *what are you think-*
find ewere gedanken? *ing on?*
Ihittet ewer herz aus *unbofome your felf*
vor einem freinde. *to a friend.*
wen redet ir an? *whom doe you fpeake to?*
er wolte fih durhaus *he would not be*
niht abweifen lafsen. *denied.*
fein mütigen zu *for fatisfaction of*
külen. feine luft zu *his mind. for fatis-*
büfsen. *faction of his luft.*
er ware blind - voll; *he was as drunk as*
er war fo voll als *a wheelbare; he was*
ein fwein. *bloody drunk.*
fi hatten zu halben u. *they had been high*
zu ganzen getronken. *a- drinking.*
wer wolte fih niht inn *who would not fall*
ein folh' artlihes fhelm *in love with fuch a*
-gen verliben? *fmockfaced rogue?*
ir hafeliret treff- *you are fool to*
lih. *the hight.*
er ift fhon über alle *he is gone and*
berge und niht mer zu feen. *paft fight.*
ir habet wunderlihe *you hold ftrange ar*
(or feizame) einfælle. *-guments.*
er hinterflihe mih. *he disftale upon me.*
mann kann euh nihts *you are too hard to*
reht genug mahen; ir *pleafe or to be pleafed.*
wollet alles zu (eben or) genawe haben.
allezeit über'n andern tag. *every each day.*

er ginge den kræbs- *he played the rope-*
gang *or* hinterrûks. *maker i. wend backward.*
ſi iſt vortrefflih ge- *ſhe goes , as though*
ſmûkket und aufge- *ſhe would ſell*
ſwænzet. *herſelf.*

ih will (mih ewer durh *i will not owne*
-aus niht anmaſen *or)* niht einmal *you.*
ſagen, daſs ir mein ſeid *or mir zu gehœret.*
ir habt's (erraten *or)* *you are in the right*
getroffen. *of it.*

es færet ime zuweil- *he takes ſome time*
en eine freude inn *or other a*
di ahſel. *frolick.*

was für ein alberer *ſilly fool that i was,*
narr (*or* einfæltiger *i gave him to*
tropf) war ih, daſs *much head!*
ih ime ſo vil (nahliſe, einræumete *or)*nahſae!
dem teufel i'm bette *to be ſtewing a- bed*
einen braten wenden *till noon.*
biſs mann mit den tellern zu tiſhe læutet.

friſh obeſt labet ein- *new fruit is refreſh-*
en des morgens. *ing in a morning.*

er læſſet ſeinen hut ver *he gets his hat*
-bræmen *or* einfaſſen. *edged.*

der neidiſhe tadeler zi *the dogged carver (or*
-jet alles durh ſeine *Momus) carpes at*
hehel. *all things.*

Gott lob *thanks to*
und dank! *God !*
lang lebe *God*
der Kœnig! *(bleſse,*
Gott erhal- *ſpare or)*
te den *ſave the*
Kœnig ! *King!*